Women of Africa
Roots of Oppression

Maria Rosa Cutrufelli

Translated by Nicolas Romano

To Deolinda Rodrigues
who died in a Zairese concentration camp
for the freedom of Angola
and the liberation of African women

Zed Press, 57 Caledonian Road, London N1 9DN.

Women of Africa was originally published in Italian under the title *Donna, Perche Piangi?* by Gabriele Mazzotta Editore, Foro Buonoparte 52, 20121 Milan; first published in English in an updated edition by Zed Press, 57 Caledonian Road, London N1 9DN in 1983.

Copyright © Maria Rosa Cutrufelli
Translation Copyright © Zed Press, 1983

Copyedited by Anna Gourlay
Proofread by Ros Howe
Cover photo courtesy of Jo Kabon, Christian Aid
Typeset by Lynn Papworth
Printed by The Pitman Press, Bath, U.K.

All rights reserved

> British Library Cataloguing in Publication Data
> Cutrufelli, Maria Rosa
> Women of Africa.
> 1. Women—Africa   2. Women—Social conditions
> I. Title   II. Donna, Perche piangi? English
> 305.4'2'096   HQ1787
> ISBN 0-86232-083-6
> ISBN 0-86232-084-4 Pbk

U.S. Distributor:
Biblio Distribution Center, 81 Adams Drive, Totowa, New Jersey 07512, U.S.A.

All quotations are translations from the Italian edition of the sources concerned.

Contents

Preface to the English Edition	1
Foreword	11
1. Colonization and Social Change	15
Traditional Africa and Colonization	15
Introduction of Wage Labour and Its Social Implications	17
Migrant Labour and the Family: the Zambian Case	20
Prostitution	29
2. The Position of Women in Traditional Society	41
The Family	41
Marriage Rites	43
Customary Marriage Town	46
Bridewealth: Traditional Significance and Latter Day Speculation	49
Divorce and Dissolution of Marriage	50
Women's Attitude to Polygamy	52
Colonialism, Neo-colonialism and Family Politics	56
Inheritance	61
Matriliny	67
The Single Woman	69
Social Change and the Conscience of the Masses	72
3. The Function of Women's Labour in Less Developed Countries	87
Women's Participation: General Data	87
Women in Industry	92
The Rights of Working Women	96
Business Women in West Africa	97
Urbanization and Womens' Work	102

Urban Petty Tradeswomen	105
Urbanized Women 'Return to the Soil'	109
Domestic Labour	111
Work in Rural Areas	115
Diet Taboos: The Nutritional Problem	123

4. Demographic Control: Tradition and Innovation — 133
- Traditional Control of Reproduction and Motherhood — 133
- The Cliteridectomy 'Mystery' — 136
- The Demographic Problem in Colonial Times — 138
- Abortion — 139
- The Family Planning Controversy — 144
- Planned Motherhood? — 147

5. Women, Education and Political Movements — 155
- Initiation Rites: The Customary Approach — 155
- Schooling — 159
- Women's Participation in Religious Liberation Movements — 162
- Women's Involvement in Social Struggles and Political Movements — 170

Bibliography — 179

List of Tables

1A	Population (%) Away from Home According to 1960–61 Demographic Survey in Upper Volta	19
1B	Population (%) Away from Home According to 1960–61 Demographic Survey in Upper Volta: Length of Absence	19
1C	Population (%) Aged 14+ Away from Home According to 1960–61 Demographic Survey in Upper Volta: Marital Status	20
2	Population Density in the Reserves of the Eastern Province: 1924 and 1942	22
3	Zambia: Population by Age and Sex, including Non-Africans: 1969	27
4	Zambia: Population Structure by Sex and Ward, 1963 and 1969	28
5	Married Women/Prostitutes, Stanleyville (Kisangani), 1944–57	31
6	Answers to: 'Can a man afford co-wives more easily in urban than rural areas?'	56
7	Percentage of Unmarried Adults (1967) by Age Group: Accra and the Northern Region	70
8	Answers to Questionnaire on African Women's Opinion of Western Women	70

9	Productive Population: 1960	88
10	Forecast on Productive Population: 1970 and 1980	88
11	Unemployed and Low-paid Labourers by Sex and Status in Nairobi: 1970	89
12	Percentage of Female Labour Force as against Total Labour Force by Economic Sector and Region: 1960	89
13	Regional Distribution of Total Population and Productive Population: 1960 (%)	90
14	Distribution of Productive Population by Region and Sector: 1960 (%)	90
15	Distribution of Population by Economic Activity: 1960 (approx. %)	91
16	Factory Absenteeism in Accra-Tema: by Occupation, Sex and Region of Origin	94
17	Borrowers Under the Small Business Credit Scheme: Ghana	100
18	Standard Estimate for the Determination of the Minimum Daily Wage: 1954	106

Other Books by Maria Rosa Cutrufelli

L'Invenzione della Donna — Miti e Tecniche di uno Sfruttamento (Mazzotta, 1974)
Disoccupata con Onore — Lavoro e Condizione della Donna (Mazzotta, 1975)
Operaie senza Fabbrica (Editori Riuniti, 1977)
Economia e Politica dei Sentimenti (Editori Riuniti, 1978)
Il Cliente — Inchiesta sulla Domanda di Prostituzione (Editori Riuniti, 1980)

Preface to the English Edition

Where cultures tend to integrate, economies become increasingly interdependent and political events may be fully appreciated only in an international perspective. Women throughout the world should now, more than ever, surmount any cultural, racial and historical divide between them and learn to know one another better.

This, I believe, will stimulate solidarity among women — though not only among women. Yet, solidarity will always be an abstract word or an infertile scion until it is grafted onto the concrete, hardy tree of knowledge: knowledge and solidarity together may well bring forth a common political hypothesis conducive to growth and able to show the way towards 'liberation'.

Writing about the condition of women in Africa meant all this to me, as it brought a geographically remote setting much closer to me and notably to my politically thinking self. Africa is not merely an immense, complex and culturally multifarious continent, it is also a fast changing world.

Hence, research into the conditions of life and the role of African women today does not only call for some regular revising but also for a continual and timely verification of previous analyses as well as of the methods employed in the research and in the analysis.

The ensuing pages claim only to offer some food for thought on a few issues which have been coming to the fore in the recent past and seem to me to be vital for understanding the reality of women in African societies.

Taking the advantage offered by this English edition of my work, I shall deal with issues such as the production/reproduction relation, the significance that the emergence and the increasingly self-assertive vindication of 'individual rights' may have for women, and the progress or the decline of women's political and economic organizations.

Far from providing an outlet for the peculiar impediments of 'traditional' African societies, black nationalism has probably exacerbated them as it has bent them to the necessities of ideological propaganda. Thus, one motif reassessed and charged by nationalism with overtones and values from the West is motherhood. Truly enough, motherhood is a 'traditional' way of defining the woman status, since 'a woman is a woman only if she is a mother'; yet, the ideas currently upheld in this regard by African intellectuals and politicians seem to be dictated by motives scarcely related to such a notion. We may even say that nationalism and liberation wars have unearthed the feminine question and put it in terms which may be defined as 'modern' by Western standards; they have revealed the thread of sex discrimination binding all women, black or white, and regardless of economic, social, cultural and traditional diversities, leading them to a common plan for liberation. The basis of such a plan to be supplied by motherhood and the production/reproduction relation, the latter being a contradictory one in any social, political or economic system.

The two terms of the question, i.e., work/motherhood and production/reproduction, have usually been analysed separately or juxtaposed, and the accent placed by turns on the one or the other according to the observer's interests. Yet, only by analysis of the relation as a whole can the profound meaning of the changes and transformations that have occurred so far be grasped, as such analysis reveals much more about the real tendencies of African development or underdevelopment than any other more complex analysis of economic and/or social politics.

The glorification of maternity is more than a 'traditional' peculiarity of African societies: in the first place it represented the social response to the depopulation caused by the slave trade and, later, by the colonial wars; a response, that is, to the high rate of sterility engendered by increasing poverty and the spread of endemic and venereal diseases. At the same time the maternity myth has been confronted with the subjective disavowal on the part of women acting on their own: abortion, as a conscious and deliberate rejection of motherhood, is not unknown to 'traditional' societies. But above all, it is the violence of the process of colonization coupled with a feeling of insecurity that has unleashed the 'dread of motherhood', as some anthropologists have expressed it. Hence, the hardening attitude in traditional societies towards the feminine role: the social duty of motherhood became more binding, even a kind of social obsession and, in allowing no option, a sentence against the woman. The customary mechanisms of control over the reproductive power of women grew harsher — and they are still harsh today.

A few years back, a Congolese young woman said to me: 'I'm 27. I got married, but my husband has divorced me on the grounds that I'm unable to have children. I've tried everything: I've been to Brazzaville and to Gabon, but to no avail. Then, my parents-in-law wanted me to divorce.'

African depopulation on the one side has accentuated the reproductive function of women, on the other it has made their participation in production necessary, thus deepening more than elsewhere and maybe in a more dramatic way the typical conflict between productive and reproductive roles. In fact, female work has become an essential productive factor, particularly in view of the fact that there has been no replacement of the natives with immigrants nor, as in Latin America, has any blending of races occurred, except to a minimal extent in few areas. Such contradictory pressures have made the demographic and labour policies of Africa rather ambiguous; rarely will a woman, with all her individual and social exigencies, be an item in official programmes: she is always a tool, never a person.

Preface to the English Edition

The new African states have generally adopted the colonial policies of utilizing the female labour force in the subsistence sector of the economy, and male force in the modern sector. During the colonial rule, women would be largely kept within rural areas whereas men would be encouraged to migrate to development areas. The situation has now changed, yet many women are still confined to the domain of subsistence economy.

Obviously, such policy of sexual division of labour has impoverished women, and not just literally: they have been penned inside a society which, rather than traditional, should now be labelled backward and subordinate, and tied down to behaviour and modes of being which impede their efforts for emancipation. Within such deteriorated social relations, women's reproductive function has been deprived of all the space for autonomy it once had, and consequently of all the social power it had gained and managed to preserve. Of course political independence could not by itself provide a way out of the predicament, mainly in light of the economic dependence of the new states; thus, revolutionary movements have found themselves bound to acknowledge the situation and go no further: the formulation of new hypotheses or diverse solutions is a long and difficult task indeed.

The issue of a more rational distribution and utilization of labour was forcefully raised at the 1976 MPLA 1st seminar on agriculture: 'Colonialism would resort to labour force migrations . . . . A modern solution calls for a different approach.'[1] Yet 'a different approach' is anything but simple to design, hence female and male labour forces are still being separately used in the traditional and in the capitalist sector respectively. In a social setting liable to abrupt changes, such a state of affairs engenders an irreducible contrast bound to affect the very fabric of the state and the power of the new national bourgeoisies.

The ascendancy of the market system along with the tumultuous process of urbanization and the break-up of the traditional family fabric have paved the way for the establishment of Western values and ways of life. A new philosophy of life, primarily catering for the needs of the individual as a 'person', has been making headway in a society still attached to a profoundly anti-individualistic *Weltanschauung*. Beyond doubt, the societal segment most directly affected by what soon appeared to be a revolutionary process was the female segment: in fact, in some strata and in particular instances, women have been the very harbingers of the new philosophy.

It is within such context that the new, characteristically urban figure, of the male-unprotected, husbandless, single woman has significantly taken shape: and, in the light of the traditional view of celibacy as a social failure, even a crime against society, the consciously deliberate rejection of marriage on the part of an increasing number of urban women appears to be a courageous, indeed daring deed. The reasons for rejection are manifold: this may well mean a 'no' to marriage arranged by kin or to polygamy, or it may be a personal and deliberate choice of freedom and emancipation through a professional career felt to be incompatible with customary marital life.

A survey of Botanga females in Cameroon has shown single women as having a solid intellectual background or being in waged employment as nurses, secretaries, waitresses — some of them even having a second job. All this prompts the conclusion that the female denial of marriage is to be associated with the prejudices, particularly strong in African urban societies, against female wage labour, whatever its level might be.

It is also a fact that African women are fiercely jealous of the economic autonomy they have customarily enjoyed within their families, and such autonomy has served them as a safeguard during the critical stage of transformation by making their position less seriously affected by the loosening of kinship ties. This has been advantageous also to women of European stock, at least in such places as the few, mostly ex-Portuguese, settlements. Maria Do Carmo Medina, a lawyer from Angola, had this to say:

> Although the woman is by and large in a position of dependence and discrimination, the Angolan woman enjoys, nevertheless, both in Africa and in Europe, a degree of economic power which is different from the one she enjoys, say, in Portugal. By means of her activities, a European woman living in Angola can afford an amount of freedom which goes a little beyond the usual limits; in other words, *de facto* situations go beyond any *de jure* conditioning. It would be hard to deny that the Angolan woman has greater social freedom than the Portuguese woman.[2]

Conversely, this very autonomy has disguised and thus been indulgent to the failure of the male to assume his own responsibilities with regard to family obligations, in particular to his children's sustenance and upbringing, which today are often left altogether on women's hands.

Thus, while modernization has helped women to voice their specific needs and problems, it is none the less fraught with perils. Marriage, for instance, has become transformed more and more from a group alliance into an individual choice for a companion. Still, the right to a love match may well lead to the idealization and uncritical acceptance of a Western bourgeois model which, among other things, involves the woman's economic dependence within the family. The introduction of the woman's economic dependence into African bourgeois families has, in fact, partly taken place without any compensation.

Truly enough, only wealthy middle-class families could afford to manage without the woman's contribution, financial or otherwise — rather, they have been compelled to incorporate female labour in the family fabric, which has been remoulded along Western lines.

The African middle-class woman now must keep track of her children's school efforts and take care of her husband and the home, just like any Western middle-class housewife. Yet, shutting up a woman who is accustomed to work outside and who, thanks to her social status, has greater access to the tools of emancipation than have other women, requires a good deal of conditioning and persuasiveness.

Preface to the English Edition

This is why these women, rather than the illiterate peasant women, have been the target of a campaign on the value of domestic labour and the duties of wife and mother. This is also why debates and seminars, like that sponsored by the National Council of Catholic Women in Lusaka in December 1974, have been organized for these women. The final resolution of that seminar, approved by the assembly of women, stated: 'The woman worker ought to know that her income is only a supplement to her husband's income: she ought to be fully aware of her responsibilities as a mother and a wife and never neglect them for the sake of extra-domestic work.'[3] The educated woman wishing to put her education to good use seems to have become a hazard for the unity and the harmony of the family. According to a woman's magazine from Ghana,

> Women who talk of liberation seem to forget that they were born to be subordinate to men. Many modern families have been wrecked by the attitude of females who have found this hard to accept. Such is the case with a large number of educated women. You can see them treat their husbands with a heavy hand, and keep the house and the purse strings under strict control: they actually dominate the man. His relations are kept at a distance, while they [educated women] become ever more arrogant.[4]

Nationalism and liberation wars were the fertile soil on which 'new' notions of the woman's role budded and the early 'modern' women's organizations took root: governments, parties and political movements were confronted with issues familiar to Western women's organizations: notably, autonomy and separatism, even though in Africa they were presented in 'historically' different terms, at least formally so — and affected by an antifeminist stance: for the image of African feminism is the folkloric one conveyed to us by the mass media.

Therefore, it makes sense, I believe, to look into the role currently being played in the new African states by women's organizations as the political countenance of the feminine conscience. Their history has not been written yet, and it surely has some surprises in store. African societies are rich in female organizations and associations. Traditional organizations are mostly of the mutual aid or guild variety, which no doubt have attained considerable social and bargaining power but, as corporative bodies are still void of real political influence.

The general trend seems to be towards mutual aid associations and away from enterprises or more directly economic units, which is hardly surprising since female trades and 'practices' — for example commerce in West Africa — will inevitably lose ground in a modern market economy.

On the whole, official political organizations are taking an active part in supporting state politics and collaborating on various projects: in authoritarian or despotic states — for example, in Mobutu's Zaire — such collaboration has often turned into 'collaborationism'. In societies of this kind there cannot be any room for autonomous female organizations engaged in a struggle for liberation: militant liberated women may solely act in opposition, well inside underground revolutionary parties and movements, and thus within the context of a more general and complex struggle.

The starting point in countries where a liberation war took place was quite different: as for instance, in the former Portuguese colonies. Then and there, women's movements originated as resistance movements, promoted by politically charismatic women such as Deodolinda Rodriguez, the founder of OMA, the Angolan women's organization. It is certainly symptomatic of a more general awareness that in Angola the woman question was, very early, a live issue: this is a common fight — said the women — and female emancipation is its main objective. The following testimonies are strongly suggestive of a climate blessed with political commitment.

Maria Do Carmo Medina, again:

> I do not believe that the emancipation of women will ever be handed over on a silver plate by some party or political movement. I do believe instead, that in order to achieve equality in the new society, women must express their will to achieve it .... It is also my conviction that in this particular moment women must stand and fight united: it would not be in our interest to separate the objectives of our struggle in this extremely delicate stage of our national life.[5]

Maria Do Céu Carmo Reis, a MPLA member:

> The struggle for emancipation of the Angolan woman is now essentially her struggle in an anti-colonialist and anti-imperialist revolutionary organization for the complete and final independence of Angola. It is only by participating in a revolutionary organization that the woman may set in motion the process of her emancipation.[6]

Lisete Antas, a member of the *Frente Socialista de Angola*:

> A primary objective of our revolution is the abolition of the colonial-fascist exploitative system, against which we have been fighting for 18 years. Our revolution purposes to create a new society in which everybody may enjoy equal rights regardless of their sex, race or religion. It is only in this perspective that the question of female emancipation can make a proper start.[7]

The Angolan Resistance saw the coming into being of the 'Deodolinda Rodriguez Centres', early forms of aggregation of women and initial reference points for them, which were repeatedly obliterated during the war. Following the proclamation of independence and the final victory of MPLA, OMA defined its political nature as being that of a women's organization acting independently of the state and side by side with MPLA.

Following is an extract from its Statute:

> OMA is an autonomous mass organization with no links with the State. MPLA orientates and directs politically the organization of Angolan women, which takes up MPLA's proposals and political line....
> Art. 4: Objectives: a) To fight beside MPLA in order to eliminate the imperialist forces and any other source of oppression of the Angolan people, and also to create a society promoting the social, political, economic and cultural advancement of the Angolan woman; b) to integrate the woman with equal rights in the life of the nation....
> Art. 7: It is the members' duty to learn MPLA's statute, programme and political line and work for their enforcement.[8]

Such full subordination of OMA to MPLA has general political reasons, among which is the need for defence against infiltrations: it can certainly be at least partly justified by the peculiar situation in Angola, which in 1976 was still rather fluid. Yet, it does make OMA's action unnecessarily problematic, not very effective and politically not very credible.

As a result, the best qualified women who were involved in a major effort to reconstruct the political and economic framework of their country refused to operate in a second-class organization, and at the same time charged OMA leaders with 'incompetence' and the organization itself with exacerbating female 'segregation'. Indeed, the leadership has been falling into the hands of urban women who have never taken part in a guerrilla war and have scanty political experience. Thus, the debate on the expediency of a separate organization, which was very much alive during the guerrilla war, has both involved and divided women.

Boavida, the Portuguese wife of an Angolan doctor who fell in the Resistance, says:

> When we first set our minds on the creation of OMA, there was a good deal of controversy. I, for one, have always believed that, since it is in MPLA's statute that men and women have equal rights, so the latter should be integrated in the policies of the movement; but others declared for a separate organization. I would now agree to this, as experience has brought home to me that there are specific feminine issues. Particularly now, after independence, women are faced with different problems to men; besides, a separate organization makes the work inside the movement easier.[9]

Whereas female leadership was aware of the instrumental approach to the woman question (reflected in the policies and modalities of the organization) and rejected it, though with profoundly different motivations, the rank and file have shown a more dramatic awareness of their role by defending the existence and the work of the organization.

Thus, a member from Cabinda:

> We just cannot leave all the revolutionary work to men. We do not only have our duties towards the home; we also have our obligations to the revolution. If women stay at home, the revolution will not make a single step forward. We want to show the world that we women are quite able to do some constructive work. Men say that OMA is not working and so it is producing nothing. We will prove that the opposite is true.[10]

Indeed, these women have been building their own centres and financing them by means of such activities as cultivating and selling the produce of collective market gardens, or the sale of handicrafts.

At the various branches of OMA in Luanda, volunteers have promoted educational courses for children as well as evening classes for adults. As soon as the courses have reached a substantial level of attendance, the women of OMA have claimed government recognition and some remuneration for the teachers.

It is above all the OMA women who have taken care of the children orphaned by the war. It was significant to note that only males were to be seen in the children's centres: 'Boys are only a burden' — they explained to me — 'girls can more easily find lodging with their kin in return for some help in the home.'

Various OMA branches have also been functioning as assistance centres for women encumbered with family problems — and there are many of them: 'It is getting worse daily', one of the leaders said to me. There, battered women turn for help, and they are usually taken to hospital or to the police by the leaders themselves, who at times even supply some provisional accommodation. Assistance at all levels and intervention in everyday issues seem, therefore, to have been a first priority in the political activities of the organization.

Such tangible and impassioned participation in the rebuilding of a nation might well be a moment of force for women, since popular, and notably female, mobilization may assume a directly political dimension transcending the aid or solidarity aims characteristic of the single initiative.

It is the same old story. Similar phenomena have occurred in other times and in different contexts. If solidarity does not become a 'message pressing the case for a full awareness of one's own rights and a struggle for them', then it may well turn once again from a moment of force into a moment of inertia ultimately bound to cause further political marginalization.

Notes

1. From a duplicated document, 1976.
2. From an interview given to ABC, No.11 (27-12-74).

3. Clara Sikaneta, 'The Progress by Women', in *Zambia Daily Mail*, 20 December 1974.
4. Matthew Ayinde, 'Who is an Ideal Woman?', in *Ideal Woman*, September 1974.
5. From an interview given to ABC, op.cit.
6. Ibid.
7. Ibid.
8. *Estatutos da Organizacâo da Mulher Angolana* — OMA, Luanda, 1976.
9. Author's interviews, August-September 1976.
10. Ibid.

Foreword

> Open this door, softly
> In you go!
> In the shadow is sitting
> A woman a mother a bride a widow
> Sobbing
> What are you doing, you fool?
> Don't go away
> Out of the shadow
> Her voice will rise
> Anon
>
> *Mweya Tol'Ande*
> (a Zairean poet)

In Italy information on the political, social and economic realities of the whole African continent is scanty.

In the March-April 1970 *Città Futura* special issue on Africa, among the reasons for such 'poor information about class struggle in Africa . . . even among left-wingers . . . in fact poorer than that about any other place on earth', mention was made of the 'direct and gigantic interests' Italy as well as the rest of Europe has in Africa. According to *Città Futura*, therefore, there is 'every good, class reason to keep so-called public opinion blissfully ignorant'.

As Fanon aptly points out, any colonial or neo-colonial politics smacks of racialism:

> Racialism makes itself glaringly conspicuous as soon as it identifies with a shameless exploitation of one group of people on the part of some other group which has attained a more advanced stage of technical development. This is why military and economic oppression almost invariably precedes, prepares and legitimizes racialism. Thus, we should abandon any notion we may have of racialism as an attitude of the mind or a psychological taint.[1]

The news and pictures of Africa in our media often have an exotic tinge, and exoticism may well be a way of expressing racial prejudice. Such an approach has frequently been endorsed by those of our left-wingers to whom Africa appears to be, in the words of *Città Futura*, 'a classless continent, fighting for generic liberties and not for socialism.' To such a prejudice we may reasonably ascribe the long silence or the hurried news, for instance, on the guerrilla war in the former Portuguese colonies: leftist newspapers, at least initially, have portrayed the struggle of the people of Angola as no more than a 'dramatic appendage' to the events in Portugal. Portugal — as leftist observers put it after 'the revolution with the carnations' — has 'left behind' its colonies, thus making the Portuguese appear to be more genuinely revolutionaries than the Africans, even though the latter have been engaged for over a decade in an anti-imperialistic armed struggle, which no doubt is the first and true cause of the collapse of fascism in Portugal.

The image of women in colonized countries, of course, better lends itself to a finding of the 'exotic', and consequently lends credibility to a racist interpretation of the African world.

Some anthropologists have used their analysis of the position of women in African cultures to argue the superiority of Western culture. In 'primitive' societies, they say, women are little more than slaves, whereas in Western societies women are treated in a 'civilized' manner. These anthropologists have simply translated the early colonists' complaints that the polygamous tribesman 'had too much land, too much leisure and too much sex. Instead of working for his master — as his proper lot would be — he grew fat in idleness and capitalized on his wives' work'.[2] Such principles on the part of these colonists were well in tune with their economic interests, notably with their hunger for land and cheap labour.

To Evans-Pritchard, on the contrary, the status of 'primitive' women is not all that different from that of modern Western women; which suggests that the generally agreed upon inferiority of women does not solely depend on surmountable economic and social factors, but rather on their 'natural' inferiority.[3]

On the other hand, tribal customs, the family and traditional morals are unreservedly extolled by some African nationalists. Henry Ngoa, a sociologist from Cameroon, suavely argues that 'the African woman has never been oppressed' and tries to prove it by comparing her status to that of the Western white woman, undeniably oppressed throughout centuries of Christianity and still the subject of political, economic, social, cultural and religious discrimination.[4]

This book is not concerned with a confrontation between diverse cultural values. Yet the very diversity of African culture cannot be ignored, since the analysis of a social structure so profoundly different from our own may quite significantly reveal the extent of interdependence, in Africa as well as in Europe, between the social position of women and their work, and also between the familial and social role of the woman and the exploitation (or utilization) of her work.

However, any attempt to grasp the nature of the problem of underdevelopment implies an analysis of how capitalism has transformed previous social and familial structures in order to use men's and women's labour in new and different ways. Otherwise, there would be no possibility of understanding the process of the restructuring of African societies by capitalism and consequently the nature of capitalism itself.

Matrilineal areas will mainly be considered as the places where cultural differences are most obvious and significant, while any 'geographical' abstraction will be avoided in the awareness that nowadays any tribe is part of a national context — a fact only too often overlooked by anthropologists.

The heterogeneity of traditional cultures makes the task particularly difficult. Also,

> the social structures of African countries are the result of at least three superimposed cultural stratifications: the traditional and pre-industrial phase, the colonial experience, and the post-colonial economico-political structure. Each of these realities varies from country to country, and everywhere the position of women depends very much on the interplay of these three elements.[5]

It is, nevertheless, possible to draw from the various cultures such common elements — whether traditional or brought about by the process of colonization — as to provide significant continuity to the theme of this book.

My analysis will start by stating that all African women are politically and economically dependent. This, no doubt, is 'a common trait to all African states as in each of them the economic system is, in a more or less direct and noticeable way, dominated by Western capitalism and is typical of a neo-colonial society'.[6]

By trying to integrate the various levels of analysis, i.e., the cultural, the economic, the jural, etc., it is feasible to attempt a judicious, general analysis of women's position in African societies. Such a way of approaching the problem allows one to go beyond the ethnographic or merely sociological data and straight to the heart of the 'feminine question' as a basically political question.

Notes

1. F. Fanon, *Opere scelte*, Torino, Einaudi, 1971, Vol.1, p.54.
2. R.S. Suttner, 'The Legal Status of African Women in South Africa', in *African Social Research*, No.8, December 1969.
3. E.E. Evans-Pritchard, *La Donna nelle Societa' Primitive*, Bari, Laterza, 1973.
4. In his 33-page booklet *Non, la Femme Africaine n'etait pas opprimee*, H. Ngoa endeavours to demonstrate that the African woman is a free and autonomous being by quoting, e.g., the fact that not only does she not lose her maiden name upon marriage but she can even pass it on

to her son, such being the case with some tribes. In conclusion, he recalls the wisdom of the Beti people, in whose eyes a woman is like 'a safe gangway between man and his origins, his ancestors and the beyond.' (Reviewed in *Amina*, No.37, July 1975).
5. M. Glisenti, 'La Donna Africana nel Contesto della Dipendenza', in *Politica Internazionale*, No.12, December 1975.
6. *Ibid.*

1. Colonization and Social Change

Traditional Africa and Colonization

An analysis of the present social standing of the African woman and the function of her activities within a developing economy must necessarily be rooted in the nature of 'traditional' African societies.

It is, nevertheless, difficult if not impossible to ascertain to what extent some social and familial structures of today are a mirror of 'tradition' rather than a product of the process of colonization. In retrospect, it is hard to justify the enthusiasm of those early anthropologists who, as they carried out their field research came to regard African societies as 'intact', that is unaffected by European influence. In fact, since 1500, well before the colonial conquest, even though the European presence was confined to short coastal tracts, it fostered profound political and economic changes; slavery had either directly or indirectly caused the breakdown of the old societies: through slave trade the Western economy had made itself felt in the remotest areas of Africa, even before the tribes of the interior had met a single white man.

About Angola, Davidson had this to say: 'Other influences, notably the increasing sale of African slaves to overseas plantation owners, conspire to bring law and order to ruin: their consequences will slowly enfeeble the social texture of these lands.'[1] This can well apply to the entire sub-Saharan continent, where the slave trade 'caused a regular loss of productive manpower, whose main effect was the thwarting of the process of development all over the continent.'[2] Contact with the West had, therefore, changed and disrupted the 'traditional' African societies well before their direct and violent clash with European colonialism.

While capitalist penetration and the ensuing colonial régime do not by themselves bring the death of autochthonous cultures, they do contribute to radical change.[3] Max Gluckman is one of the few anthropologists who has fully highlighted this phenomenon. When in the 1940s he studied the economy of the Lozi, an influential tribe of present-day Zambia, he stressed the fact that:

> as soon as British sovereignty was established on the Lozi kingdom, and even more later, when the minerals of Northern Rhodesia, the timber

and the soil were subsequently exploited by the Whites, the Lozi became part of a large economy based on different social relations which radically altered their internal relations. In effect, so great were the changes that an entire social system has now become the object of our study.[4]

Naturally, the colonial conquest caused different reactions in different societies (depending, *inter alia*, on whether or not the area became a settlement colony) and variously affected the process of social change. Yet the consequences of colonization and the ensuing phenomena are all similar or comparable.

One of the most frequent consequences was the breakdown of the family structure and the traditional, kinship grouping, followed by a transformation of the social function of the family that inevitably, primarily affected the traditional sexual division of labour: such transformation took place under the violent pressure of the forces of colonialism. The residential structure for instance which mirrors and supports the tribal socio-familial organization was profoundly and irretrievably upset, first by the military conquest and secondly by the politics of the colonial administration.

In analysing the residential structure of the Ngoni — another influential tribe of Zambia, formerly living in the Fort Jameson district which is now Chipata — Barnes explains:

> The physical dispersion of the people vis-à-vis the British troops was followed by an even larger dispersion in mining villages . . . . Large villages, once the very heart of the old residential system, were burned down and their inhabitants never came together again . . . . [After the 1898 diaspora following the anti-colonial war] people lived in small settlements made up of just a few thatched huts on the hill or in the wood. Later they gradually reunited in villages, yet what a structural change from the early village people! . . . About 1912, the white administration resorted to the policy of reducing the number of villages by amalgamating them in spite of the fact that they had nothing in common except their being neighbours. From about 1920 onwards, new immigrants, mostly from the Cewa tribe, began to move in following their eviction from the land in favour of the Whites . . . . These villages became the local administrative units.[5]

In the former Belgian Congo too, the colonial administration opted for a policy of greater concentration of the population, with a view to more easily controlling them, politically and physically. In fact the population grouping mainly carried out in the 1920s made it easier for tax-collectors and administrators to pay frequent visits to the villages and thus 'establish normal relations with them'.[6]

At all events, 'the villages of today are by no means a faithful image of the past'.[7] Even though among some populations, clusters showing the characteristic ring-like arrangement and scattered dwellings still claim to be a federation of small, clannish villages, most people have lost the habit of grouping their dwellings by lineage. Likewise, the replacement of the traditional, with Western style houses — that is to say, built for a 'stable' working population and only destined for small families — does not take place by means of a peaceful and gradual process. In other words, it is not a case of a mere *cultural* (even if more or less traumatic) and only indirectly political change, but of a violent imposition of a different way of life and a different domestic organization.

> The ground house with a 2/3/4 -slope thatched roof, the only type to be seen nowadays, was introduced and imposed throughout the Congo by the Belgian colonial authorities . . . . We don't know if a specific law concerning it is in force: all our researches to this purpose have yielded no result so far; but at the turn of the 1940s we did see sanitary officers demolish thatched houses. The people were then ordered to build themselves new ground houses whose minimum dimensions had been fixed by the authorities, and to burn down the old houses. The traditional dwelling was indeed right-angled yet entirely built with plaited or woven straw, and resting on a timber framework.[8]

The significance and the real scope of these measures become clear if we consider the 'traditional' familial organization of such societies, in which kinship is an element of the economic infrastructure. It is first and foremost by means of various 'marriage rights' such as the husband's right over his wife's or wives' work or the right of the parents-in-law-to-be to the son-in-law's labour, that the necessary work for social reproduction is secured: kinship relationships express production relationships, and vice versa.[9] Moreover, as we shall later see, the social control of production takes place through kinship relationships. The woman, namely her work and her function as a reproducer of labour force, is naturally at the centre of this system.

The changes, the contradictions and the tensions inside the traditional family structure are not simply a reflection of economic transformations but a primary cause of them: thus the aggression wrought upon the family organization makes up the first chapter of the Western economic penetration into Africa.

Introduction of Wage Labour and its Social Implications

The colonizing process means the introduction of cash economy and wage labour upon a basically common pattern in the whole of Africa. The African farm labourer's 'response' to the 'stimulus' of taxes imposed by colonial governments and the replacement of local goods with European goods which can only be acquired by cash, was the quest for wage labour either in European-owned plantations or in mines. Yet in Africa, wage labour originally took the form of forced labour. The fact is that the availability of a local labour force was an obvious prerequisite for the capitalist exploitation of mineral and agricultural resources and, as A.J. Hanna puts it on Rhodesia, 'on realizing that the African labourers they wished to take on preferred to spend their days chatting under a tree, the early colonists turned to the governors and invoked coercion'.[10]

Another problem was the density of the local population, generally low and inadequate to meet the demand for workers on the part of mine owners and plantationists. This led to compulsory recruitment of manpower, either directly by colonial administrators or through special recruitment bodies, causing the shifting *en masse* of adult males.

Out of compulsion or out of 'free' choice, men shifted from country to country and from workplace to workplace, sometimes covering long distances:

> Year after year, from either side of the continent, hundreds and thousands of men move from one territory to another. . . . Boundaries and borders, open or closed as they may be, do not make much difference for these men ceaselessly roaming in search of some wage labour. . . . A map of all these annual migrations throughout Africa would show a web of paths as they were traced by these labourers on the move.[11]

At times, mass migration may be a way of escaping from the various forms of colonial, local exploitation. During the colonial period, for instance, people staged a mass emigration from Upper Volta, driven into it by the system of forced labour brought in by the colonial authorities to carry out such of their 'development' projects as the construction of ports, bridges, roads, or the Abidjan-Niger railway and the Bamako-Thiès railway. Migrations are also largely the result of forced recruitment. It has been reckoned that in 1936 the European companies operating in the Ivory Coast were employing about 20,000 workers from Upper Volta, only half of whom could be described as 'voluntary' migrants, the rest being supplied by recruitment officers.

In fact, still in 1936, as soon as the French authorities introduced some reforms and, at least on paper, abolished forced labour, many people left the plantations and the 'labour centres'. By about 1947, the flow of work from Upper Volta had dwindled to the extent of becoming inadequate for the needs for manpower in the Ivory Coast plantations; the effect was that in 1951 the plantation owners were forced to set up an association for the supply of workforce, whose main task was the actual recruitment of workers in Upper Volta for the Ivory Coast plantations. In other words, it was back to some form of forced labour, albeit in disguise.

In 1960 the government of Upper Volta put an end to such activities and on the 9 March an agreement was reached with the Ivory Coast to regulate the recruitment and employment terms of its workers. In spite of this and other more specific agreements, the vast majority of emigrant workers remain without the protection of any law or regulation — and 'over 12 years after independence the pattern of the Upper Volta emigration is basically not different from that of the last years of the colonial history, except for the fact that financial considerations play a bigger role in the decision to emigrate.'[12] Obviously, all this constant mass shifting around was bound to exert some influence upon the tribal societal structures as well as upon the customs and the way of life of the African peoples.

It has been argued by more than one observer that a migratory stream mixes people and thus can help break ethnic barriers. Actually, migrant labour coupled with mere subsistence wages, has, by strengthening the ties with their ethnic groupings and making them compete with workers from other areas only increased the material and psychological dependence of the migrants on their native villages. This system has been instrumental in exacerbating or even creating tribalism and racial rivalries.[13]

A glance at the data supplied by the 1960-61 demographic survey in Upper Volta (see Tables 1A, B and C) will suffice for anyone to realize what the system of migrant labour really means in social terms. The migratory flow is mainly made up of adult males: unmarried men appear at the top of Table 1C as those who are away from home more often and for longer periods, divorced men are second, and polygamous men last. Women stay away for shorter periods and basically move within the country, that is to say, not far from their birthplaces. Thus migration is 'generally' conducive to a marked imbalance of the sex and age population structure. In economic terms, this has primarily meant a precipitous decline of the rural areas.

Table 1A
Population (%) Away From Home According to the 1960-61 Demographic Survey: Upper Volta

Sex	In Upper Volta	Abroad	Residence Unknown	Total
M	5.4	6.2	0.2	11.8
F	5.0	0.9	0.2	6.1
Total	10.4	7.1	0.4	17.9

Table 1B
Population (%) Away From Home According to the 1960-61 Demographic Survey: Upper Volta: Length of Absence

Length of Absence	M	F
1 month	23.3	40.2
1-5 months	26.7	23.7
6-11 months	6.7	6.1
1 year	14.3	10.4
2-3 years	22.7	15.4
4 years and over	7.0	4.2

Table 1C
Population (%) Aged 14+ Away From Home as Shown by the 1960-61
Demographic Survey: Upper Volta: Marital Status

Marital Status	Males Away from home	Males Away for over 6 months	Females Away from home	Females Away for over 6 months
Single	29.8	18.3	6.4	2.8
Widowers	6.6	2.9	6.3	2.1
Divorced	17.2	7.3	2.7	0.7
Married	9.5	3.5	4.1	1.3
Monogamous	11.3	4.3	—	—
Polygamous	5.8	1.9	—	—
Total	16.4	8.6	5.9	1.9

Source: A. Songre, *Mass Emigration from Upper Volta: the Facts and Implications*, in various authors, *Employment in Africa*, Geneva, ILO, 1973.

It has been maintained by some that this decline was due to the preponderance of adult women in rural areas, which would consequently lower the standard of economic activities. This sounds somewhat simplistic, and I am inclined to believe that it is not merely the use of unskilled female labour that should be blamed for the poorer productivity, but the disruption of the female/male ratio and thus of the sexual division of labour. In fact women are customarily responsible for food crop farming, men for cash crop farming. It follows that when many men are away, cash crop farming will invariably decrease. This affects the rural people's capacity for making money by farming — which is the only means they have in their areas — and consequently, the supply of money in rural areas will become more and more dependent on the remittance money from workers' wage labour. The attempt in many areas, well before independence, to stabilize the migrant labourers in labour centres often led to the disruption of the supply sources and to the cutting or weakening of the rural-urban ties.[14] At the same time, the lack of development plans brought many a rural area to collapse, as will be shown later.

The stagnation of agricultural production and the disorderly yet unstoppable 'boom' in towns, largely due to women flocking into urban centres around the 1960s, are no doubt among the major socio-economic problems of the newly independent states.

Migrant Labour and the Family: the Zambian Case

The European Penetration into Zambia
Western penetration into Zambia was not the effort of groups of pioneers,

but rather the deed of private companies which directly administered the country for years.

Upon settlement, the British South Africa Company bargained with the local chiefs for a formal acknowledgement of their own authority and managed to win a few of them over: in 1890 F.E. Lochner, for instance, acquired the exclusive rights of subsoil exploitation and trade from Lewanika, the Barotse supreme chief, against an annual payment of £850. Probably upon the advice of a French missionary, Lewanika succeeded in leaving the Barotse valley proper out of the definitive concession of 1898. Under his authority, this became a native reserve and later the Protectorate of Barotseland. To all appearances, however, the company's scant interest in the area was due to its dearth of minerals, and its unhealthy climate, rather than to the king's dubious political cleverness.

The BSA Company administered North-East Rhodesia and North-West Rhodesia (which were to form Northern Rhodesia in 1911) directly through an administrator appointed by the Company and liable to them. Only in 1924 did the Company make the administration over to the Colonial Office.

The so-called process of modernization of present day Zambia, through the introduction of a cash economy and wage labour, was not all that different from that of other African countries: forced labour and 'voluntary emigration' played a major role in such a process. In fact, in order to secure a regular supply of African manpower, recruitment bodies operated up to 1932, when such a policy was abolished as by then there was enough 'voluntary' manpower. The Rhodesia Native Labour Bureau, established by the BSA Company in 1903, was the main body active in Zambia; the creation of 'reserves' mainly served to control and channel the movement of the local labour force. Such policy of internment and segregation of the local populations had disastrous effects on the traditional African economy. Much of the land 'reserved' for the Africans was actually uninhabitable and miles away from any stream or perennial water source, and since the population tended to concentrate in the few inhabitable areas (see Table 2), the reserves were soon over-crowded.

In its turn, the pressure from over-crowding made the land poorer and poorer — a fact which was summarily blamed upon the 'primitive' farming methods of the Africans. In the Abercorn region 'things were made even worse by the fact that the millions of acres the Africans were forced to evacuate were not occupied by Europeans, and in the absence of human occupants they were invaded by the tsetse flies.'[15] The gravity of the situation in the reserves called for a 'resettlement', which took place in the years between 1940 and 1947 and once again produced arbitrary and forced movements of whole village communities and even entire populations.

During the first decade of this century some projects at a high occupational level, such as the Livingstone-Katanga railway (1904-1909), the lead and zinc mine at Broken Hill (now Kabwe) from 1902, and the copper mines at Kansanshi from 1908, were the major sources of work in the country. Nevertheless, on the whole the local employment opportunities were very low indeed and many workers moved to Rhodesia, South Africa, and

Women of Africa

Zaire, which they were to leave again on the occasion of the 1931 crisis: no strong flow of local labour was underway in the copper mines before 1925.[16]

Yet in Zambia a remarkable concentration of wage-earners took place after the 1920s: in 1927 there were 11,000 African workers in the local mines, and by 1930 their number had increased to 30,000. In 1937, some 20,000 Africans from every part of the country were working within the Copperbelt. As might be expected, no women were among them.

Table 2
Population Density in the Reserves of the Eastern Province: 1924 and 1942

Reserves	Area (sq. miles)	1924 Population Number & Density		1942 Population Number & Density	
Msandili	264	15,151	57	22,539	85
Ngoni	784	42,961	55	63,561	81
Chewa	756	37,045	49	53,350	70
Zumwanda	177	5,707	32	9,800	55
Fort Jameson reserve total	*1,981*	*100,864*	*51*	*149,250*	*75*
Nsenga	960	38,450	40	43,218	45
Lusandwa	172	5,000	29	6,213	36
Petauke	293	5,500	19	6,666	23
Wambo	44	1,050	24	2,308	53
Chilinga	16	500	31	1,263	79
Petauke reserve total	*1,485*	*50,500*	*34*	*59,668*	*40*

Source: G. Kay, *Changing Patterns of Settlement and Land Use in the Eastern Province of Northern Rhodesia*, University of Hull, 1965.

The Emigration of Women in the Colonial Period

For a better understanding of the vicissitudes of female migration,[17] we should distinguish an early stage when only primary production, namely the exploitation of mining resources by means of a high turnover of labour force, was vital to the colonial capitalist system — from a later stage, such as in Zambia now, during which an attempt was made to stabilize the local labour force.

In the early stage the colonial government tried very hard to discourage female migration by enacting specific ordinances and prompting the native authorities (particularly after Indirect Rule was introduced in 1929) to forbid or restrict the movement of women, and especially of single women. The aim of this was both to have a frequent replacement of migrant labour and consequently keep labourers toing and froing between labour centres, and to hold women as near-hostages in their villages so that their husbands would be lured into going home and thus a regular and foreseeable ebb and tide of manpower would be ensured.

The native authorities willingly submitted to the pressure from the colonial government; very likely they were even more interested than the government itself to control the movement of the female labour force, as their power was essentially based on the rural areas and the control of the traditional economy. Heisler comments that: 'The policy before 1953 has an obvious meaning: the native authorities wanted to make sure that the men away from their villages would go back.'[18]

Yet, keeping the women within their tribal areas had first of all an economic significance of paramount importance: it was mainly the women who kept the fundamental sector of the traditional village economy going, which was expected, among other things, to reabsorb the labour force when they were ill, old or had been ejected from the advanced, European economic sector: women conventionally tied to farming represented the core of the labour force occupied in subsistence farming. With this in mind, the native authorities were stricter than the colonial authorities in anticipating the movements of the female labourers; likewise their sentences upon any woman who contravened their proclamations were more severe. For example in 1924, the sentence passed by a native court[19] upon a woman found guilty of disobeying a proclamation dating back to 1916, to the effect that neither a single woman nor a wife unaccompanied by her husband was allowed to leave the Mumbwa district unless in possession of a special authority, was quashed by the High Court of Justice.

Legal restrictions on women were much the same in every ward: among the Ngoni, for instance, women were not allowed to go outside the tribal area without their husbands, or a pass issued by the native authorities; likewise, among the Chewa, in the Eastern Province, women going out of the Province were expected to be in company with their husbands or to produce a proper marriage certificate.

Up to 1953, the native authorities exercised their control over the women's movements by the use and open political manipulation of the marriage institution. Formally organized as local governments, native authorities were in fact based in rural areas, never in towns; and, since they had the exclusive right to register marriages, these had perforce to be celebrated in rural areas: a legal marriage in town was very difficult if not impossible to obtain. Thus, a husband-to-be was bound to return to his village, while a woman could not leave it except on clearly specified conditions, such as her legal marriage well proven by a certificate (and marriage registration is still optional), her husband's agreement, and so on. Moreover, the native authorities would not grant any certificate concerning unions they regarded as irregular, such as, in their eyes, the marriage of a couple from diverse tribal areas.

In 1939, the recently created Urban Native Courts applied to the government for permission to register the marriages of those urbanites who could prove that their rural kinship approved of their marriages. Their application was rejected. Only on 16 April 1953, on the strength of an administrative circular, were the Urban Native Courts granted the authority to issue marriage certificates, but only after they had ascertained that any applicant had broken off 'all normal relationships with rural areas', or when the native authorities were unable, because of their administrative inefficiency, to issue certificates themselves.

Of course such an abnormal situation led either directly or indirectly to disturbances and riots. Following the investigation on the 1935 tumults in labour centres, the regulations concerning women's movements were reviewed and made even more restrictive. The colonial administrators decided that they should help the native authorities to enforce the rules of female migration; also, any woman clandestinely working in a labour centre should be sent back to her village, in spite of the Commission on Native Labour's explicit advice to the contrary, which was ignored. This resolution was officially confirmed in 1945 along with the government's pledge to encourage repatriation by supplying free transport. Lastly, the practice of combing out urban women and taking them back to their villages under the escort of a native authority was made legal.

In its report on the workers' conditions in Northern Rhodesia issued in 1938, the Commission on Native Labour had also pointed out the presence of 'delinquent children' in labour centres: this prompted the authorities to deal with them more rapidly than they had with the women.

The Department of African Education carried out a survey of the infant population on the Copperbelt, especially with reference to its educational needs, and resolved to appropriate £1,000 . . . for the repatriation of the children who either were not under the direct control of their parents or were not school children! It was the mining companies who resisted the radical proposal to send back all the African children, regardless of their parents' wishes: at all events, by May 1942 several hundred children had been repatriated. Needless to say, such 'family politics' did not even contemplate divorce: getting married was hard enough, divorcing was even harder. 'Divorce may not actually give a woman the freedom to migrate, but it may well dampen a man's desire to go back to the rural system.'[20]

In a study on the Luvale people it has been argued that the prolonged absence of a migrant husband can justify only seven out of 100 divorce proceedings. Such a low percentage cannot solely be explained by the oft-quoted fact that many of the migrants were young bachelors and only few of them stayed away for more than four years, plus the fact that, besides farming, women had an income of their own. Actually, 'among the Luvale the percentage of divorces caused by labour migration would perhaps have been higher had it not been for the attitude of the rural authorities.'[21]

The Native Courts proclaimed that it was their duty towards a tribe's migrant not to grant his wife an easy divorce. Even though different tribes had different ways, it was generally taken for granted, within the first two or three years of absence, that the man would be back, even if he had never sent any word home meantime: therefore a desertion of less than two years could never be a cause for divorce. Thus, among the Lozi a woman could claim a divorce for desertion only at the end of a three year absence, since the Court had decreed that she was married to 'a man, not to a blanket'; in the Northern Province, in the 1950s a woman could get a divorce only at the end of 'five years without help of any sort', whereas a Tonga woman in the Southern Province could apply for a divorce after a short time on the grounds that 'she had married a man, not a remittance'.[22]

Women living in an uxorilocal residential system were less dependent and better protected, whereas those living in their husband's village grew more and more dependent on his kin. These women could earn money only by brewing beer, making vases, or by working on the plantations. But plantation work meant escaping the surveillance of their husband's kin, who could accuse them of going in search of a lover or a new husband. The husband's kin would keep an eye open for these women in order to prevent them committing adultery or to denounce them if they did. If the relatives were in touch with the man, they would write to him about their suspicions: sometimes the man paid no attention, but at others he might send instructions or show up at the village unannounced.

Labour migrants often sent money, and some of them sent blankets or various other goods to the village by their friends who went back. Sometimes these presents were sent directly to their wives, though more often they thought it wiser to send them to their fathers or brothers, who would pass the presents on only if they felt that the women had behaved well enough to deserve them. By accepting a gift, a woman would indicate that she regarded herself as still dependent on her husband. On the other hand, if she applied for a divorce on the grounds of desertion, his kin could produce the gifts as evidence that he had no intention of deserting her. The woman would then go to court wearing her oldest and shabbiest clothes, both to show that her husband had defaulted on his traditional duty to provide her clothes and to show that she did not wish to attract any other man. It was, nevertheless, easier for a woman to prove desertion when her man was still living in the country than when he was working in town and wrote to her only rarely.

In pre-colonial days, divorce was granted by the village assembly; Native Courts were a colonial institution. As Barnes notes: 'My impression is that women are less favoured in courts than they are in villages.'[23] In fact courts would set greater store by the formalities of the customary marriage and the rights related to the diverse kinds of bridewealth than would village assemblies. The chiefs, councillors, officials and the police, all of them court members, were men, while in a village assembly old or important women gave their opinions and were attentively listened to. Also with regard to this, the colonial administration proved to be less inflexible than the native courts: often in fact the administration even urged the courts to proceed with cases about women long deserted. Barnes mentions the remarkable case of a district officer granting the divorce to a number of deserted women who had applied in vain to the Native Courts.

The native authorities' control was enforced in 1933 by an Ordinance on the employment of women, youths and children, which aimed not just at keeping women and children within their villages, but also at making clandestine migration impossible by depriving women of any legal opportunity of finding a means of supporting herself in town. Such policy found its 'moral' motivation in attitudes regarded as 'traditional'. The Mambwe notion of 'dignity', for example, forbade women to find work by themselves: a woman showing such degree of independence was assumed to be immoral, as would a single woman going to stay in town.

As we have seen, married women, too, found it difficult to follow their husbands to town; this was not due to legal restrictions but to the fact that, as we shall see later, men's wages were calculated on the basis of the presumed bare essentials of a bachelor. Some traditional customs also influence a wife's freedom of movement. In the Southern Province, for example, the Ila-Tonga and the Gwembe-Tonga, who traditionally were allowed to live with their wives soon after marriage, have shown themselves more 'willing' to have their wives with them in town, while it appeared to be less simple for women in uxorilocal populations. Here too, a breach of tradition frequently occurred: a husband could pay of his own accord if he so wished, and thus obtain the authority from his wife's family to take the woman away before the time allowed by tradition.

The system of migrant labour eventually emphasized the customary sexual division of labour by creating two different and often contrasting worlds: the one made up of adult males working in the 'advanced' sector of the economy, the other made up of women plus the usual appendage of the old and the very young, working in the traditional sector of the economy. This sector was also expected to take upon itself the work of the labour force expelled for longer or shorter periods from the capitalist sector.

Soon, however, mining companies realized that the quality of work in the mines could have been higher, and that productivity depended on the extent of stabilization of the labour force. Thus, from 1931 onwards, some mining companies ceased discouraging their workers from taking their wives with them at the expense of the companies themselves. Yet not all of them supplied a home for married couples, and those who did so, since it was necessary to follow some guidelines for the housing allotment, insisted that applicants should produce marriage certificates. Thus their marriage policy ended up by contradicting itself and also being at variance with their 'housing policy'.

As late as the 1950s only one third of the men living in urban areas had been joined by their wives. But at Broken Hill, as early as 1940, 45.8% of the miners lived with a wife, while in 1948 less than 40% of the miners living in the Copperbelt labour centres were part of a family unit. In 1951, however, when the family housing project was almost complete, the proportion increased to 60%, and in 1954, still within the Copperbelt, to 78%. This trend spread to all the major towns, where by 1960, 87% of the miners were living in family units.

Nevertheless, if some companies, such as those of Luanshya or Mufulira, opted early for a stable and thus more productive manpower and, therefore, encouraged family settlements, some other companies were for long in favour of a labour force that would be temporary, cheap, easily replaceable and virtually impervious to trade union propaganda.

The Migration of Women after Independence

> Husband, my husband
> Let us go together
> And love each other
> Like doves, like doves!
> (A popular Nyanja song)

The present, apparent sexual disproportion in the distribution of the Zambian population, according to the latest national census, can be still justified by the predominant male migration to urban areas or labour centres. Yet, the number of women migrating to towns is growing fast. Over the 12 months prior to September 1969, when the latest census was taken, the urban population as a whole — African, white and Asian — increased by 12.9%, only 2.5% being due to a natural increase: the proportion of women migrating to the major urban centres over this period was even higher. With regard in particular to the Copperbelt, over the same 12 month period a specific increase of the female population of 13% occurred, rising from 313,588 to 354,463 units; in Lusaka there was an increase of 15.9%, i.e., from 146,376 to 169,662 units. This seems due to the fact that after independence, women were free to join their husbands in town. The Central Statistical Office has suggested that this influx of wives is largely responsible for the extremely high rate of the urban population growth, which is, therefore, expected to decrease in the future.

The 1969 census supplies no information on the family structure in urban and rural areas, but it does supply the sex ratio in both areas. In the rural areas the ratio is 895 males per 1,000 females, while in towns it is 1,113 males per 1,000 females. The difference clearly demonstrates that, predominantly, it was the males who were moving from their villages into towns (see Table 3).

Table 3
Zambia: Population by Age and Sex, including Non-Africans, 1969

Age	Female No.	%	Male No.	%	Males per 1,000 Females
0-14	930,198	44.9	928,630	46.7	998
15-19	183,880	8.9	172,676	8.7	939
20-44	698,098	33.7	578,234	29.1	828
45-59	170,943	8.3	207,607	10.5	1,214
60+	86,865	4.2	199,864	5.0	1,150
African population only	2,042,223		1,956,421		958
Total	*2,069,984*	*100.0*	*1,987,011*	*100.0*	*960*

Source: *Census of Population and Housing* — 1969, Lusaka, Government Printer, 1973.

In 1963, the year of the previous census, however, the ratio was 1,280 males per 1,000 females in urban areas; the decrease in 1969 indicates that, contrary to what had happened during the colonial period, many men tended to take their families with them when they left their village.

If we analyse the census data per district, we will note that there is a tendency towards equalization of sex ratios in the areas of immigration and low emigration, while in the areas of higher emigration, namely in the poorest, 'rural' areas, the unequal ratio of men to women is growing (see Table 4).[24]

Table 4
Zambia — Population Structure by Sex and Ward, 1963 and 1969

	(M per 100 F) 1963	1969		(M per 100 F) 1963	1969
Central Province:			Northern Province:		
Kabwe - Urban Ward	127	110	Chinsali	93	90
Kabwe - Rural Ward	107	102	Isoka	94	86
Lusaka - Urban Ward	126	123	Kasama	93	89
Lusaka - Rural Ward	102	83	Luwingu	90	86
Mkushi	105	102	Mbala	93	88
Mumbwa	95	97	Mpika	86	87
Serenje	92	93	Mporokoso	89	94
Copperbelt:			North-West Province:		
Chililabombwe	141	114	Kabompo	83	88
Chingola	128	110	Kasempa	92	94
Kalulushi	126	112	Mwinilunga	92	89
Kitwe	134	112	Solwezi	96	96
Luanshya	119	108	Zambesi	85	87
Mufulira	118	110			
Ndola - Urban Ward	125	112	Southern Province:		
Ndola - Rural Ward	103	100	Choma	100	94
Eastern Province:			Gwembe	85	86
Chipata	89	87	Kalomo	106	98
Lundazi	83	80	Livingstone	138	122
Petauke	86	84	Mazabuka	99	99
			Namwala	93	94
Luapula:			Western Province:		
Kawambwa	95	92	Kalabo	86	84
Nansa	100	93	Kaoma	84	84
Samfya	106	92	Mongu	81	85
			Senanga	81	90
			Sesheke	98	96

Source: M.E. Jackman, *Recent Population Movements in Zambia*, Lusaka, Institute for African Studies, University of Zambia, 1973.

This seems to suggest that the greater the distance from the urban areas, the lower the 'propensity' to migrate on the part of women. In fact the majority of the women who migrated into urban areas came from adjacent districts where they were only slightly outnumbered by men. The lesser

Colonization and Social Change

inclination of women to migrate and the continuing importance of the movements country-town-country indicate that the work and the permanent residence of women in rural areas are still a fundamental issue.

The reasons are obvious. A few years after independence, Kay wrote:

> It seems that the labour force of Zambia is gradually becoming stable: men tend to stick to their jobs for longer periods or at least to stay as wage labourers for most of their lifetime, although doing different jobs in different places, and more wives and families live in towns. Nevertheless, there is still many a year to go before the system of migrant labour will be abolished or reduced to negligible proportions. Leaving any other consideration aside, the cost of a rapid change would be so huge that it could not be faced without reducing the necessary development plans. Not only should salaries be increased to allow a man to keep his family at a decent standard of living, but a whole range of social services now provided by the rural economy and the rural society should be transferred either to the employers or to the local or central governmental authorities in labour centres.[25]

As far as services and work are concerned, the surplus women in the rural system, therefore, have crucial social relevance besides being a politically balancing factor.[26]

This accounts for the lack, underlined by several field researchers, of independent migration of the female labour force: women go to town to join their husbands or their families rather than to achieve their own economic advancement. Many women, however, do migrate to free themselves of their familial dependence, but 'women living singly or without a legal husband and in economic independence . . . represent one of the most striking peculiarities of the African towns in contrast to the rural areas.'[27]

What drives these women to town? One good reason may well be the constant decay of the female status, which renders situations formerly susceptible of improvement and restoration inside the rural society itself quite intolerable. The instability of marriage is another reason. In more than one study the connection between marriage breakdown and migration has been clearly pointed out. Barrenness is another factor that may well induce the rural woman to migrate: a barren woman would feel useless in a rural system, since she cannot strengthen her relationships and create property rights for herself. Here too, the migrant woman is endeavouring to find a way out of social frustration even more than out of financial straits.

Prostitution

> Let me try
> to grind the millet
> Let me try
> to grind my way

> A few bananas
> in my compound . . .
> My breasts were taut
> The lads would look
> and look as I ground
> Mother sent 'em away:
> "Child, thou art too young
> Thou knowst not how
> to heat the water
> Thou canst but grind
> the whole of the millet"
> Now I've grown up
> and I've forgotten . . .
> My husband, you know,
> deserted me
> so long ago
> He will be back
> tomorrow, I think . . .
> He's divorcing me
> Street girls appeal to him
> more than I do
> I wanna go home.
>
> (Song of Kaonde women pounding the millet)

Urban Prostitution

The uprooting of thousands and thousands of adult males from their native places led to prostitution, that is as an exclusive, permanent, full-time and remunerated job.

Before long, the migrant workers' tracks came to be known as 'the whores' tracks' — some of them, such as the track from Muloberi to Mongu in the Barotseland, rising indeed to notoriety. The people living in the villages along this track would lure the migrants through promises of beer and women, in return for cash of course. In 1940, in five Mawiko villages on the Sonso river there lived 97 women, 41 men and just 33 children: needless to say, they were villages of whores. Prostitution became then a measure of the urban female status. Nevertheless, when the policy of stabilization of the labour force, and hence stabilization of the family, took off, things improved to some extent.

In 1945, just before the demolition of labour camps began,[28] 63% of the urban adult male population of Zambia were in a position to set up permanent heterosexual relationships. In 1951, in the Copperbelt 'towns for Africans', which had replaced the labour camps, the proportion of possibly permanent sexual unions went up to 80%; in 1963, when the 'towns for Africans' had been built, it was 82% for the whole urban system.

The growing possibility of a permanent heterosexual relationship in towns has been linked with the growing numbers of married women joining their husbands. Nonetheless, in the 1950s, at least half of the women who had migrated to the 'towns for Africans' could not be said to be wives joining their husbands as, at the time of their migration at least, they were not married to urban males.

Being denied wage labour, these women were often obliged to cohabit with men for survival. There ensued peculiar forms of prostitution, such as the one we have looked into at Broken Hill (Kabwe), where a woman would agree to cohabit with a man in exchange for money. A relationship of this sort might well become transformed into a domestic union: after a while the woman started cooking for the man, and in return the man maintained her. Some of these liaisons have ended up in legal marriages, but quite a few go on very precariously. The fact is that inter-tribal unions to which people are well disposed in towns, do not usually receive the blessing of the rural village; therefore, when a man resolves to go back to the village, he feels bound to abandon his woman, thus putting her in quest of a new partner. Naturally, the case of Zambia is not in the least unique, witness the increase in numbers of married women and prostitutes at Stanleyville, now Kisangani. (See Table 5)

At Elisabethville, now Lubumbashi, 'soon after 1950, an intelligent Belgian administrator reckoned that a quarter of the African urban women were *femmes libres* earning a living' through prostitution.[29]

Table 5
Married Women/Prostitutes, Stanleyville (Kisangani), 1944-57

Year	Married Women (1)	Prostitutes (2)	(2)/(1) %
1944	4,265	2,093	49.1
1945	4,506	2,155	47.8
1946	5,294	2,266	42.8
1947	5,640	2,527	44.8
1948	6,122	2,739	44.7
1949	6,943	2,993	43.1
1950	8,015	3,256	40.6
1951	8,249	2,976	36.1
1952	8,840	3,420	36.7
1953	10,229	3,751	36.7
1954	11,312	3,409	30.1
1955	—	—	—
1956	12,169	3,211	26.4
1957	13,081	3,574	27.3

Source: A. Romaniuk, *La Fecondité des Populations Congolaises*, Paris-The Hague, Mouton, 1967.

It was the same story elsewhere, though with one or two variations. Lubumbashi was set up as a mining town in 1910. Since the number of the locals was not up to the requirements of industry, a planned immigration policy became necessary. The recruitment of manpower was first carried out by private organizations and subsequently by state-created or state-supported bodies.[30] The available statistical data show that the immigrants were usually men and it was next to impossible to find a family unit among the workers.

> Why such a shortage of women? It can be accounted for thus: the short-term contract imposed by the recruitment bodies made families unnecessary burdens; besides, the demographic policy of Northern Rhodesia — namely Zambia, from where many migrants came — required the unconditional return of its workers as soon as a three or four month contract expired.[31]

Also, the quality of life in the camps by no means encouraged workers to have their families join them: 'The unhealthy climate and the unnatural life of the migrants caused many health problems . . . Malnutrition coupled with over-drinking which seemed to be the only leisure activity available to them.'[32]

The Permanent Commission for the Protection of the Natives, growing uneasy about a state of affairs that was adversely affecting productivity, suggested some measures which appear to be the first effort on the part of the public authorities to revise the recruitment terms. In the first place, the Commission asked the recruitment bodies to ensure that there would be more of a family pattern in the labour-camps and that more women should, therefore, be sent to Lubumbashi.

> Among the recruiters who tried hard on that score we may mention the OTCK and the UM. The OTCK made an impressive contribution to the sending of family units to the labour-camps: OTCK's statistics for the years 1928, 1929, 1930 and 1931 show a 50% increase in the despatching of families. As to the Union Minière, they too sent a few women to their work-camps. Their stabilization policy was a success, even more so because it was adopted by other local, small companies. This policy inevitably produced the long-term contract, which was to give the workers a greater stability and therefore a greater capacity for work . . . . Anyhow, up to 1950, which is as far as our study goes, no demographic balance had yet been achieved.[33]

The number of families 'despatched' varies in accordance with the economic situation: if there was some decline during the 1930s, there was on the other hand some increase during World War II, as shown by the labour-camps statistics. On the whole, the family presence ratio is growing, and the greater the number of families, the lesser the number of prostitutes. This appears to be invariably the case with all the African labour centres.

At the end of the 1950s, although prostitution had far from disappeared in the urban areas, yet it was no longer the sole condition of life for urbanized women, but increasingly the preserve of a somewhat restricted milieu. It was well on the way to becoming a trade or profession, according to the Western model. Nevertheless, either overtly or covertly, prostitution is still the main if not the only source of work for African women.

An investigation carried out in Kinshasa shows that prostitutes enjoy a higher income than any other women and even than many men. But their wealth, which is relative and always precarious, can be maintained only by a 'continuous effort and constant worries about their standard of living and the satisfaction of their daily needs.'[34] The following interviews demonstrate the conditions of these 'free women':

> Yes, 'free women' suffer more than other women. But I am all right. You can see how much and how well I spend for my daily food. If I say that I'm doing fine, this is because I only receive serious people. If a man happens to be broke and yet wishes to go to bed with me, first I examine him thoroughly. If he is an old customer, I give him my body, and at the end of the month he will pay his debt. You know how it goes in shops, where old customers do not always pay promptly, and credit is almost always the rule. Well, the same thing applies to some of my customers.
>
> My children and I eat a bit better than the average because I am a single mother and I can cope by asking my family or my friends for money. You see, in a job like mine you cannot afford to stay in all the time; you have to go out, preferably to a bar. If you get somebody, you should never make him pay for too many drinks, because if he spends a lot in the bar, the morning after he won't leave much money. If someone treats me to a lot of drinks, after a while I take some of them back to the barman saying that I am off; and if the barman gives me some cash in return, I may as well go home and sleep on my own. The morning after I won't be short of the money I need to feed my kids.
>
> There are men who don't pay women well: we call them *Mabanga*, which means 'hard like a stone' or 'bad payers'. Yet, if we happen to have no opportunities and walk the streets without any man calling us, well, if we then give a thought about the food for the following morning, we can really go crazy, especially if it is already eleven in the evening.[35]

As the cash income becomes more important, wives too go into prostitution as a 'prop' to their husbands' wages. The investigation above quotes prostitution by wives or other relatives as an appreciable source of income.

> This woman is half-married and half-'free'. She has a double life. She is a married woman because she brings into the world children who

will be nurtured by their father. She is 'free' because whenever she is in straits, she will get help from other men. The difficulties of this family are overcome thanks to the work of the husband and to the double life of this woman.[36]

'Traditional' Prostitution

Prostitution, whether premeditated or not, can hardly be seen as an act of female emancipation, as Davidson seems to argue.[37] It may well be experienced by some as an act of defiance and rebellion, but it is never a way of shirking the 'Morality and Order of the Family'; it is rather a way of escaping from a hopeless economic situation.

The African prostitute's status is quite different from that of the Western prostitute. Prostitution in Africa is never seen as a permanent way of life and as such juxtaposed to a normal life style; nor is it organized as a *racket*.[38] In certain circumstances it has appeared to be a way out of traditional conditions and situations that women found hard to bear. Among the Nigerian Hausa, for instance, prostitution has long been established, and now it is an institution. It has always been the way to salvation for women secluded by Muslim laws and forced to marry against their will.

> Such women, usually members of the ruling class subject to the strictest seclusion, if they could successfully make a hazardous journey in those days of slave raids, could move to some other emirate and turn for help to the local chief whore who could help them, give them money, and lodging, and find customers for them.[39]

The position of these women is entirely different from that of the more recent 'street-walkers', a product of modern life. They usually earn a living by practising some craft and in addition engage in a peculiar kind of prostitution by picking up a small number of men with whom they tend to keep a steady relationship: this is not just a business rapport, since no immediate or standard payment is proferred or requested; these women are approached by men through presents, as in courtship.[40]

Here, prostitution is the 'price' a rebel woman must pay: her rejection of the marital institution, and in particular of the forced marriage, is made socially acceptable, fairly harmless and finally institutionalized. Yet, for many Hausa women prostitution can also be

> a provisional status between two marriages. A young widow or a divorcee who for some reason has not been able to go back to her family or, wishing to be autonomous, has no desire to do so, more often than not ends up resourceless. Without any false shame, she will then consider prostitution, which is not without its own attractions after all. The prostitutes we happened to meet lived, as most of them do, in a large concession endowed with single dwellings. They would do the cooking together and spend whole days looking after their children and chatting while in a very relaxed atmosphere they waited for

visitors .... A visitor would join in the chat, make merry, show his gifts, and only after a while retire into a room with the woman of his choice. But then, a visitor might well leave the place without making any overtures; in fact he might happen to be a friend who had popped in only for the pleasure of a conversation or to relish an atmosphere for once different from the usual, in the company of 'emancipated' women with whom he could freely express himself. Certainly we did not see there the degrading face of the induced prostitution peculiar to a big city.[41]

There are a few other forms of prostitution which may be said to be practised along 'traditional' lines. Among the Nupe of West Africa, for instance, there are women traders who go on long trips, away from the control of parents or husbands; it is taken for granted that these women traders prostitute themselves for extra money.

Prostitutes and Housewives

In a study on the Hausa population that migrated to Yoruba towns, particularly those who went to Sabo, an Ibadan quarter, we find an interesting comparison between the position of prostitutes and that of housewives.[42]

In Sabo, in 1963, out of 4,184 people, 1,753 were women; of these, 483 were girls under 15 years old; 950 were housewives; 250 were prostitutes, and the remaining 70 were either old widows or recent divorcees. This partition between prostitutes and housewives represents one of the most striking peculiarities of the societal organization at Sabo.

No social stigma but rather respect and admiration seemed to attach to prostitution in Sabo. In the course of research, male informants did not hesitate to define the prostitutes as ideal wives in all respects. There were two 'ideal types' of a woman in the Hausa society; the prostitute, who leaves her native community and follows a man to his new place; and the housewife who, once her man had settled down at his new place, maintains the family, rears the children, and does many a good service to the family economy. When the Hausa men began to migrate and install themselves at Ibadan, they were soon followed by prostitutes in growing numbers. Among the Hausa of northern Nigeria an adult female is customarily married, therefore, all the prostitutes who migrated to Sabo were former housewives who had either divorced or left their husbands.

At the time of the study, all the housewives of Sabo, except the very old ones, were strictly secluded from public life, secular and religious, of the quarter as well as from any contact with men other than their husbands.[43] Such seclusion was quite uneconomic, even as far as housework was concerned. Only 10% of the Sabo houses had piped water, the remainder getting their water from two street taps. Their husbands were thus bound to provide water for the recluses with the help of Yoruba young girls. Similarly, their dirty linen could only be washed in a brook outside the quarter, and was usually handed to professional washermen — there were over 50 of them at Sabo.

Even in town prostitution was still an 'institution'. Prostitutes were organized under a chief, a woman, the *magagiya*, officially installed in her position by the chief of the quarter. The *magagiya* dealt with problems and disputes among prostitutes and represented them before the chief. Two prostitutes acted as her official messengers.

Prostitutes carried some weight in the political life of their quarter: the research at issue shows that they were organized in female sections separate from the two main parties of southern Nigeria, namely the NCNC (NEPU) and the Action Group. While housewives were secluded from public life, did not vote in the federal, regional and local elections, and were not politically active, prostitutes were among the first to register in the electoral roll and to play an active part in the electioneering of the 1960s. On the other hand, housewives played an important role in the economy of the quarter: all of them, unless too young or too old, were in some trade or other. Paradoxically, Sabo women who were secluded housewives could go into business, but not 'free' prostitutes. A third or so of these housewives controlled the retail sale of fruit, while the other two thirds were in charge of the local food vendors, serving thousands of the local unmarried men, and travellers who stopped at the two lorry parks of Sabo. They also cooked for other families on request.

Prostitutes were confined to about 11 houses and, since there was no pimping, they could retain their earnings but the high cost of living made it virtually impossible for them to save any money. Housewives, however, could easily pile up their earnings from trading which was rightly theirs; they paid no rent, were clothed by their husbands; as were their children and above all they could rely on their customers. Nonetheless, secluded as they were, they were in no position to invest their riches in business expansion or to compete with men.

Since the 1950s there have been relatively fewer prostitutes, but they still served as a source of wives for Sabo men. For this reason and also because of the frequent divorces which made them available for prostitution, many Hausa women hovered between the mobility and 'freedom' of prostitution and the seclusion of housewifery; and they did so again and again during their married lives.

The fact that although strictly separated and defined, the roles of prostitute and housewife are interchangeable causes a good deal of confusion when it comes to an official report and makes inquests and official statistics unreliable. In 1916 for instance, among the Hausa who had settled in Sabo, out of a total of 394 people 122 were women; 114 of these were officially labelled 'petty traders', but informants have made it clear that the majority of them were really engaged in prostitution; conversely, the married women registered in the 1962-63 Nigerian census as housewives were really 'petty traders'.

Notes

1. B. Davidson, *L'Angola nell'Occhio del Ciclone*, Torino, Einaudi, 1975.
2. *Ibid.*
3. According to Fanon, 'the aim of imperialism is not so much the utter disappearance of a pre-existing culture as its prolonged agony. Thus a culture, once alive and liable to growth, ends up atrophied in the colonial statute and deep into the grip of oppression . . . . Archaic, inert bodies are created, bound to operate under the oppressor's surveillance and to ape, as if in a caricature, once fertile institutions; such bodies, though they claim to respect the tradition, the cultural peculiarities and the identity of the enslaved peoples, in reality identify themselves with a most uncompromising brand of contempt and a most sophisticated sadism'.
4. M. Gluckman, Economy of the Central Barotse Plain, in *The Rhodes-Livingstone Papers*, Manchester University Press, No.7, 1968 (1 ed. 1941).
5. J.A. Barnes, Marriage in a Changing Society: A Study in Structural Change among the Fort Jameson Ngoni, in *The Rhodes-Livingstone Papers*, Manchester University Press, No.20, 1970 (1 ed. 1951).
6. H. Hochegger, La Structure Lignagère et les Relations Interlignagères d'un Village Yansi, in *L'Organisation Sociale et Politique chez les Yansi, Teke et Boma*, (various authors) Bandundu, Publications du Centre d'Études Ethnologiques, 1970.
7. Such was one of the geographer H. Nicolai's considerations in *Le Kwili - Etude Geographique d'une Region Congolaise*, Bruxelles, 1963. The quasi-complete disappearance of the traditional dwelling means that villages are no longer architecturally different, or negligibly so: only the building material still is.
8. E. Munzadi, Le Village Yansi, in *L'Organisation Sociale et Politique*, op.cit.
9. How interesting G. Dalton's analysis in La Produzione Tradizionale nelle Economie Primitive Africane, in *Antropologia Economica*, (ed. Tullio Tentori) Milano, F. Angeli, 1974. Also see P. Scarduelli, Lévi-Strauss e il Terzo Mondo, in *Quaderni di Terzo Mondo*, Milano, 1974: 'Lévi-Strauss's careful reconstruction of the kinship structures in primitive societies and the dominant role acknowledged to them within these societies do not mean a devaluation of the production relations: in fact, in these societies kinship relations dominating social life act as production relations.'
10. A.J. Hanna, *Storia delle Rhodesie e del Nyasaland*, Firenze, Sansoni, 1963.
11. B. Davidson, *Which Way Africa?*, Harmondsworth, Penguin Books, 1973.
12. A. Songre, Mass Emigration from Upper Volta: the Facts and Implications, in *Employment in Africa*, (various authors) Genève, ILO, 1973.
13. According to Kay, 'The variety of ethnic groups in towns is today a potential source of conflict' in G. Kay, *A Social Geography of Zambia*, London, University of London Press, 1967.

14. See A.M. O'Connor's interesting analysis: *An Economic Geography of East Africa*, London, 1966.
15. A.J. Hanna, *Storia delle Rhodesie* . . . , op.cit. See also O. Guitard, *Les Rhodesies et le Nyasaland*, Paris, Presses Universitaires de France, 1964.
16. P.O. Ohadike, *Development of and Factors in the Employment of African Migrants in the Copper Mines of Zambia 1940-66*, Lusaka, Institute for Social Research, University of Zambia, 1969.
17. We have singled out Zambia also because the migration of labour force there has been extremely well documented, from Godfrey Wilson's study dated 1930 to H. Heisler's study published in 1974.
18. H. Heisler, *Urbanisation and the Government of Migration*, London, 1974.
19. The legal systems of Africa prior to the colonial rule fell into two categories: the first based on traditional laws, the second based on Islamic laws, which nevertheless acknowledged many customary laws. Despite the introduction of European laws, the colonial power accepted indigenous laws in many cases, which were thus still enforced as for the legal relations among the African populations. At the same time, at least in the British colonies and protectorates, the traditional courts were acknowledged as having jurisdiction over disputes among Africans; these were the Native Courts. This caused a duality in the legal and judicial system: the Native Courts had jurisdiction only with regard to cases concerning Africans, and the native customary law was solely enforced in respect of disputes among Africans. The non-African was exempt from the jurisdiction of the Native Courts and was also not subject to the customary law, yet the opposite did not apply: the African was subject to the Territorial Courts and to the territorial law brought in by the Europeans, notably the criminal law. At independence, every African country tries to abolish the court duality as soon as possible; yet such duality is extant in the law. On the subject see A.N. Allat, The Place of African Customary Law in Modern African Legal Systems, in *Proceedings of the First International Congress of Africanists*, (various authors) Accra, 1964.
20. H. Heisler, *Urbanisation and the Government of Migration*, op.cit.
21. *Ibid*.
22. Betty Kaunda relates: 'In 1900 my mother, Milika Musata, was given in marriage to a very adventurous fellow who soon after the wedding left her at the village — Kamoto was its name — and went to Johannesburg in search of work and further adventure. For many a long year mother yearningly waited for him to return. He never did, nor has anyone heard of him any more. During the First World War, and particularly in 1915, men and women had to carry containers and sacks of corn meal from the village to the regional office. They would carry them on their heads, walking in single file throughout the one-day or so journey to Fort Jameson. It was during one of these journeys that a local youth by the name of John Chinuza Kaweche Banda noticed Milika. More than that, he went up to her parents and asked them to allow him to marry her. Milika's parents said no: it was out of the question, they said, because Milika was a married woman, her husband had left to go

to Johannesburg only five years earlier. They still believed that he would come back some day. What would then happen — they wondered — if he found his wife married to somebody else? He would kill them and no mistake. In spite of these objections, John Kaweche and Milika kept having secret rendezvous and finally decided to elope. They planned the whole thing properly. John Kaweche left his own village of Jumbe and went to seek work at the Mission Station, known as Miezi. As soon as he settled there, he sent his friend Thomas Koloko to Kamoto in order to abduct his sweetheart and take her to Miezi. Koloko did as he was told. A few days later Milika and John Kaweche were man and wife. Yet John Kaweche had already a wife who lived at Jumbe. When she heard that her husband had taken a second wife, she grew very angry, especially with Thomas Koloko for carrying out the plan. Time — they say — heals all sorrows. It healed also the angry sorrow of John Kaweche's first wife. She joined Milika at Miezi, and the two women lived together as the wives of John Kaweche.' (From S.A. Mpashi, *Betty Kaunda*, London, Longmans of Zambia, 1969.)

23. J.A. Barnes, *Marriage in a Changing Society*, op.cit.
24. We note *en passant* that sometimes the depopulation in some areas is due to political rather than economic reasons. For instance, the fact that the Chinsali district has lost 10% more of its population than any other district in the country was certainly due to the 1964 clashes between some followers of the Lumpa Church, a Messianic movement founded by a woman called Alice Lenshina, and UNIP, the nationalist party of Kaunda. As the clashes went on, very many Lumpa left the country and by the time of the 1969 census they had not returned.
25. G. Kay, *A Social Geography of Zambia*, op.cit.
26. The imbalance between the sexes caused by the migratory flow also bears heavily upon the demographic situation, as it badly affects the capacity for reproduction of the populations. In a society leaning towards monogamy, such as Zambia is at present, the fact that men are more disposed to migrate than women means that the actual number of family units is lower than it could otherwise be.
27. Colson as quoted by H. Heisler, *Urbanisation and the Government of Migration*, op.cit.
28. The labour camps, i.e., the traditional clusters of immigrants around the labour centres, were, in the context of the policy of stabilization of the labour force, turned into the characteristic 'towns for Africans', the *blackbelts besieging* the urban residential nuclei of the whites, wherein also offices, shops and so on were to be found. But for some countries in West Africa, such as Ghana, this is the typical layout of all the African towns.
29. B. Davidson, *La civiltà Africana*, Torino, Einaudi, 1973.
30. In 1927 the former *Bourse de Travail du Katanga* became the *Office du Travail du Katanga*.
31. Malizia, Regard sur la Situation de la Citoyenne Lushoise avant 1950, in *Elima*, 25 May 1975 (extracted from Likundoli, Département d'Histoire, Campus de Lubumbashi).
32. *Ibid*.
33. *Ibid*.

34. J. Houyoux, *Budgets Menagers, Nutrition et Mode de Vie a Kinshasa*, Kinshasa, Presses Universitaire du Zaire, 1973.
35. J. Houyoux, op.cit.
36. *Ibid*.
37. 'These *femmes libres* were themselves, somewhat obscurely maybe, part of the great transition, because they often represented a deliberate act of female emancipation . . . . Generally their behaviour is an extreme challenge to the Morality and Order of the Family.' B. Davidson, op.cit.
38. There are, nonetheless, all the prerequisites for a development of the kind, such as the brothel chains or the hotels permanently accommodating groups of prostitutes of their own, and so on.
39. Lucy Mair, *African Marriage and Social Change*, London, 1969.
40. In the Hausa societies of northern Nigeria, but also among the Hausa who have moved to the south, prostitution is associated with the *Bori* cult, and therefore there is also a ritualistic side to it. On the subject see J. Nicholas, Senso di Colpa, Somatizzazione e Catarsi in un Culto di Possessione: il Bori Hausa, in *La Donna — Un Problema Aperto*, (ed. Ida Magli) Firenze, Vallecchi, 1974.
41. J. Nicolas, op.cit.
42. A. Cohen, *Custom and Politics in Urban Africa — A Study of Hausa Migrants in Yoruba Towns*, London, 1969.
43. 'Islam has often been associated with the seclusion of women, yet the nature of this seclusion is not always clear. Married women's seclusion at Sabo, for instance, considerably differs from that in Arab villages or in the Northern Hausa lands, in the sense that it is public and not individual (whereas among the Arabs as well as the Northern Hausa some men seclude their wives and others do not), and the men are under a common constant pressure to keep their wives isolated from public life.' A. Cohen, op.cit.

2. The Position of Women in Traditional Society

The Family

The social organization of production in traditional agricultural societies is closely associated with the familial organization.[1] The ideological strength of traditional kinship therefore rests on a complex 'concrete hinterland'. Social control over access to women, i.e., the marriage mechanism, is the very keystone of the system. The woman, as a 'producer of producers, constitutes the most powerful prospective means of production.'[2] Controlling women thus means controlling the reproduction of the production unit. In political terms, control over access to women legitimizes social hierarchy, namely, the authority of the old over the young, of the dominant over the dominated lineages, of one caste over another, and so on.

By disrupting the traditional family by separation, the colonial system led to an overall instability of the local system. The modern nuclear family does not stem from the evolution of pre-existing family structures but from the forced integration of traditional societies into a capitalist economy: it arises along with the need for a geographical mobility of the labour force of the individual. In Africa, where imperialism has used migrant labour on a continental scale, the nuclear family has appeared as a necessity, a sort of Hobson's choice, and yet alien to the existing social structures, and opposed to the various forms of traditional family.

The transition from a traditional family system to a 'modern Western' system, still in progress, seems to be one of the most difficult problems now confronting African states. The two family systems are governed by two different legal systems and the problem of transition becomes more evident and dramatic where, in towns, the family fabric has largely changed while the laws have not.

Naturally, the diversity of African peoples implies a diversity of customary family laws. The division between matrilineal and patrilineal societies could well be the watershed, although the laws governing them do have much in common. For example, in contemplating marriage, the man may be already married but the woman must be single, a widow or a divorcée: in other words, both systems admit polygamy.

41

Likewise, for both systems marriage is never just a union between husband and wife but rather between two groups, which, through marriage, start a 'complex system of interrelationship bound to operate for a long time'.[3] The nuclear or restricted family is thus seen as relatively ephemeral; there is a saying that, 'Marriage and ashes will strew at a gust.' Not the conjugal family but the lineage secures the stability and continuity of the group: 'the hard conditions of life . . . call for a societal framework whose solidity may compensate for the frailty of the basic family.'[4]

Thus in Zaire, among the matrilineal, patrilocal Yansi peoples, the elders judge any conjugal controversy from the standpoint of the lineage, to which precedence is always granted. There is, nonetheless a tendency for restricted families to be more independent, manifested by a growing sense of responsibility on the part of the father towards his children, whose schooling, for instance, is entirely dependent on the father's initiative as he will bear the cost of it. Another positive index is the increase in the marriage payment to the bride's father. 'This evolution is yet very limited because the economic conditions force the elemental families to keep faithful to their lineage group which is anyway a warrant for the traditional social security.'[5]

With one exception the initiative in a marital alliance is taken by the man. Besides being classified according to their age, the Yansi males are in fact stratified by lineage, and may thereby form really privileged classes.[6]

Only girls who belong to a dominant lineage are allowed to openly express their marital choice.[7] This provides scope for some selection of the fathers-to-be of the future chiefs, besides bestowing upon women of such lineages and their children, a fair degree of independence vis-à-vis their husband's lineage. No bride-price is accepted for these women; by refusing to accept a marriage payment, the members of the ruling lineage secure all the rights over the offspring born to a woman of their lineage. Men who marry such women (and marriage in these circumstances is regarded with disfavour) are granted a number of privileges by the lineage chief, as compensation for the restrictions enjoined upon them — one of which used to be monogamy.

Officially, Yansi women, like the men, are classified by age; in practice their modest role in public life makes such classification wholly theoretical and thus ineffectual. A Yansi woman is linked with her husband's age class, and by this she is less subject to the severe restrictions binding upon him. Her quality as a bride or mother seems to have an edge over her membership of any particular age group. Such status, conditioned by her husband's age group, emerges clearly in some of a woman's activities and in social gatherings. On the occasion of a collective fishing session, for instance, a wife of a notable man aged over 55 years — even though she may be only 18 years old — has equal rights with her mother. Whereas, usually, her married brother will not be in any position to claim equal rights with his father whilst the latter is still living. In a sense, a woman marries her husband's influence, as well as the consideration due to the group of which he is a member. For example, a notable's wife is allowed to exorcise a sick person, or to act in lieu of her husband to remove an interdict.

Marriage Rites

Let us now consider in particular the marriage ritual of the Bemba, a Zambian matrilocal and matrilineal people.

The Bemba term *uku-upa* has been rendered as 'getting married', but it actually refers to a very different kind of relationship, legally and socially, between a man and a woman.

The Bemba traditional marriage cannot be described as a single act, accomplished once and for all through a ceremony or a property transfer. It is a multi-stage event, mostly ritually stressed, whereby a young man becomes incorporated into his wife's family group as he takes up residence with them and gives his services in return for food and maintenance. The ritual also extends over many years and is so closely related to the give-and-take of gifts and services which are integral to the marriage contract that it would be difficult to separate the two aspects of the marital relation.

The ceremonial aspect is particularly complex if it relates to the first marriage of an adolescent girl, including, as it does, the initiation ceremonies, which in fact is regarded as the 'typical' marriage. In its modernized version, the ritual is much shorter and probably the 'typical' ceremonial is no longer observed anywhere.

The consent of a girl's parents and next of kin is not a mere formality in a village respectful of tradition. Father, mother, maternal uncle and paternal aunt will discuss the matter very seriously with the girl, who may well turn the proposal down.

Bemba informants particularly emphasize the point that the bride is expected 'to use' the marital bed gradually, in much the same way as the bridegroom gradually gains his other rights.[8] They disapprove of forced intercourse and criticize the European custom of forcibly and painfully rupturing the hymen on the wedding night.[9] The sexual relationship varies according to the degree of the girl's physical maturity. She may be 'pledged' to a man from childhood, but intercourse must not take place before the initiation ceremony at puberty, namely the *chisungu*. This ceremony used to be probably the most important stage in the whole ritual: the bridegroom would then acquire legal rights over the bride, and both would accept legally binding obligations.

The marriage payment made on the occasion of the *chisungu* still appears to give the husband legal and exclusive rights over the sexual life of the girl: if the girl is seduced before the ceremony, he cannot claim damages. Conjugal duties are expressed ritually: one of the ritual songs a girl must learn for the ceremony underlines the fact that if before marriage she was entitled to refuse to serve in the home when she was tired or bored, after marriage she may no longer do so; if she does, her husband is entitled to apply for a divorce.

The *chisungu* has 'magic' overtones pertaining to purification, the teaching of beauty care, and fertility control, but it also possesses generally 'moral' overtones. According to Richards, in fact 'the *chisungu* purposes to hammer into the girls' minds social and conjugal morals rather than technical teachings ... such as cookery or gardening, which the girls have learned from their mothers since childhood.'[10] It also serves to create social bonds, since the girls join the caste of the initiated as well as of the married young women.

After *chisungu*, marriage can be fully consummated. In European eyes, this may be no dramatic event, given that premarital intercourse has already taken place. But to the Bemba post-*chisungu* intercourse is an entirely different act — legally and ritually. For the first time, the sexual behaviour of the girl has a 'magic power': on that night she begins to take up the usual conjugal duties and now, for the first time, she is allowed to produce offspring. The *chisungu* was, and largely still is, the most important act of consecration of women's reproductive power;[11] so much so that the abduction of a prepubescent girl is looked on as of no consequence, even if she is already betrothed, whereas a heavy compensation is usually claimed for the abduction and seduction of an initiated girl. Similarly, premarital relations are tolerated, but adultery is not. Before the advent of the whites, adultery was punished as a crime if it concerned the wife of a chief or a man of high standing.[12] Nowadays this attitude has survived only as superstition and sorcery: thus an adulterous woman is expected to die in childbirth, unless she confesses her lover's name; if a man commits adultery while his wife is pregnant he is feared as someone who is endangering his wife's life.

The sexual rites of the Bemba were part and parcel of the old marriage contract. The disappearance of this ritual has inevitably changed the whole marital system, the very notions of parenthood, as well as the relations between man and wife, and between the two kinship groups concerned. Goods and money have taken the place of the son-in-law's services and work, thus totally transforming the relations with the affines. Now, in return for money, a young man is in a position to take his wife from her people before the time set by tradition, and the European influence has brought in the *patria potestas*. All this is bound to sharpen conjugal tensions: 'the men who scold their wives and occasionally beat them are, as far as I can say from experience, young, not old'.[13] To some extent, this may have always been so. The insecure position of the son-in-law and the early, trial stages of the marriage are likely to provoke tension before a permanent, conjugal relationship is established, 'yet the novel situation [now] has entitled young husbands to show an arrogance they would have never dared to show before'.[14]

Polygamy is relatively little known in this area. Unlike many Bantu people it has never played any part in Bemba family or economic life. The polygamous family is based upon quite different principles from those of the Southern Bantu. The position of the second wife oscillates between wifehood and concubinage, although her children will enjoy the same legal status as those of the first wife. However, if she is so inclined the first wife may not recognize the second, in which case the husband must choose between them. Usually women do not willingly marry a polygamist, unless he is a headman or very wealthy.

The marriage ritual of a patrilineal society differs very little from that of a multilineal society except in one important respect: marriage implies the permanent transfer of the woman's fertility to the husband's group. For example, the Ngoni of Zambia, who share their political and 'national' area with the Bemba, regard the marriage rites as sanctioning the transfer of the woman's fertility, and of the agnatic affiliation of her offspring, as well as of the reciprocal rights and obligations of the affines.

A ceremony and (as will be shown in detail below) ritual payments betoken the beginning of a marriage. One year later, another rite takes place: for the first time, the wife cooks for her husband. Previously she has relied for her food upon any other wife of her husband, or upon his mother or his grandmother; it should be noted that among the Ngoni a woman cannot prevent her man from taking a second wife, but she can make his life so difficult as to convince him to change his mind.

The passing of time also gradually brings to an end the avoidance taboo pertaining to the mother-in-law, according to which her son-in-law must not speak to her and, if he should see her coming along a path, he must detour into the bush until she has passed. The final ceremony, when they eat together signifies the mother-in-law's acknowledgement that he is properly performing his double role as a son-in-law and as a husband. Betrothal will take place only if the girl has had an offer of marriage before puberty, and the marriage will be celebrated some years after that. In the past, the Ngoni expected an unmarried girl to be a virgin, and it seems that girls were examined before the marriage ceremony in order to detect any evidence of defloration.[15]

There was a time when young people could in no way object to a marriage arranged by their parents. Nowadays, parents can still exert some pressure in order to prevent or impose a marriage, but it is almost impossible for them to force their daughters into an undesired marriage, and quite impossible in the case of their sons. Confronted with parental pressure, a son may emigrate to town, while a daughter, if the pressure continues, may go and stay with relatives. The colonial administration often voiced its opposition to forced marriages, yet there are no cases on record of any steps taken to prevent them.[16]

A father who opposes his son's or his daughter's marriage can refuse to sanction it, and the couple may start their life in common without one or even any of the prescribed ceremonies. Today, the absence of these ceremonies does not invalidate the couple's legal rights, it still means that the couple is less sure of their relatives' support, namely that they are deprived of the family solidarity which here identifies with 'social security'.

There is another type of marriage in which none of the prescribed ceremonies are performed. This is known as the 'shaky marriage', and places itself between a proper marriage and concubinage.[17] The instability lies rather in the peculiarities of the couple in question, such as their flightiness or litigiousness, than on the absence of ceremonial or of bridewealth. Divorce in such cases — particularly because of the absence of bridewealth

— can be easily arranged. Marriages unaccompanied by payment, however, are not necessarily 'shaky': due to poverty, absence of payment can be easily forgotten in the daily flow of village life.[18]

Adultery incurs social censure and magic practices are resorted to with an eye to punishing or preventing it. The men who migrated to Rhodesia without their wives appear to have made much use of such practices: well on record is that performed with a view to making it impossible for a lover to withdraw after the coitus and, as a result, the adulterous couple was bound to turn to neighbours for help.

Despite the disruptions caused by mass migration, the customary marriage remains an important reference point in society: it is such an institution that ensures 'the local stability of social relations against all the flux'.[19] To this day 'a man moves from village to village and from mining town to mining town; he may sleep with a prostitute for a night or live with a concubine for years. What is relatively stable in the end is his rapport with his wife and the children he was given by her.'[20]

Customary Marriage in Town

As one of the inbuilt mechanisms of a local group, marriage is necessarily part of the general political scene and as such is bound to change accordingly.

If traditional marriage was linked to a well defined residential system where rights and duties were clearly distinguished, nowadays the forces maintaining kinship ties appear to be declining, hence the danger of a group disintegrating because of quarrels and so on is greater. The break-up and dissolution of the customary marriage and consequently of the related traditional political and societal framework is, inevitably, more rapid in towns in the context of a novel social and political situation.

As soon as the African *citizen* gains access to the monetary system, the conventional economy goes topsy-turvy: because of the money income, the sex division of labour is disrupted. As the wage-earner, the man is now the 'essential' element of the family, and obviously, this affects his relationship with the woman.

> Far from being a dynamic member, the woman now appears to be unproductive. Resenting this, she endeavours to earn a living by horticulture or sewing or, more frequently, trading. Wage labour, the ambition and hope of many a young woman, is actually accessible to only few of them.[21]

The economic dependence of women in urban and suburban areas therefore creeps into the marriage relation. In 1934, a Luanshya woman told her interviewer: 'Yes, my husband beats me, but what can I do? You see, I am

The Position of Women in Traditional Society

totally dependent on him as my employer. Who else would give me work here?'[22] Similarly, a few men tried to justify their violent behaviour towards their women by saying that they 'were paying' them — and this was especially the case with provisional unions. Nonetheless, the traditional family solidarity, which betokens the continuation of kinship in towns, has not yet disappeared. On the contrary, it is an indispensable element for the survival of the individual in a big town.[23]

Naturally such solidarity manifests itself in a manner that is no longer traditional. In Kinshasa, for example, it is a widespread custom for a young man's first wages to be given to his parents, or the head of the family. Part will then go to the family members who have contributed to the youth's education, and part will be given back to him. The family (mainly the father and the uncle) continue to play a major role in town when it comes to marriage; not only for the ceremonial aspects (the dowry, the rites and the speeches) but also in the choice of the future spouse. This can provoke conflict especially in the case of the young man, often torn between a more congenial, educated girl, and the girl chosen by his parents, who may well be still staying at the village. 'It has been openly admitted that the main asset of a country girl is the fact she does not question the superiority of her husband in the home, and this means harmony. As soon as she marries him, he becomes a second father to her . . .'[24]

It is noteworthy that many of the migrants who, at their village have a wife whom they married with the customary rite (namely, without her consent) remarry in town often with mutual consent. Such situations emerged in the course of a recent survey in Kinshasa. Here are some interviews by way of example.

A 30-year-old graduate holding an important public position says:

> I meant to marry a Kinshasa girl but my parents didn't let me. Father had already decided to marry me to the woman you can see, when she was still a boarding schoolgirl. As soon as he had paid for the dowry, he let me know that he was about to come to Kinshasa with this woman. Now I live with her, and I can tell you that so far it's OK with me.

A high officer's spouse relates that:

> It was not my husband that came and asked for me in marriage. It was his sister, his elder sister, his brothers and his parents who chose me from among the girls of our village as a wife for him. They chose me when I was still a child. As soon as I reached marriageable age, I joined my husband. Things have been fine with me all this time, and he treats me as any woman should be treated. His family and mine get on very well together.

Sometimes things are altogether different.

> Mr X wanted his daughter to marry either one of the clan or some rich man, but his brother-in-law objected to this, as he wanted his niece to be free from any engagement so that she might choose the man to her liking and therefore her father should not oblige her to marry this or that. Mr X retorted to his brother-in-law that when his daughter was still at school, had he never given her anything for her clothes or her books; now that it was a matter of picking a fiancé, he was coming forward, obviously with the only purpose to get some money. The brother-in-law resented the remark, stood up and said: 'Well, you do as you choose, but I'm telling you that when this girl is with her husband, she will not bear [children].'[25]

As things are, it is obviously difficult, if not impossible, for the sort of 'comradeship', which is characteristic of the 'modern' Western marriage, to develop between a married couple. Yet it is not so much the social inferiority of the woman that makes such a 'relationship' impossible in the customary marriage as the real 'lack of intimacy between the sexes'.[26] Boys and girls are separated at a very early age. Brother and sister never play together, and from puberty they are required to live in separate huts. The Basengele of Zaire never allow a boy to go into the fields or fishing with his pubescent sister, unless they are accompanied by their father or mother. Adult males and females eat and socialize separately; additionally during the early years of married life most couples have no independent life, not even as an economic unit. The traditional familial and communal organization precipitates men and women into separate everyday lives: a young wife is more in touch with the other women of her own clan or her husband's than with her husband himself. She still stays, works, eats and talks with the other women of her own or her husband's family, whereas he can eat and work with men from outside. Man and wife only share their house by night. The Bemba girls are being taught that 'a good wife does not talk with her husband. A good wife is expected to go to her man's bed early in the morning and ask him if he has anything to tell her.'[27]

This situation is little changed in towns. At Accra, say, the Ga have kept their customary habits, and men and women live in separate houses or, at least, in separate parts of the house. The woman takes food to her man or sends it through her children and only stays with him overnight. A study by Margaret Peil shows that 82% of the women of Tema, an industrial town in Ghana, live on their own, and 58% of the married women of Accra do not live with their husbands.[28] Significantly, only within the wage-earning stratum is a marked change to be noted: only 7% of the married workers have women who live elsewhere in the same town. The men, more readily than the women, say that they willingly live with their partners, although this is probably due less to a feeling for comradeship than for reasons of personal comfort.

Bridewealth: Traditional Significance and Latter Day Speculation

This is a hotly debated aspect of the African marriage, and its value as well as its customary significance are in many respects far from clear.[29]

It should be noted that in traditional marriage, those goods whose transfer represented the bridewealth, would primarily serve as a sanction of the social order. They had no *exchange value*:

> Marriage goods are not for exchange; actually, by being moved one way or another, they sanction the control of one side over the offspring of a woman from the other side. It is not a matter of 'exchanging' women for dowry items: what is at issue in this circulating process is the offspring anticipated from a woman. It would probably be more accurate to say that dowries circulate not contrariwise to women but to their children. Truly, it can be observed that in case of divorce often the dowry is not rendered if the children stay with their father.[30]

The dowry was thus an essential element of the societal control system: its amount never reflected 'the qualities, to a higher or lower extent appreciated, of the woman in question'.[31] Marriage payments were indissolubly tied to the ceremonies marking the various stages of a marriage: here, for instance, are the basic payments required of a Bemba husband:
1) The engagement gift (*Nsalamu*), which served as a request to the potential parents-in-law to consider the offer of marriage.
2) The main payment, called *mpango*, given to the girl's parents during the preliminary negotiations or sometimes later, to legitimize a union.
3) The payment for the girl's initiation, called *ndalama shya chisungu*, when as it used to be, initiation ceremonies were one part of marriage ceremonial. A common feature to all these payments was their scanty, real value: payments in goods made of natural fibres were preferred, because they could easily be made and easily returned in case of a marriage breach. Nevertheless, Richards stated that by 1919-23 the *mpango* value had already been increasing and there was a good deal of anxiety about its repayment in case of divorce.

Possibly the bridewealth was quite substantial among other Bantu populations. For example, the *Lobola*, in South Africa, was such that to repay it would not be so easy, and thus a marital breach was less attractive. Even in this case, however, bridewealth was not a lucrative business.

The case with patrilineal peoples is not all that different. In the *Ngoni* customary marriage there are two principal stages, marked by two distinct cattle transfers. The first is called *mfuko* and consists in the transfer of one head of cattle. This gives exclusive sexual rights to the man, in so far as he can take legal action in case of adultery, although he has neither the right to remove his wife from the village nor to rear any children she may bear him. The second stage, called *malowolo*, consists in the transfer of some one to a dozen head of cattle; according to the status of the spouse's father, and this gives the man the right to take his wife with him.

The significance of bridewealth comes out clearly in the procedure followed on the occasion of a marriage in which it is not paid. If a man pays the *mfuko* but dies before paying the *malowolo*, any children born in wedlock belong to his wife's kin and not to his own. One of his brothers might take the widow as a wife and legitimize the children as members of his clan segment by paying the bridewealth. In such an instance, the woman can refuse to go and stay with her late husband's brother, but she cannot refuse to yield her children to those of her husband's kin who have paid the bridewealth. If the bridewealth has been paid and she marries another man, any children she bears him will belong to the deceased husband's kin.

Among the Ngoni, bridewealth is manifestly associated with political events. Three phases may in fact be identified: one prior to 1898 — when a war against the Europeans was fought and lost — during which the payment was made in terms of cattle; the second, 1898-1930 phase, characterized by a low-level payment; finally, the post-1930 phase, marked by a constant increase in the pecuniary value of the payment. The majority of marriages without any payment, therefore, took place after the 1898 war and until 1938; it seems reasonable to associate this fact with the extreme poverty of the people during the period of colonial conquest and settlement, but also with the general uncertainty about the sort of society the white administration was building for the Ngoni. An accurate assessment of the divorce rate for this period would be difficult, yet we do know that a lot of women from other tribes, such as the Chewa and the Nsenga, who had married before 1898, left their husbands and went home as soon as British rule was established over the area.[32]

Following the stabilization of the political situation, the transfer of cattle has increasingly been replaced by cash transfer and accordingly the woman has increasingly become a commodity.

> The dowry used to represent the marriage deed, but in a colonial economy and under the pressure of a growing poverty, the girl's parents have found a way to ask for money, in fact for sums which have grown higher and higher, mostly too high for the youth to cope with.[33]

Thus, the dowry or bridewealth, which originally sanctioned the marriage alliance (but also the social hierarchy since it would be distributed only among the elders), has, after the introduction of the money market, degenerated into 'womanwealth'. And, like any other price, it depends on the fluctuation of business, demand, supply, and speculation.

Divorce and Dissolution of Marriage

> O, I am done for
> Fori Gyaama, I am done for
> O, Fori Gyaama, alas!

> The trap has sprung up
> When the trap springs up[34]
> I must go back home
> When my marriage is over
> I must go to the Boadwo[35]
>
> (A popular Ghanaian song)

Some anthropologists have denounced the instability of marriage in traditional societies; others, on the contrary, maintain that such societies hardly knew divorce. Here, too, there is such a discrepancy between the institution of divorce as we see it and African customary divorce that to make an assessment of it is difficult.

Among the Bemba, for instance, a conjugal separation might be due to quarrels between a betrothed boy and girl, to an inter-familial agreement when the marriage was at an early stage, or to the provisional or permanent return of the wife to her village. The Bemba call these modes of separation *ukuleka* (to leave) or *ukulekana* (to leave each other), commonly translated as divorce. The terms are also used with reference to the divorce of the colonial period, which was obtained either by mutual consent or upon application of either party to the Native Courts.

The results of Richards' analysis of the grounds on which the Native Courts would grant a divorce are as follows: a man can obtain a divorce if his wife is a confirmed adulteress (22.8% out of 229 divorce cases in the sample); if she is barren (9.8%); if she neglects her domestic duties or is unruly, untidy, or a bad cook (7.5%); if she has deserted her husband and returned to her family (7%) or if she is too old to have children and wishes to go back to her village.[36]

A woman can divorce her husband if he is impotent (2%), or is not providing for her (6%) or has deserted her (18% out of 87 marriages) or has been persistently cruel to her, say, through regular maltreatment. Either party may get a divorce in case of some contagious disease such as leprosy, or because of madness, mutilation or if either party is an invalid (4%).

In some patrilineal societies, such as the Ngoni, a woman may not divorce her husband for any reason,[37] while a man can do so at any time. It will suffice for him to send her back to her family with a little present meant to indicate that he has divorced her. If he has already paid bride-price, the woman's kin are expected to send him another wife as a substitute. The customary law of matrilineal societies is usually characterized by a large degree of tolerance towards 'human frailties'. Among the Yansi, occasional unfaithfulness by either party does not justify divorce. Thus, if a woman abuses her husband, the elders of the lineage consider the case carefully and, if it is revealed that the woman despises her spouse or the 'allied' group, the marriage is annulled. But if it is only a case of a fleeting emotional outlet, reconciliation will ensue. Also, barrenness of a woman does not necessarily call for a divorce, even though in such cases the man is allowed to take a second wife.[38]

Violence, even in self-defence, is a serious matter. Any physical violence used by a woman against her husband is a grievous affair tantamount to a public injury.[39] Divorce will probably take place if an angry wife breaks her husband's possessions and throws them outside.

In some cases the lineage elders may dissolve a marriage even against the spouses' wish. The main reasons for this may be the sterility of either party, or the death of a child, both of which are ascribed to sorcery; and even an extremely good understanding between the parties, which would be seen as a threat, since it could result in the couple eluding lineage control.

Marriage, as we have already said, is an affair concerning two groups and not just two persons, so much so that among the vast majority of the tribes the death of either party does not by itself imply dissolution of the marriage.

By European laws, death means the end of the marital status: from the moment of the death of either partner every marital duty ceases and the widow or widower is free to remarry, even immediately. By a great many African customary laws, this is not so. Obviously, the marital relation will no longer exist as a physical relation, but for women some marital obligations survive the husband's death. Most significant is the restriction of her right to remarry or to have a sexual liaison. The necessary steps to free the widow from all ties with her deceased husband differ according to the various customary laws; some common points may, however, be identified: 1) ritual purification through ritual intercourse of the widow with the successor to the deceased husband;[40] 2) a period of mourning ending with the ceremony of dissolution of the marriage; the length of mourning, as well as the elements of the ceremonial dissolution, may vary; 3) any sexual relation or the marriage of the widow before the ritual purification are tantamount to adultery: the dead husband's relatives may approach the man for damages, and in some areas the woman also.

In colonial times, ritual dissolution of the marriage led to various and serious abuses. The purification ceremony was soon replaced or accompanied by payment to the deceased's relatives of a certain amount in cash or in kind, by the surviving party. At other times, the relatives would put off *sine die* the appointment of the purifying substitute; this was apparently done to keep the woman tied to the man's family in the knowledge that her labour was vitally important, and even more so in a rural area. Nowadays all the women's organizations, including the most traditional ones, agree in denouncing these customs as degrading and frustrating for the woman and in urging their abolition.

Women's Attitude To Polygamy

The Woman I Share With My Husband
I won't deny
I am a bit jealous
Lying is no good
We all suffer

The Position of Women in Traditional Society

> From a touch of jealousy
> Jealousy seizes us
> And makes us feverish
> (Okot p'Bitek, an East African poet)

Polygamy is an almost universal institution in Africa. The patrilineal system, whereby children belong by rights to the paternal clan, favours polygamy: the clan will be more willing to make the necessary sacrifices for the acquisition of other wives if it feels sure about the legal possession of the children.

The matrilocal systems view polygamy much less favourably. It would be difficult for a polygamous husband to exert effective control over wives scattered in various villages, or to fulfil his conjugal and paternal obligations. Also, the matrilocal system is frequently characterized by the husband's status of relative dependence on his wife's family and consequently on his wife herself. Thus, among the matrilocal peoples of South Katanga, if a man decides to take a second wife, he must have the consent of the first one; this, at least in principle, is never required among the patrilineal peoples.

In polygamous unions, each wife is traditionally supposed to have a hut of her own next to those of the co-wives. The man will consider his principal (usually first) wife's hut his headquarters and will keep his monies and possessions there. The principal wife welcomes a guest in her husband's absence; on his coming back, it is she who has admittance into his hut first. These 'respects' apart, a man is supposed to be impartial to his wives: in reality, unity and harmony in this respect rather belong to Utopia.

> Polygamy creates serious problems to African women. If it is true that it involves the husband's impartially sharing out the cohabitation among his wives, it is also true that it makes the women enter a world of jealousies and uncertainties, since the favourite wife may be pushed aside at any time to make room for another wife .... Some of them do adjust themselves reasonably well to polygamy as they find some comfort in their work or in their child-rearing or in their marital obligations, but many others feel very uncomfortable about it, whether they share the concession with the co-wives or they experience loneliness in town.[41]

It is the city loneliness above all that drives these women into some romantic escapade or love affair. A woman journalist from Zambia writes:

> In many African countries, like in many Western societies, the accusing finger is constantly pointed at women: for centuries men have considered themselves above faithfulness. They have apparently looked upon [adultery] as a sort of birthright or a divine privilege of theirs .... What could, indeed, sound more ironical than the comment in the *Daily Graphic* of the 20th July to the effect that 'quite a few women nowadays believe that indulging in adultery is no misbehaviour, while

men contest such outlook'? With whom pray, may a woman commit adultery? . . . If a man wishes to have two or more wives, it is his responsibility to have intercourse with each of them, even concurrently . . . . If he does not do so, and any of them happens to be unfaithful to him, he has only himself to blame for that.[42]

Relations between co-wives are usually bad, no matter what the supporters of the customary polygamous family say. Reciprocal accusations of witchcraft as well as practices of magic intended for one another are commonplace. In West Africa, for instance, magic 'drugs' are used, which are thought to prevent a man having an erection with any woman but the one who has administered them to him. Rivalry with other women and emotional insecurity often turn into hatred for the husband and for the children she had from him. Such hate, which if expressed would provoke the censure of society, frequently drives the woman to madness. Emotional instability worsens, primarily during pregnancy, when the woman is removed from her husband, who cohabits with another wife.

In October 1974, a significant news item was reported by *Drum*, a popular monthly magazine in anglophone Africa: Patience Onyege Ogbonnaya, a 'pretty housewife' from Abakaliki in Nigeria and a childless wife for 13 years, agreed to become the third wife of a polygamist. Twice she was made pregnant by him, and twice miscarried. Her doctors say that the third time will be lucky, but the other two wives object, claiming it is now their turn, and that Patience should go and stay with their husband's parents in a remote village of the interior. The husband gave in and fixed the date when she will leave, in spite of her begging to stay since she is pregnant again, for the third time, and so in need of help. The man would not relent, and Patience, hating to leave, hung herself.

Instances of family conflicts ending in the madness of one of the wives are also reported in a study on Senegal:

> I am not ill: I am only the victim of witchcraft meant for my death. My husband's co-wives and lovers are to blame for it; you see, he's a lady-killer, but it's me he wants . . . . They have made some plots against me, so that he would leave me. And a proof of this lies in the fact that my husband has had no sex with me since when I was in my first month of pregnancy . . . .
> (From the case history of a 31-year-old woman, a mother of four, admitted to hospital for miscarriage in the sixth month of her pregnancy.)[43]

The introduction of wages has also affected the relative economic equality of co-wives, generally by favouring the first wife, in terms of law. Today, money provides an easy and accurate way of measuring services: co-wives can work out the allocation of their husband's earnings among themselves and they can also more easily notice any partiality, however little it may be.

The introduction of cash economy is nevertheless responsible for a certain decline in polygamy.

According to a local adage, if all African men are polygamous by aspiration, they are less so today by destiny. This 'destiny' is the unbridled speculation on the bridewealth, which has made marriage more difficult; and above all, urbanization, which has made the maintenance of the extended family increasingly difficult. An extra wife is not a problem by herself, because a woman can well support herself both in the rural and in the urban areas, yet in towns it is more of a burden to pay for the children's school fees as well as to provide them with medical attention and all that it is customary for the father to pay.

Indicative of this are the answers given to a questionnaire (see Table 6) by hundreds of urban and rural Ghanaians. Caldwell comments thus:

> In a town the polygamous family may have to face many problems, notably 'physical' and economic. The housing cost may be devastating, and particularly so if the woman must live separately: an additional house used to be built through collective help, while today only rarely can an urban extended family find cheap accommodation, a thing easier to achieve for a restricted nucleus.[44]

Yet, even in villages maintaining a polygamous family is becoming more and more difficult:

> My study on the rural population of Ghana shows that the extended family is causing economic difficulties to parents also with respect to agriculture, and to a growing extent in the far-away rural North, too. It had caused no problem in an entirely subsistence rural economy, as it used to be mostly the case, but the spread of cash economy, the growing desire to purchase a vast range of goods and the large extension of schooling facilities have radically altered things . . . .[45]

Despite increasing difficulties, in Ghana, half the rural labourers aged over 40 and a quarter of these in provincial towns still practise polygamy, while only 12% of the urbanites within the Accra-Tema complex do so: but the percentage falls dramatically if we take wage-earners into account. Margaret Peil's already quoted study on the wage-earners of Accra, Tema, Kumasi and Sekindi-Takoradi, i.e., the chief towns in Ghana, reveals that only 8% of these labourers are polygamous out of a total of 26% of married males.

A crucial factor in the decrease of polygamy is doubtless girls' schooling: an educated female will, as a rule, reject polygamy and if she does not, it probably means that she is not sufficiently educated to earn a living as a skilled or a professional worker. An educated male may well spurn polygamy as it was practised by the elders but as a rule will be in favour of concubinage or prostitution.

As to the woman, the polygamous marriage – which is not legally

Table 6
Answers to: 'Can a man afford co-wives more easily in urban than rural areas?'

	Rural Survey		Urban Survey	
	No.	%	No.	%
In town	177	10	33	6
In a village	1,432	80	420	72
'There is no difference' or 'There are difficulties in both cases'	56	3	67	11
No answer*	117	7	65	11
Total	1,782	100	585	100

*Mostly unreliable answers they were in fact as they came from village people without any experience of city life or of an urban polygamous marriage as well as, vice versa, from urban families without any experience of village life or of a village polygamous marriage.

Source: J.C. Caldwell, *Population Growth and Family Change in Africa — The New Urban Élite in Ghana*, Canberra, Australian National University Press, 1968.

recognized in many countries — appears to her to be 'the lesser evil':

> if you question these wives, who are concubines in the eyes of the law, they will invariably reply that they prefer polygamy to prostitution: 'You win more respect if you are somebody's wife than if you stay single, whatever your rank may be'. If you go on to say that they are not official wives and consequently unprotected by the law, they will rejoin that a customary court may yet settle a quarrel. . . . The co-existence of two judicial authorities thus supports polygamy . . . which could be abolished only by means of a guaranteed wage to women.[46]

Colonialism, Neo-colonialism and Family Politics

The colonial administration opted for a family policy aimed primarily at strengthening particular rules of the customary laws, twisting their original meaning to accord with the exigencies of the colonial economy, while purporting to comply with tradition. The earliest measures of the Zambian administration for a marriage statutory law were the 1903 *North-Eastern Rhodesia Marriage Regulations* and the 1918 *Northern Rhodesia Marriage Proclamation*: since then, the only legally binding African marriage in the eyes of the administration would be one according to the native law and customs — not even a Christian marriage qualified for official recognition. In order to implement the native customary law, it became necessary to find a way of defining a 'native customary marriage'. The crux of the matter was whether the essential and final act of a marriage contract was the payment in cash and kind — and if so, which payment — or was it some particular ceremony or the marriage consummation itself? This was never precisely defined, but two 'formalities' soon became the sole prerequisites for a legal marriage, namely the consent of the girl's parents and the delivery of whichever was the most substantial payment.

The colonial administration thus on the one hand intensified the customary female subordination whilst making use of the dowry on the other. Operating in the same way as they did in respect of compulsory taxation, thus ensuring that people would become more deeply enmeshed in the cash economy.

The colonial administration's 'marriage laws' were carried out with the complicity of the native authorities. The only deliberate and constructive act related to the marriage law seems to be the law enacted by the native courts in 1944, which bade the Ngoni pay at least 30 shillings for the legalization of a marriage; unfortunately, there was so much speculation that the colonial administrators felt obliged to fix a maximum for the dowry payment. This was often circumvented by means of inter-party arrangements. The high bridewealth imposed by the native authorities, which served as a safeguard to the social importance of marriage, in the end served as a safeguard to the authority of the local notables.

> Within the context of the colonial cash economy, the money circulating as retail trade and the money circulating as bridewealth have a diverse qualitative content. The conversion of the one into the other will therefore be resisted. The bridewealth is determined by the elders by an amount which grows as the young gain access to money income. Any attempt made by the colonial administration at reducing such amount came up against the fact that *such restriction would enfeeble the authority of those notables who were enjoying the support of the administration.*[47]

Only after independence, that is to say from 1964 onwards, were the Zambian people allowed to marry according to the *Marriage Ordinance*, which was a more faithful mirror of the needs of the new times. Yet the number of African marriages complying with the *Marriage Ordinance* was still very low. From 1964 to 1970 there were more than 7,000 'ordinance marriages' involving Europeans, Indians and Euro-Africans, against approximately 954 involving Africans. The following figures refer to the latter: 41 in 1964; 89 in 1965; 122 in 1966; 195 in 1967; 252 in 1968; 225 in 1969; 30 in 1970 (end of March).[48] Thus in modern Zambia there are marriages according to the *Marriage Ordinance*[49] along with customary marriage; such duality, far from being a trait exclusive to Zambia, applies to the whole of Africa.[50]

This duality is at the root of many social problems, particularly those related to the rights of women. Some rights can only be obtained by 'ordinance-abiding' married women (in effect, the customary marriage has no full statutory status: e.g., only recently has a woman married by customary law been exempted from being compelled to witness against her husband in court). Furthermore, the uncertainty as to the moment when a customary marriage may be regarded as 'definitive' — and we have seen that such uncertainty was introduced by colonialism — becomes very serious indeed in cases such as when a woman is, or is not, a widow, and consequently if she is entitled to social security benefit, pension, etc.

We have also seen how the colonial marriage policy in Zambia was linked to migrant labour and how it tended to keep women tied to the rural system and the customary family, denying them any autonomy. This seems also to be the way of the new, post-independence régimes born out of the nationalist struggle, all of them generally reluctant to grant much autonomy to women.

> Women have a constitutional full right to vote in 29 nations south of the Sahara, including Madagascar . . . and this is no sheer formality. These women do use their polling rights; they are elected to the legislative bodies of many independent states, they do attain to high positions in their governments and gradually enter professions [yet] the political status of the majority of African women is by far more advanced than their social status as it is sanctioned by individual and familial laws.[51]

This is clearly manifested in the fact that the consent of some matrilineal relatives is still essential to the customary marriage. Traditionally, assent would depend upon the maternal uncle in matrilineal societies; but almost everywhere now it is the father. Assent is requested regardless of a woman's age or any previous marriage experience. To remarry, a widow needs her father's assent, unless she marries her husband's successor, to whom the original consent is automatically transferred (in the ordinance marriage the father's consent is not required if the woman is over 21 or is a widow).

Some 'local courts'[52] also require that a plaintiff or a defendant wife in a divorce case should be accompanied by a male relation — father, brother, or uncle. Women have also been put at a great disadvantage by the absence of a maintenance order system on the part of many local courts — with some recent exceptions coming from urban local courts.[53]

A woman's rights on marriage over her pre-marriage possessions are assured; also, by customary law she usually has a right over her earned income, from the selling of beer or handicraft items for example. Uncertainty arises when a wife is a' full- or part-time wage-earner. Ten members of a district court in the Southern Province, all of them belonging to the same ethnic group, expressed the following discordant opinions of a woman's rights to the earnings and

possessions accruing through extra-domestic work:
1) Man and wife shall share the wife's earnings, including the savings, even in case of marriage dissolution.
2) In the course of marriage the wife may use part of her earnings for her sustenance, but in case of dissolution of the marriage she has an exclusive right over her savings.
3) As the head of the household, the husband shall control all his wife's earnings.
4) The wife has a right over all her earnings.[54]

The court's justification for the ruling that a wife should share her earnings with her husband was that her absence would be a disadvantage to the man if he was not compensated by a supplementary income; also, her absence meant an increase in the family expenses. The members of the court also stressed that a woman should have her husband's consent before taking a job.

Polygamy calls for a brief, separate discussion. *In appearance*, it has been a constant feature of the colonial policy to modify the customary marriage along monogamous lines. In 1904 the Commissioners for the indigenous territories, i.e., the administrative officers in charge of the districts of the two Rhodesias, increased the per capita duty by ten shillings after the first wife on the assumption that more than one wife 'was a clear indication of an above-average wealth and therefore of an aptitude to pay above-average contributions.'[55] The tax remained into the 1960s and 'consequently [became] a less onerous and decreasingly important item of the administrative budget of the territory as the earnings have gone up and the economy has developed.'[56]

In effect, polygamy was always tolerated by the colonialists, who did nothing but superimpose laws of the Western type which, far from abolishing it, have simply lowered the status of the 'supplementary' wives. For example, in Zaire, polygamy was sanctioned by the law until the end of 1950. From 1 January 1951, a decree came into force that 'nobody shall go into a customary marriage before the annulment or dissolution of the preceding marriage(s).' But here, as elsewhere, the law does not apply to polygamous marriages contracted prior to its enforcement, but neither does it apply to those contracted afterwards. Polygamous marriages are ignored by the law, with the result that from a legal standpoint they have become concubinages. Thus, only the first wife of a polygamist is officially acknowledged. From the above decree onwards, widespread 'clandestine' polygamy has altogether escaped statistical estimate.

According to the 1955-57 demographic survey, polygamy is the actual status of 31% of married women and 17% of married men in Zaire; but, this is exclusive of the various forms of clandestine polygamy. A survey conducted in 1967, in the Manzasay parish, which covers about 30 Yansi villages, shows that 9.22% of the local families were officially registered as polygamous; yet, according to the survey, 'there are at least as many clandestine polygamous families, especially among the Christian tribes.'[57]

There is nowadays some hovering between an official position inclining towards monogamy and a 'traditional' position extolling polygamy as the sole 'genuinely' African family pattern. An article related to this appeared in a Zairese periodical, condemning the 'monogamous hypocrisy' and giving an idyllic portrait of polygamous family life. Of course everybody knows that monogamy is only a 'legal proposition' properly counterbalanced by prostitution, but it is also a fact that polygamy is by no means a gratifying proposition for a woman.[58]

In any case, polygamy continues to be a *legitimate* family form, above all in Muslim countries, albeit not *legally* acknowledged by many states. Now and again 'rumours' of a legal reinstatement of polygamy arise, only to be regularly denied. Nevertheless, 'if there is no way of going back on what appears to be a woman conquest . . . , it is a fact that polygamy is today practised in the majority of African states, even though everybody pretends not to know that.'[59]

The promulgation moreover of new and up-to-date family codes represents the recent culmination of a slow and painful process, notably in countries won over to Islam.

Caroline Diop recounts the Senegalese women's efforts to have a pro-women family code accepted:

> The adoption of a Family Code in 1972 on the part of our National Assembly was a really crucial achievement. Needless to say, it was a hard struggle . . . . Here, marriage is based on the Koran's precepts, since 80% of the people are Moslem. There have been some awkward and sorrowful moments of mutual misunderstanding when women have been accused of mocking the traditions and principles of the Koran. Yet, we have in this country a tradition which allows us to solve our problems: the 'dialogue' tradition. Like in old days, when sentences were issued under a baobab and instead of brutally assaulting each other the notables would come to an agreement by means of 'dialoguing' at length, we have resorted to this custom which makes the strength of our country. The government has started a dialogue with the religious leaders for a combined study in detail of the controversial terms and paragraphs. And the leaders seem to have finally understood that those points in the Family Code that appeared to them to be incompatible with the Koran gave instead its true significance back to it: the truth is, they had simply been misinterpreted.
>
> Yet, the promulgation of a Family Code does not mean by itself that women will understand its rules and become suddenly aware of their rights. A law is frequently passed without the people it is meant for knowing about it. It was with such knowledge in view that well before the Family Code members of the Women's National Movement took the pilgrim's staff and went even to the tiniest villages to inform and talk with women all over the country. Still, we cannot reasonably assume that all the Senegalese women became straight away convinced of the utility of the new dispositions.[60]

The Position of Women in Traditional Society

The fact is, in practically every African country the customary law is the only one most women know, they are even unsure that there is such a thing as a statutory marriage. This is why, on 2 February 1975, the *Sunday Times* of Zambia thought it necessary to explain in detail the procedure of the ordinance marriage, since it was obviously almost unknown. This is also why Margaret Peil, in her study on Ghanaian workers, remarks that civil marriage is virtually unknown: in fact, 'not one of the workers interviewed about it mentioned it.'[61]

On the other hand it is true that African women, and above all women's organizations, have just started to discuss these problems. Never, up to very recently have marriage and succession questions been the subject of a serious and detailed debate in any of the several conferences of African women. Commenting on such an 'extraordinary fact' on the occasion of a seminar on women's rights held in Zambia, H.J. Simons notes:

> There are, I believe, various possible reasons why women are reluctant to examine their position under the customary law. They are probably under the impression that the final result would be some antagonism with men, who 'will take it as a rebellion', in the words of the *Tanzanian Union of Women*! Yet, maybe the leaders of the women's organisations marry according to the French or English law which they make use of as regards property, and therefore they are less oppressed than those who live under the customary law ....[62]

Such very serious and certainly not groundless indictment brings well to light the division caused, also within the female masses, by the colonial and neo-colonial family politics.

Inheritance

Inheritance and hereditary rights are among the most outstanding problems stemming from the change of familial and marital forms, and in particular from the conflict between forms of matrilineal succession and the imposition of a societal organization and patrilineal laws after the fashion of the West.

Briefly, this is the position: in matrilineal societies, the next of kin and heir is the brother born of the same mother, then comes the eldest sister's son and, failing this, the next nephew in the descent line. In a nutshell, the children may not inherit from the father, as they do in patrilineal societies, wherein the inheritance often passes down to all the offspring.

This concerns traditional African societies as well as Western societies. The Ngoni inheritance system, for instance, strongly resembles the old English system. By Ngoni customary law, property, either personal or real, passes on to the heir according to the principle of primogeniture. Thus, on the father's death, his property will pass on to the eldest wife's eldest son or, in the event of his decease, to the second eldest and so on; in case of no progeny, the property will go to the eldest living nephew or brother. The position of the widow, too, is similar to that laid down by English law: a widow may continue to occupy the house and the land of the deceased for the rest of her life providing she does not remarry.[63] Likewise, by Lozi patrilineal customary law, a man's property is transmitted to his children, males and females alike — although a married daughter, as long as she stays married, will have no right whatever over her deceased father's land.

What happens if a man belonging to a matrilineal ethnic group marries a woman belonging to a patrilineal ethnic group? The progeny cannot inherit from their father because this would be against the paternal custom, neither can they inherit from their mother. Should a case like this occur in a traditional society — though it very rarely does — an interfamilial agreement would be reached. Now, instead, the frequent intertribal marriages and the evolution of the matriarchal family towards patriarchy have made the position of women and children less secure, primarily in town, where the woman ever more frequently finds herself in a new situation of dependence on her husband.

In present-day Zambia, a widow's rights depend on the existence of a written will. If the husband dies intestate — as happens in all the cases in virtue of the 1966 *Local Courts Act* — property will be transmitted according to the customary law, which states that in case of a conflict between matrilineal and patrilineal rights the widow may be deprived of everything by her husband's kin. If a will exists, the pre-1911 English law, outdated even in England, will apply. Miss Lombe Chibesakunda points out that this creates a dual system very much like the colonial one: the husband's customary law will apply to an African widow, whereas the English law will apply to the widow of an African domiciled in Zambia.[64]

There is, nevertheless, a number of important and significant restrictions to the customary law. According to the *Workmen's Compensation Ordinance*, the widow, or the children under age, of a man killed or made disabled by a work accident have a right to compensation: here, the customary law is not enforced, neither is it enforced when civil servants' pensions or other pensions and social security funds are at issue. 'If a widow is deprived of these benefits, it is not so much a question of inadequate legislation as of inadequate consciousness of one's own rights: in other words, it is a question of education.'[65]

Surely enough, the uncertainty of the woman's position is even greater in towns, but here women have on the other hand a better way of defending themselves and knowing their rights, as a recent study on some Zairean towns reveals.

> The economic value of a house is well known to the women of Inongo.... Unlike their provincial sisters who tend to leave the house as soon as their husbands die, they claim either personally or through their brothers, the house as a heritage. Should this be denied to them, claiming damages is their right. As a rule, the husband's family finds a

way out by handing the woman about one third of the house value.[66]

In Kinshasa, hereditary succession is governed by a set of rules specifically created by the judiciary to face the new economic and social conditions in town.[67] Such rules, which make up what Kinshasa customary judges have termed a 'progressive custom', generally oppose the customary rules. Article 7 of the 10 February 1953 decree, which constitutes the basis of Kinshasa progressive customary law, states: 'In the absence of a will, real property shall be inherited by the children or their descendants. No contrary clause withstanding, the partition shall be carried out in equal proportions among the children . . . .'[68] The enforcement of this article has come up against many difficulties: people tend to make only verbal wills and then, more often than not, they know nothing about the decree: therefore they will not settle their quarrels through the ward courts but rather through the customary arbitration. Banks and savings banks, nevertheless, under pressure from the National Bureau for Hereditary Succession, have taken adequate steps to protect legal and not customary heirs. Regarding the activities of this Bureau: in 1969 there were 37 either urban or ward courts having already ruled in 3,782 civil cases and 2,281 criminal cases. Conflicts related to inheritance made up about 50% of the civil lawsuits.

Yet, it does occur that, before the issue of decrees and specific rules aiming at codifying a new situation, traditional societies give themselves new moral rules — presumed to be better in tune with the societal reality even though carrying no legal weight — which will reflect the contrast between matrilineal and patrilineal law.

Consider, for example, the Ashanti people of Ghana, a matrilineal society, politically and jurally sophisticated. Already in the days of Rattray's celebrated and classic research,

> any adjustment of the normal order of succession must be implemented via a public will, and only in such way was a father allowed to pass property on to his son. He must declare his will in the presence of witnesses, to whom the son or other beneficiary would give the *aseda* in the form of money or palm wine, and upon acceptance of the *aseda* the disposition became valid. Wills of such kind were called *samansie*, meaning 'what the soul has put aside'.

Yet, the will was not bound to have a follow-up, since no jurally binding force was attached to it. The Ashanti people Rattray approached had this to say for that matter: 'If the deceased has unfairly allotted his (private) property, the living will proceed to a new allotment. In effect, if the maternal kin did not approve of some decision, they would promptly make it void.'[69] Albeit the laws of the Ashanti society still favour the maternal lineage descendants, 'the Ashanti fathers are fighting hard against the dictates of the maternal principle',[70] and this they do by imposing new rules and also by resorting to popular beliefs, religious or magic as the case may be. It thus happens that the new rules are observed, not because they are legal or more 'just', but for fear of often more imaginary than real sorceries or revenges.

In 1942, a man on his deathbed made an eleventh-hour donation of one of his cocoa fields to his son, and took an oath binding his succeeding brother to implement the donation:

> 'If you don't give the field to him', said the dying man 'I'll summon you before our ancestors, and they will judge our case.' After the man's demise, his brother, aided and abetted by the other members of the family, denied the field to his nephew. As it happened, there was a fire at the village two months later, and the brother fell from the roof while giving a hand to quench the fire: a wound in his right leg ensued, and finally death. Before dying, he told his folks he did believe that he was being summoned by his brother to the world of the dead to answer for not complying with his oath on the point of death. Everybody in the family seemed to share his belief, and so it happened that the second successor felt bound to give the cocoa field to the man to whom it had been originally bequeathed.[71]

Issues related to succession are being hotly debated in all the matrilineal areas. In Accra, in August 1974, the People's Educational Association of Ghana and the Young Women's Christian Association sponsored a seminar on the subject. Here is an excerpt from the contribution of Kate Abbam, the editor of *Ideal Woman Magazine*:

> The matrilineal system has caused a good deal of suffering to many people .... Women are subject to every sort of humiliation upon the death of their husbands. Often they are driven out of the marital house and deprived of even the smallest portion of the inheritance .... Ghanaian women have always worked hard. In the rural areas, they help their husbands with the sowing of food crops and cocoa. Coastal women married to fishermen take care of the fish caught by the men. They sell it fresh or they cook it before sending it to towns or other villages .... What happens when a woman farm labourer loses her husband? She cannot work on the farm any longer nor can she gather the crop because her husband's nephews (and nieces) have inherited it all .... Is then an ordinance-married woman in a better position as regards inheritance and succession? I would say that this hinges wholly on the type of relatives and even on their mood when her husband dies .... The negative aspects of the matrilineal system seem to outnumber the positive ones. We should never forget that our mothers had no chance to fight against this system. Now we have one.

Kate Abbam seems to be well aware of the unfavourable position of women within the matrilineal system, yet she is wrong in ascribing it to the system itself rather than to the introduction of the monetary and supply and demand economy which, as it calls for a new type of familial organization,

The Position of Women in Traditional Society

pushes toward a patrilineal system and thus imposes a profound change of the societal structures.

This stance, common to many African women's organizations, does not contribute towards clarification of the actual position of women in Africa but only towards solving the more acute contradictions inherent in the position, mainly by supporting or passing proposals for a change in the law. Valuable though this may be, it still represents a limited and limiting approach, above all because the trend is now towards a Western-type family, which certainly cannot be regarded as an 'ideal model'.

As a conclusive example, we give here the complete text of the motions for a reform of the law on intestate succession, as they were put forward by Philip Archer, Chairman-in-charge of the Law Reform Commission, on the occasion of a press conference.

Since the beginning of this year, as part of its IIIrd programme, the Law Reform Commission has been considering the reform of the rules concerning intestacy in Ghana. A quick look at the present position of our relevant law will suffice to reveal a few flaws.

Customary Law
a) The widow is in an unsafe position. She has no right whatever to any portion of the deceased husband's property despite the fact that through her manifold (and unpaid) housework she has in no small measure contributed to make the home comfortable for her husband. After toiling with him to acquire some property, looking after him when he was ill, being a solace to him when he was sad, now that he is gone she has been left destitute, with the insecure right to live in the house they both purchased and the rarely granted right to some maintenance money. In brief, she is at the mercy of her husband's successor.
b) In matrilineal communities, the children only receive a life annuity or, though less frequently, they are allowed to stay in the house acquired by their deceased father. They are so treated because, as regards the succession to property, they are not looked upon as members of the paternal family. If minors, they have moreover the right to be maintained by means of the paternal patrimony.

Section 48 of the Ordinance Marriage (Chapter 127)
In this section we find once again the rules of the 17th-Century English intestacy law, rules which have been repeatedly amended in England itself.... Another shortcoming in the section 48 of chapter 127 is that when the deceased is the wife the same rules of distribution will not apply, so that if a woman married according to the ordinance marriage dies intestate, her husband will inherit two-thirds of the whole patrimony, her family one-third and the children nothing.

Section 10 of the Muslim Marriage (Chapter 129)
According to this section, the devolution of the property of a Ghanaian

Muslim male, who married in conformity with Muslim rites but has had his marriage registered, must be in accordance with the Islamic law. The precepts of Chapter 129 are being violated rather than observed, and this may well be due to the fact that the Ghanaian Muslim in question is ignorant of the precepts above or maybe he is not but he finds the procedure complicated and irksome. By the Islamic law, an infidel, i.e., a non-Muslim, is not entitled to succeed a Muslim. Thus, when a Muslim dies intestate leaving children, or parents or other kin dependent on him, any of these who happens to be a non-Muslim will have no rights over any portion of the patrimony. Also this second precept is as a rule not complied with.

The Purpose of the Above Precepts
Our present endeavours for a national integration require that every attempt should be made to achieve uniform rules on intestate succession. The norms we propose in this regard, aim, therefore, at putting an end to the present-day multiplicity of systems as well as at making sure that justice is done to the people depending on the intestate. The Commission has only *suggested* that there should be such a change as to hand on to the surviving spouse as well as to the children of the intestate a portion of the inheritance, and it has consequently submitted some proposals for the eventual consideration of our government. Nevertheless, in Ghana, succession, notably customary succession, is a very delicate issue, therefore the Commission feels that, prior to submission, an exhaustive public debate on our proposals is necessary.
The Commission thus invites the audience to express their ideas and opinions on the following proposals:
1) Ghana should have one system of intestate succession, regardless of the ethnic group, religious creed or form of marriage.
2) The new norms should apply to the Ghanaians and also to non-Ghanaians married to Ghanaians or having a Ghanaian progeny, and dying intestate.
3) The new norms should solely apply to the property purchased by the intestate. They should not apply to family, clan, tribal or communal property, or to any position in these institutions.
4) If the deceased leaves a spouse and/or children, then all the family moveable property purchased by the deceased, such as a refrigerator, a television set, a radio, furniture, knick-knacks, earthenware, kitchenware, books, etc, all this should go to the surviving spouse and to the children (if any) in absolutely equal parts.
5) The remainder of the deceased's property (both moveable and immoveable) should be partitioned as follows: a) one quarter to the deceased's family (the customary family — that is to say, the family deriving from the deceased, whether a member of a patrilineal or of a matrilineal community); b) one quarter to the surviving spouse; c) half to the surviving children in equal parts.
6) If the deceased leaves a spouse but no children, then the surviving spouse should have half of the whole property, the other half going to the deceased's family.

7) If the deceased leaves children but no spouse, then three-quarters of the property should go to the children and the remaining quarter to the deceased's family.
8) If the deceased leaves neither children nor a spouse, the whole inheritance, inclusive of the moveable property, should go to the deceased's family.
9) If the deceased leaves neither children nor a spouse and his family has not been traced within 12 months, then the inheritance should go to the state.
10) If the deceased was the holder of some form of insurance against death, such as a life policy, or he was the beneficiary of social security contributions, a pension or other social security funds, but he made some designation to the prejudice of the spouse or of the children, upon application of any of the above parties, the Court may rule that a specific portion of such funds should be given to the applicant, unless the Court is satisfied that the applicant would not suffer from any undue deprivation in case the application is rejected.

The Commission has not yet decided what constitutes the deceased's family, as concerns the partition of the property. Any suggestion about the following questions will therefore be welcome:
a) Whether it is a matrilineal or a patrilineal family, should the suggested partition concern the deceased's extended family or only the next of kin, often referred to as the 'immediate family'?
b) If the deceased belonged both to the matrilineal and to the patrilineal system respectively, through the mother's and the father's side, will both families, either extended or immediate, make up the deceased's family? (E.g., the deceased's mother is a Fanti, but the father is an Ewe: then, both maternal and paternal kin can claim to constitute the deceased's family.)

Matriliny

At this stage we can assert that matrilineal *jus*, as it stands today, is *in fact* against women. It does not necessarily follow, however, that patrilineal *jus* is instead in their favour: rather, we have more than one proof to the contrary.

It is not our intention to embark here and now on the debate, so much beloved of anthropologists and sociologists, upon the qualities of either descent system. But a few comments on the subject are essential here, because this is no abstract academic issue but a real and dramatic topic closely affecting very many African populations.

Perhaps it is not pointless to underline once again and in the first place the fact that matriliny has never implied by itself a real social power of the woman, even though it has bestowed upon her a distinctly better status than patriliny has ever done.

In a traditionally patrilineal society, a woman has no inheritance rights; also, she is neither entitled to own any land or cattle nor is she allowed to participate in any debate or negotiation concerning property. As a permanent 'minor', she does not qualify for a legal action and certainly not so in person, not even if she is directly involved: she must always be represented by her father or brother or husband or son. On appearing as a witness in a public assembly, she must put on a subdued demeanour, speak quietly and clearly but with downcast eyes, and constantly stay on the edge of the assembly. Needless to say, all this is in sharp contrast with the male bearing.[72] Furthermore, in some patrilineal societies, even a mother has only a limited influence over her son.

In matrilineal societies instead, say, among the Ashanti, a woman enjoys precise inheritance and property rights, besides being the custodian of the community treasures.[73] Before taking a decision, the community always consults an elderly woman: 'Inferior as an Ashanti woman may appear to be to foreign eyes, she is really the final decisive factor in all the activities of the man as well as the arbiter of good and evil for the entire community.'[74] And yet the Ashanti woman appears to be, and in fact is, socially inferior to the man.[75] Thus, in the Ashanti region, unlike other regions in Ghana, there is a marked trend to keep educated women in the villages and to use female education solely for marital purposes. As a rule, unlike boys, girls are discouraged from spending their time in contests and sports. As a rule, sport is considered to be 'out of their depth': their force and drive should be 'preserved and kept for the strenuous maternity life in store'.[76]

Taking the initiative with a marriage in view is for the man. No girl would accept an offer of marriage without the consent of her parents: many Ashanti women have known their spouse only when the two of them have met as man and wife. It is, nevertheless, true that even a man's marital choice is limited: it is really his parents who choose for him.

Men and women are not allowed to 'dip their hands into the same plate' or, in other words, to eat together; this social barrier is mostly due to the taboos surrounding menstruation as well as to the basic 'uncleanness' of the woman.[77] The wives carry the evening meal, which is the main meal of the day, to the place of their father or of their husband's uncle for the communal meal where all men, married or not, meet. The women eat instead each in her own house or, at most, with other women who live in the same house.

The introduction of industrial crops such as cocoa has been accompanied by the breaking up of the family community as well as of the subsistence farming and the common ownership of the land. The Ashanti say: 'cocoa kills the family', and it is a fact that it has turned the clan property of the land into private property, thus breaking up the extended nucleus and the very basic principles of the matrilineal family.

The matrilineal law has been, and still is, a hindrance to the introduction of the private ownership of the land. The transition from matriliny to patriliny has not occurred peacefully but has been punctuated with social struggles betraying contrary interests on the part of rich Africans supporting private ownership and hence opposing matriliny, and poor Africans advocating communal property.

Such contrast certainly antedates the colonial intervention, which nevertheless represents a crucial factor in the outcome of the struggle. In fact, quite a few African kings found it advantageous to join the colonial forces, not only because this would ensure that they maintained certain privileges, but also, primarily, because they soon realized that the power of the newcomers might be used to oppose the matrilineal law and the common ownership.[78] Colonialism therefore strengthened the patrilineal law, as it denied the matrilineal family structure of all its positive significance, first of all by depriving women of their customary rights.

A typical case in point is what happened as the Kariba dam was being erected in the mid-1950s. In the (matrilineal) Tonga valley, a woman has the same access to the land as a man: on inheriting some land from her lineage or from her father, she has the same rights over them as a man. These rights were seriously jeopardized by the redistribution of the land carried out by the colonial administration during the construction of the Kariba dam, as this was accompanied by a shifting of the local populations. The land was subsequently redistributed but allocated exclusively to the male heads of the family.[79] Since then, the reduction and breaking up of 'free' land have facilitated the progressive discontinuation of the habit of diverting land to women too. At this stage, matriliny is no more a way of social organization, but *sic et simpliciter* a way — ever more outdated, contradictory and counterproductive as regards women — to settle the lineage.

Nowadays it is no longer a question of choosing between matrilineal and patrilineal law, for the choice is between a capitalist social organization and a *new* social organization no longer founded on exploitation: a new organization still to be constructed and perhaps even invented.

The Single Woman

An adult woman who was single was rarely to be met in traditional societies. Various studies on Ghana have made it clear that local women were more easily married than men and, in tune with tradition, this is still so today. In Ghana, it still falls to the woman's lot — as indeed the only one open and acceptable to her — to be a bride and a mother. (See Table 7)

Customary marriage is mainly regarded as an institution for the control of procreation, and is seen as a social act endowed with religious values and one from which nobody should shrink. For this reason, celibacy is deemed to be an actual 'social failure': a bad marriage is by far better than no marriage. (See Table 8)

The attitude illustrated by Table 8 is clearly reflected by Ghanaian tribal songs. Besides being a *comment* on various aspects of everyday life and current affairs, these songs help to rectify any 'deviant' individual behaviour on which public attention happens to focus.

Songs of this kind are a form of direct social control, sometimes used to

Table 7
Percentage of Unmarried Adults (1967) by Age Group: Accra and the Northern Region

Age Group	Accra District M	F	Northern Region M	F
15 plus	43.4	14.0	24.1	2.6
15-24	86.4	34.2	72.2	8.0
25-34	35.4	3.6	21.7	0.9
35-44	10.0	0.9	6.9	0.3
45 plus	5.8	1.1	2.1	0.4

Source: A. Tetteh, Marriage, Family and Household, in *A Study of Contemporary Ghana – Some Aspects of Social Structure*, (various authors) London, 1967, Vol.2.

Table 8
Answers to Questionnaire on African Women's Opinion of Western Women

Question: There are many unmarried and childless women in the Western countries. Some of them have interesting jobs and claim to be happy. What do you think of that?

Answers	F (331) No.	%	M (296) No.	%
Approving without any qualifications	9	3	1	0
With the following qualifications:				
That's right if they are happy	66	20	29	10
That's right if due to particular reasons such as medical advice, disappointment in love or desire to avoid a specific marriage	38	11	28	9
Other reasons	16	5	1	0
Disapproving without any qualifications	37	11	95	33
Disapproving with the following qualifications:				
Not congenial to the Ghanaian way of life	118	35	92	31
A mark of egoism	10	3	24	8
A mark of immorality	30	9	17	6
Other reasons	2	1	0	0
No answer	5	2	9	3
Total	331	100	296	100

Source: J.C. Caldwell, op.cit.

change non-conformist behaviour through ridicule, reprimand or an even more direct penalty. They may also be used against anti-social conduct, especially sexual offences: thus, they may be directed at some female member of the community guilty of bestowing her favours too easily or of indulging in slander or adultery; additionally, perhaps directed at sterile or unmarried women, both being significantly associated in the same censure and contempt.

> Young woman, go and seek some drug
> You have been ill long
> Get yourself some drug
> So that somebody may marry you.[80]

Here the singer displays little sympathy for the socially pathetic position of the woman at issue: 'not much patience with these unfortunate members of the community is shown, rather indifference towards them as human beings.'[81] The song may, nevertheless, serve the woman as an outlet, a token of her awareness of a difficult and unjust social situation.

> As to this sort of marriage
> I'd have done better to stay a spinster
> If you marry, you'll have problems
> If you stay single, they'll abuse you
> This question of marriage
> Has plagued society
> Nothing vexes me so badly
> As this question of marriage.[82]

As African societies became gradually Westernized, however, things inevitably changed, notably in urban areas. Unmarried women have become so numerous as to create a social problem. In fact the unmarried state often arises due to an individual and deliberate choice of freedom and emancipation.

Mambou Aimée Gnali confesses that: 'For a long time I believed, no doubt under the influence of my African upbringing, that in order to prove and express herself to the full, a woman should marry. Only experience has made me conscious of how vast a prejudice my belief was.'[83] At times, women, especially if highly educated, relinquish marriage to take up a professional career, which they feel would not fit in with a customary marriage. On opening a series of lectures upon women's rights in Zambia, Betty Kaunda said:

> In 1968 the United Nations sponsored a seminar in Ghana on women's civic and political education. On that occasion it was said that in Africa 'there is little recognition and appreciation of the contribution a single woman may give to the wellbeing of society.' There has never been much room for a single woman in our society. Now, many women, determined to push on with their careers, choose not to marry or at least to marry much later than by tradition they are expected to do.[84]

But the option for celibacy may also be due to the rejection of marriage as an 'imposition' rather than to career problems.[85] Nowadays, however, it is not so much a question of an 'unmarried' woman as of a 'single' woman, whether she may be a celibate, a widow or a divorcée. This relates not only to towns, but also and probably mostly to rural areas where increasingly the once unknown phenomenon arises of a woman deserted by her husband and now head of the family: the 1969 census in Kenya revealed that in the rural areas 31% of the families had a woman as a head; 20% in a rural district of Botswana, and 16% in Mali. Betty Kaunda explains:

> In the traditional society a woman or a divorcée would have been taken into the extended family by a new marriage or other arrangements. Now they face the difficulties of life staying single. The single woman plays an important role in society and thus she deserves respect like anybody who is contributing to the wellbeing of everybody else.[86]

Social Change and the Conscience of the Masses

We have so far analysed some of the problems stemming from the forced modernization of African societies and the warping of customary rites.

> Nothing is more dangerous than rites robbed of their significance and surviving in a changing world. Men clutch these empty forms with even a greater determination as they feel that the earth is shifting under their feet. Feeling uncertain about what is now and what is to come, they stubbornly cling to what is left of their past, unaware that they are clinging to mere corpses.[87]

This comment by Jacques Vignes is correct only in part; we believe that in order to survive, men must adjust and respond to economic changes by seeking new modes and models of living. The African peoples themselves have not always given a progressive response; they may well have won the nationalist battle but they have so far lost the class war. Hence they cling to the tradition which various local chiefs have given a brush-up for the occasion and then put forward again for conservative purposes. The 'rites emptied of their significance' serve now as a prop to the few authoritarian régimes, as well as the compulsory return to the 'authentic tradition' — actually non-existent and impossible, anyway — serves as a mass subordinating *anchor*. Nevertheless, the response of the masses to the problems brought by social change is not merely an appeal to the past: despite a good deal of wavering and backing down, they have definitely embarked on the quest for new ways and new prospects.

The torment of the private as well as of the collective conscience is manifested in African literature, more so in the oral than written forms. It is here that we find the dramatic tale of a shift from the values of village life to the new issues of 'modernization'. The following stories from the Boma peoples, collected and transcribed between January 1971 and May 1972, are particularly revealing.[88]

These stories touch upon all the questions we have dealt with so far, notably the decline of the authority of the elders, and primarily of the father: on the one hand, Westernization advocates *patria potestas* in matrilineal as well as patrilineal societies; on the other hand, as it makes youth more independent, it takes them away from this *potestas*. The consciousness that traditional institutions may be finally shattered is there, but so also is a 'propaganda' of the new values; values that is, such as monogamy, 'free marriage' and marital love (see the beautiful story below *The Woman Saw that Everything had Gone Wrong*).

A favourite theme is also how financially difficult it is to find a wife, or how hard it is to make two wives get on well together, especially if they are bound to share the hut they live in — once an unthought-of arrangement. In these tales we also find the condemnation of female adultery and the exaltation of motherhood, but at the same time the anguish and the rebellion of the woman, as they are portrayed in the poetic tale *A Drop of Rain Touched the Girl*, in which a young woman, although well aware of the peril she is about to face, tries to liberate herself from the suffocating security of village and home.

Up the River there is a Chief who has some Girls for Sale

Narrator: Niango; Village: Mushie Pentane

There was a young villager who had made friends with a local cook. Both were bachelors. One day they heard somebody say: 'Up the river there's a Chief who has some girls for sale.' They jumped into a pirogue and rowed to the place where the Chief lived. He asked them: 'What are you looking for?' 'We're looking for girls', they said. 'Are you bachelors?' 'We are bachelors'. And the Chief said: 'Stay here overnight. Tomorrow I'll give you two girls and you'll leave with them; you don't have to pay for them. I'll give you them for nothing.' The next day the Chief made two large parcels and gave one to the cook and one to the lad. They took the parcels, put them in the pirogue and left for the village.

'How now', said the lad, 'we went for brides and he's given us these parcels. Let's open them.' But the Chief had said: 'as to these parcels, don't open them along the way, but only in your sleeping room.' The cook said, 'Don't! He told us not to open them on the way.' 'I'm going to open my parcel now' the boy said. 'I want to see what there is inside.' 'No, no, let's open them at home', insisted the cook, but eventually he gave in: 'All right. You open your parcel now, I'll open mine at home.'

The boy opened his parcel and no sooner had he done so than he cried: 'Oh!', for his bride fled in haste out of the parcel, and he had to go back to the Chief. When the cook saw that the lad had opened his parcel and lost his bride, wisely he restrained himself. At home, he opened his parcel and the girl stayed with him.

Meanwhile the Chief was questioning the boy. 'Have you followed your woman?', 'Yes', replied the boy. 'So, you've opened your parcel on the way. Now, you have to pay for your woman if you want her back.' The lad paid 1,500 for his bride. Now, can you see, friends, why the cook had his bride for nothing while the lad had to pay for his?

I Will Have some Monies to Pay for my Marriage!

Narrator: Besak; Village: Mbaya

A country mouse and a house mouse struck up a friendship. 'My friend', said the house mouse one day, 'now the two of us are comrades. Come with me, will you, and let's go fishing in the river. If we catch some fish, we will then be able to wed our sweethearts.' 'My friend, I'm not coming fishing', replied the country mouse. 'Why not, my friend?' asked the house mouse, and he added: 'You see, when I've caught some fish, I'm going to sell it at the mart and so I'll have some monies to pay for my marriage.'

The house mouse took his fishing-rod and went. He cast and a fish bit: it was a big catfish. The mouse pulled as hard as he could but, small as he was, he could not pull that big fish out. There and then a hippopotamus came along and inquired, 'Well, what's wrong?' 'A giant fish has bitten but I can't pull him out', explained the mouse. 'What will you give me if I do that for you?', asked the hippopotamus. 'You do that for me, then come to my place and I'll give you something', the mouse promised and gave way to the hippopotamus who drew the catfish out.

'Dear hippo, you're a true friend', cried the mouse, then he cut the catfish and put it into his basket. And then he grumbled: 'How can I, a little thing, carry this basket?' 'You carry it for me, will you please, hippo, and I'll give you something.' 'Have you a beautiful present for me?', asked the hippopotamus. 'Certainly', replied the mouse. And they went to the village. 'My friend, have you caught such a big fish?', asked the country mouse. 'Sure I have', replied the house mouse. 'Tomorrow I too will go fishing', the country mouse decided.

The house mouse sold the fish and got married. The day after, the country mouse went fishing; he cast and a big fish bit. The mouse pulled and pulled, but so did the fish. Before too long, the mouse was dragged into the water and drowned. The house mouse also wed the sweetheart of the country mouse who had died because of his foolishness.

How Beautiful, I have Found a Husband for Me!

Narrator: Mundon Martine; Village: Nkowa

Two girls went in search of wild peppers. One went up and down but didn't find any. The other one did. The one who had found nothing was about to go back to the village when she spotted an extraordinarily big pepper. She picked it up only to realize that a boy was lying inside. The girl took him to the village crying: 'How beautiful, I have found a husband for me!' Back home with him, she said to her grandmother: 'Grandma, don't have this boy scurry here and there. If you send him somewhere, you'll answer to me for that.'

One day the girl went fishing with other women. Grandmother stayed in; she said to the boy: 'Go get some pepper at the back of the house.' The boy did so and then took flight. But the girl saw him and went after him singing:
Dear friend, wait for me! Husband I've finally found!
Wild little pepper, hullo!
Dear friend, wait for me! Husband I've finally found!
The boy sang back:
How now, I must run all the time!
How now, as soon as the sun is up!
I rather go back home!
I rather go away!
The girl pursued him for quite a distance and finally caught him up. They went back together. But what had happened already happened again. The grandmother said to the boy: 'Keep an eye on this pot on the fire, will you.' The boy did as he was told, but then 'I must go', he said, and took flight.

When the girl knew that her husband had gone away again, she chased him for a while, but this time she couldn't reach him. Then she returned home, locked her grandmother in and set fire to the house. Grandma died. 'You've killed your grandmother', said the villagers. 'We don't want you here any longer.' They drove her away, and the girl stayed in the forest until she became ill and died alone, deserted by one and all.

The village folk threw her body amid the grass. There, the jackals devoured her.

The Woman Saw that Everything had Gone Wrong

Narrator: Lonzi Kesandere; Village: Mbaya

A man had begotten two children. One could speak, the other one was dumb. One day the former called to his dumb brother, 'Let's go and look for some girls we can marry.'

Off they went, up to a village. They boy who could speak sought and found two girls. The dumb boy stayed motionless. When his woman took his meal to him, he just looked. The food stayed untouched. The following day his woman saw that everything had gone wrong. She threw the food away. The other woman was left wondering. The dumb boy's bride pondered a while and then said to herself: 'This marriage is no good. I'm serving the food to my husband but he's not eating it, and the food is going rotten. Things being as they are, I'll send a message to the village. Father and mother have given me in marriage; now, let them come and see for themselves.'

And so she sent for her parents. They came and asked for an explanation. 'My husband, whenever I give him food, does nothing but stare', the woman explained. Father and mother talked at length and concluded: 'This boy had not touched food for a long time, but we have succeeded in having him eat again. If he refuses to touch anything done by his woman, this is because he does not love her.' The village elder had given that woman to the elder boy, but he had not wanted her. You cannot force a marriage. A good marriage requires that the woman loves the man, and the man the woman. Forced marriages are no good.

The Polygamous Man Took the Woman of the Monogamous Man

Narrator: Kakesa; Village: Bunsumi

One man had two wives, another only one. The polygamous man took by force the wife of the monogamous man. Left alone, he said to himself: 'How is it that this friend has two wives and now he has taken my only one? He has done so because I am no real man. If I was he would not have dared to do so. Well, now I want to see which of us is going to die, if it's going to be him or me.'

The moon was shining. The man left his village armed with three spears and went towards the polygamist's village. At dawn he arrived and hid himself near the path along which the other man was expected to pass. The polygamist appeared and with him was the woman he had abducted from his friend. She was walking ahead of him. The lurking man leapt out, and the other tried to escape but the first cast his spear and — *kabou*! — it hit him in the thigh. The wounded man cast his spear and his assailant fell; but he rose immediately and returned to his village.

'My friends', he said 'yes, the man who abducted my wife, I've wounded him with a spear thrust. I don't know if he's dead or alive.' He was dead, and his woman cried loudly. People came and saw that he was dead. The monogamous man was cured of his wounds.

Your Wife's Going Out with other Boys

Narrator: Munoko Zo Mikodem; Village: Bunkulu

A man married a woman and the two lived together. One day the woman went to the market, the man to work. While at work, he realized that he had been hurt by a scrap of iron. He consulted a seer.

'It is not without a reason that this scrap has hit you', said the seer, 'your wife's going out with other boys. This is the *leshir*, an accident caused by unfaithfulness.'

The man decided that: 'This marriage shall be dissolved.' But the woman's relatives objected, saying: 'This marriage shall not be dissolved.' 'It will be as I have said', the man insisted.

The woman took her husband's possessions and sold them. When he came back from work, he found an empty house. He started weeping. 'What shall I do?' he wondered. 'She has taken away all.'

Then the man said to his wife: 'You have stolen my property. Now you will be a property of my family for ever. If you go back to yours, none of your children will grow up: they will all die. You shall live here and see only my family. You will stay here till you die. If you return to your family, you will surely die.'

This is Our God-given Task
Narrator: Adolofin; Village: Nkowa

A woman went to live with her husband. She soon realized that her womb was growing day by day. The woman thought: 'There must be a reason for this.'

In the ninth month she was delivered of a child. Instead of being two, now it was three of them. The child went through the crying-time, then it went on all fours, and finally it stood up. 'How beautiful!' said the woman, 'it was only the two of us before, and now we are three.' And she resumed her marital relations.

An unmarried friend of hers said to herself: 'How marvellous! My friend used to be on her own, and now she has a child.' She too got married, went to her husband's house and became pregnant. Nine months later a baby came into this world. She bore it in her arms, she nourished it, and soon the child was walking. It had just been the two of them, and there, they were now three.

Another friend of theirs wedded and the same thing happened. Those who were three became four. And they said: 'Marriage is a marvellous thing. This is the task God has given to us who are here below, on this earth.'

She Took the Child and Threw Him into the Water
Narrator: Ntango; Village: Busuka

A man had two wives. Whenever he rebuked either, he would beat her hard. Yet the two brides would come to blows daily. One said: 'I will no longer eat the meat my husband brings me.' But the other one ate it. One day, the husband slaughtered a pig, then he called to his women: 'Come, let's go and cut up the beast.' They went and cut up the beast. Back home, one of the women quickly ate up her portion, the other still had some left. The one sent her own child to the other's so that he would dine with her.

'Why is my friend's son eating here?', the woman wondered, 'Has he not been given his share by his mother?'.

Now, this child and the co-wife's child slept together. The woman got up and thought: 'How's that, my friend's child is here, he is eating and sleeping here.' At midnight she took the child and threw him into the water. Then she returned to the village saying to herself: 'I've thrown my friend's child into the water.'

Nobody could find the child. Everybody was asking: 'Where's the child?' His mother couldn't find him; so, he must be dead. Everybody was weeping.

Suddenly, the woman realized that it was her own child she had thrown into the water. Out of jealousy she had committed evil and had been punished at once: her child was dead.

If She Has No Eats, I'll Give Her A Licking
Narrator: Nkakiwa Pasikali; Village: Mbaya

Once two men lived in a village similar to our village here, Mbaya. Both of them had a wife. One day they went hunting but found nothing. On the way, they plotted against their wives. 'If, when I go home, my wife has no food for me, I'll give her a beating', one said. The other said, 'And if my wife has nothing for me to eat, I'll give her a beating, too.'

Finally, they were at home. One of the two fellows was a sly old thing. He called his wife and told her what he and his friend had decided, and then said, 'But if you haven't cooked a thing for me, I won't beat you. But when I strike the wall, then you get crying.' He struck the wall and the woman cried: 'Oh, I'm dying! Oh, I'm dying!' But the other man did beat his wife. The village Chief questioned them both: 'Why have you beaten your wives? Come here and let us consider the matter.'

The first one said: 'I've not beaten my wife: I've beaten the wall instead.' 'Why have you cheated me?', said the second one. 'We agreed on the road that we would give our women a bit of a beating if they had no food for us. I've beaten mine but you, why did you strike the wall instead?' 'Well', the other replied, 'If you get married, you should never strike your wife on a question of food.'

A Drop of Rain Touched the Girl and She Died
Narrator: Ngola Setrid; Village: Ito

Once upon a time a woman gave birth to a baby girl. Not a single drop of rain must touch the girl. Whenever the mother went into the fields, she would give the girl some food and lock her in.

One day some friends of the girl came and called 'Kananga, Kananga! Come fishing.' 'No', she replied, 'Mother has left food for me here.' 'Your mother said you'd come fishing with us. Why d'you say no?' 'I'm not saying no, but I'm locked in', said the girl. A girl in the courtyard said: 'Your key is just like ours.' So they took the key and opened the door. Kananga got out, and off they went fishing.

A big thunderstorm threatened. The mother went home and saw that her girl was not there. In a flash she left and sang as she went:
> Kananga, Kananga, Kananga, the rain will splash over you!
> At our village, the rain does not splash over anyone!

The girls sang back:
> I'm coming, I'm coming!
> At our village, the rain does not splash over anyone!

The mother took her child, and they returned home. Some time later, she locked her daughter in again, and again her friends came and called. She replied: 'Mother's gone to the fields and I'm locked in.' 'We have a key just like yours', they said, and they went away with her.

The sky clouded over. The mother went home in anguish. She opened the

door, but her daughter was not there. And she left and called as she went:
> Kananga, Kananga, Kananga, the rain will splash over you!
> At our village, the rain does not splash over anybody!

The girl called back:
> I'm coming, I'm coming!
> At our village, the rain does not splash over anybody!

The mother ran and ran, and finally got hold of her child. But on the way home, a drop of rain touched her and she died. Her mother wept and went into mourning. The girl was buried.

The village notables were called in and the girl's friends were summoned. They were tried and found guilty, and their fathers were sentenced to the payment of an indemnity for the death of the girl.

A Father is like a God

Narrator: Malotshi Sozefu; Village: Nkowa

A lad went to work in Boma. He worked and he worked, and then he said to himself: 'The money I've earned is enough: I'm going back to the village.' And back he went.

'Father', he said, 'I've come back to take a wife.' 'Very good', his father replied. The boy turned to his mother. 'Mother', he said, 'I've come to take a wife.' 'Very good', said the mother. 'Here's a house for you to sleep in.' The father took the boy to the house and gave it to him.

The boy went to sleep. And he slept the whole night. Daylight came, it was six o'clock, but the boy did not stir. The father grew uneasy. 'Why does my son sleep so long? It's past six, it's nearly seven and he's not made a move yet? What manners are these?' He went to the house and knocked. 'D'you sleep so long?' he asked. 'Yes', the boy replied. 'Give me water to wash myself.'

The father fetched water and gave it to him. The boy washed and used the water up. When he had finished, the father went out and waited for him. He waited and waited; it was nearly eight o'clock by the sun. 'Does my boy want so much time to wash himself?', he wondered. He asked: 'How does it take so long for your washing?' 'I'm dressing now', replied the boy.

'Ah, my son must be dressing to the nines', he thought. 'D'you need so much time for dressing?' he asked. 'Certainly', replied the boy.

'Son, when you return to work leave me your clothes, will you', the father suggested. 'How now, father', the boy retorted indignantly, 'I wore these clothes well before you begot me, when I was still in my mother's womb.' The father cried out, 'Woman, have you heard the way your son is talking now?' But the boy was unrepentant. 'Yes indeed', he said, 'I bought these clothes when I was still within your womb, mother.' 'Very well then', said the father, 'it doesn't matter.'

They fell silent. Then the father fetched a cock and gave it to the boy; they prepared and ate it. Then they slept well into the next morning. The father went and knocked at his son's door. 'Let's go, son, the cock I gave you yesterday is not enough; let's go hunting.'

They went and entered a forest, but there was no game there, so they turned to another forest. There, they saw some buffaloes wagging their tails. 'What now?' asked the boy. 'You stay here', said the father, and he crawled near the buffaloes. Then he shot at one and – koo! – the buffalo fell. They cut its tail off. 'Go and get your mother, quick!', urged the father. 'Let all the villagers, let the men come and cut the buffalo up.'

The boy ran fast. 'That's a good one', he said to himself, 'I've cut the buffalo's tail and now I'm taking it to the village.' But when he was there, he saw his mother weeping. She was wearing yam leaves fastened with lianas and throwing ash onto her back. She only carried a *cache-sexe*. 'What's wrong?' asked the boy. 'Your father's dead', she replied. 'What? Father's dead, did you say? We've just killed a buffalo together. So, how can he be dead?' the boy objected. 'Just as you say, but your father is dead,' his mother repeated. 'It's a lie', said the boy. 'Not at all. If you think I'm joking, go into the house and see for yourself', the mother said.

He peeped into the house and saw his father lying with thin legs and skinny calves, his teeth jutting out, his mouth half-open, his nose pointing upwards.

'Woe to me!' he cried, 'What's the meaning of this? Did I not go into the wood with my father?' And he set off running as fast as he could. Then he saw his father sitting next to the buffalo, waiting for him. 'Son, where are the men?' he asked. 'Father', the boy sighed, 'I've had enough of it. Nice things I've seen today! I've seen them crying for you as if you were dead. Mother was casting ash onto her back and wearing yam leaves. I told her that she was telling lies. But then I looked into the house and there you were, lying down.' 'Oh, son what a pack of lies! Go and call the villagers, tell the men to come.'

Quick as lightning, the boy returned to the village. 'Mother, come and see. Father is in the wood.' 'You're lying, you're only lying to me', replied the mother.

The boy went back to his father. 'Father, at the village, one can see that you are dead.' 'Let's go', said the father. And they returned to the village. The boy went inside the house, and he didn't see the corpse any more. 'Son, you told me you bought these clothes when you were still in your mother's womb. Well, you meant to put me to the test, I believe. What have you seen?' 'I understand', said the boy.

They quartered the buffalo and brought the meat to the village. When the day came for the boy to go back to work, the father gave him a wife. 'Son, give me these clothes, will you?' asked the father. 'Father, these clothes I'll never give to you.' 'Never?' said the father. 'Well then, the woman you're about to leave with will never bear a child.' 'Not true!' the boy retorted. 'I will beget with her.'

The youth lived with his bride, but six months later she had not conceived, whereas all the women of his friends had. The youth returned with his woman to his father, and gave him his clothes. The father put a string on his arm as a token of his benevolence.

One month had scarcely gone by when his woman conceived. Nine months later, she was delivered of a boy. Her husband shewed him to his father saying: 'Truly, a father is like God in Heaven.'

Notes

1. For an exhaustive analysis of the question we refer to C. Meillassoux, *L'Economia della Savana – L'Antropologia Economica dell'Africa Occidentale*, Milano, Feltrinelli, 1975.
2. *Ibid.*
3. E.E. Evans-Pritchard, *La Donna nelle Societa' Primitive*, op.cit.
4. H. Hochegger, *La Structure Lignagère* . . . , op.cit.
5. *Ibid.*
6. The unprivileged classes are mostly made up of descendants of domestic slaves.
7. 'An easily manipulable privilege, though', H. Hochegger comments in *La Structure Lignagère* . . . , op.cit.
8. For example, he will not have any right to a field or a barn of his own before one or two years' service in his bride's house.
9. The Bemba talk about the sexual relation more frankly than the Western people do; also, they give the adolescents a straight education and elaborate ceremonials so that they may understand the tribal attitude to it. Nevertheless, petting in public or dancing in each other's arms, as the whites do, is shameful in their eyes.
10. A.I. Richards, *Bemba Marriage and Present Economic Conditions*, Manchester University Press, 1969, 1st ed. 1940.
11. Among some Bantu peoples marriage is so closely related to the reproductive purpose that it is taken to be incomplete till after the birth of one child, or even more; it is on the occasion of such event that the ritual payments to the bride's family are made.
12. We find the same custom among other tribes. Among the Teke, for example, adultery with the chief's wife is regarded as a very serious crime and thus punished with the most severe fine of three or four zairis, a goat, a sack of salt, and a piece of fabric. If adultery is committed with the wife of an ordinary villager, the man is required to pay 20 makutas, a goat, two chickens, and a piece of fabric. (B. Schweizer, *Analyse Sociologique d'un Village Teke, Kingala Matele*, in various authors, *L'Organisation Sociale et Politique* . . . , op.cit).
13. A.I. Richards, *Bemba Marriage* . . . , op.cit. Another source of conflict in the Bemba society is provided by the relation between the father and the maternal uncle. The father is the head of his family group and has the highest authority over the early life of his children. He gives them education until they are of marriageable age and leave home to reach their brides' villages; and he has well defined rights over the marriage payments concerning his daughters as well as over his son-in-law's work. The father's sister too has some rights over the children, and she can ask one of her nieces to be an extra wife for her husband or

one of her nephews to be a husband for her daughter (cross-cousin marriage). But in the face of this, the maternal uncle is the legal ward of the children; he has a right to receive services from the males and a portion of the compensation money concerning the females. In return, he is obliged to keep them, if they so need.

14. A.I. Richards, op.cit.
15. In areas where premarital relations (except defloration) were allowed by tradition, the Church has modified such customs. For example, the *Women's Association of the Bantu Presbyterian Church* has reintroduced the virginity test in the guise of a premarital examination, and non-virgin brides are not permitted to wear the veil upon wedding.
16. In French West Africa and in French Equatorial Africa, the 1939 Mandel decree required the women's consent to the marriage: yet, the decree would not apply to a woman who had cohabited with the husband imposed upon her. In declaring the woman to be of age at 21, the 1951 Jacquinot decree gave her freedom to marry, 'nobody being allowed to take advantage of her either upon engagement or during the marriage.' (Sr. Marie-André du Sacre Coeur, *La Condizione Umana nell'Africa Nera*, Torino, EMI, 1958). Of course not only did such decrees remain unknown to most people, but also they could hardly be enforced, alien as they were to the local social realities.
17. Among other tribes there is a sort of 'trial union'. The relatives though, endeavour to offer the couple every opportunity for a successful marriage. The trial period preceding the proper marriage usually lasts up to the first childbirth, following which the union may be regularized. One should not fail to distinguish these *second class* marriages from the consensual unions not regularized through the customary marriage, which are also frequent. Such consensual unions are often essential for the woman: a barren woman, say, will be happy with her inferior status as a concubine with a polygamist.
18. Some women become the concubines of Europeans or Indians. These unions lack the substance of marriage, albeit sometimes the man gives a present to the woman's relatives, and this is seen as a marriage payment. The colonial administration did assist these concubines in order to secure the children's sustenance, yet they would not recognize these unions as legal marriages. The locals instead refer to these unions as marriages, even though of a peculiar sort, and show no contempt for the concubines. A woman who has lived a few years with a European can leave him and still enter upon a regular customary marriage.
19. J.A. Barnes, *Marriage in a Changing Society*, op.cit.
20. *Ibid.*
21. J. Segers, A. Habiyambere, *Les Conditions de la Croissance Économique, Kinshasa*, Centres d'Etudes pour l'Action Sociale, 1973.
22. J.A. Barnes, *Marriage in a Changing Society*, op.cit.
23. 'Some observers have found apocalyptic tones to denounce the consequences of such solidarity: the wage-earners, and above all the intellectual workers forced to divide their incomes and thus thwarted in their "natural" propensity to saving.' G. Althabe, *Les Fleurs du Congo*, Paris, Maspero, 1972.
24. *The Plight of our Women*, Zambia *Daily Mail*, 24 January 1975.

25. J. Houyoux, *Budgets Ménagers* . . . , op.cit.
26. A.I. Richards, op.cit.
27. *Ibid.*
28. M. Peil, *The Ghanaian Factory Worker: Industrial Man in Africa*, Cambridge University Press, 1972.
29. A fundamental work is the analysis of the economic and social meaning of the marriage alliance goods made by C. Meillassoux in *Saggio d'Interpretazione del Fenomeno Economico nelle Societa' di Autosussistenza*, in *L'Economia della Savana*, op.cit.
30. *Ibid.*
31. *Ibid.*
32. As a sort of contradiction in terms, kinship ties attain now a greater 'psychological' and social importance. Villages used to be part of a residential system and their structure was sustained by a central power which manifested itself through the real village governors and rested on the common notion of the rights given by the bridewealth. Where the governors have not much power and the bridewealth is not paid, the village is held together by kinship and affinal ties between the villagers as well as by the restriction of movement from village to village, namely by the control exercised by the colonial administration through the system of registering the adult males — a system which proved effective only in the Resettlement areas. The old marriage alliance, therefore, seems to be the only bulwark against the total disgregation of society.
33. *La Donna in Africa*, in 'Terzo Mondo Informazioni', V, No.3, March 1974.
34. An idiom referring to divorce.
35. *Bo-adwo* literally means a place where peace of mind is to be found.
36. Formerly, a man of high standing was entitled to send his wife back once she had become aged and ask for one of her younger relations in return. He would say: 'Go back to your brother's. You have grown old. Now you are just like a man. Let your people send me a girl instead.' This peculiar sort of divorce was known as *mpokoleshi* (A.I. Richards, op.cit).
37. Among the Ngoni, not even the husband's madness or contagious disease is accepted as valid reason for granting divorce to a woman, on the grounds that, instead of divorcing, she should try and look after her sick husband.
38. If the man is sterile, often, following his request, the wife is fecundated by a friend or a relative and the husband becomes the legal father of the child.
39. This is due to the social inferiority of the woman. The men of Kwaya, a Yansi village, refer again and again to the inferior status of the woman. *Bakar bar e lo*, meaning 'women are not human beings'. A statement often heard in the course of conjugal tiffs.
40. Among the Bemba, for instance, either party is legally bound to solemnize the ritual breaking of the mystical ties binding the couple by means of a rite referred to as the 'chasing out' or 'taking away' of death (*ukutamfye* or *ukubule mfwa*). The widow shall have ceremonial intercourse with the heir to the deceased husband or with his substitute

so that the dead man's spirit may return to his family. The husband's kin are required as soon as possible to appoint the substitute entrusted with the liberation of the widow from her bond with the deceased. On his part, the widower shall have intercourse with a girl provided by his late wife's kin. The girl is usually particularly anxious to perform this rightful act failing which no man will dare to marry her knowing that, for violating a taboo, he risks a disease or death.

41. R. Guena, Ch. de Preneuf, Ch. reboul, *Aspetti Psicopatologici della Gravidanza in Senegal*, in *La Donna — Un Problema Aperto* . . . , op.cit.
42. M. Kwakwa, 'Causes of Infidelity', in *The Mirror*, 2 August 1974.
43. R. Guena, Ch. de Preneuf, CH. Reboul, *Aspetti Psicopatologici* . . . , op.cit.
44. J.C. Caldwell, *Population Growth* . . . , op.cit.
45. *Ibid.*
46. Assiatou Diallo, *Recrudescence de la Polygamie*, in 'Amina', No.38, August 1975.
47. C. Meillassoux, *L'Economia della Savana*, op.cit. The speculation on bridewealth becomes thus a feature of customary marriage, yet not just of this one. In Zaire, say, even in case of a civil marriage (still a rare event) the registrar requires the presence of witnesses to the payment of the bridewealth confirming that it was actually received.
48. W.T. McClain, *The Legal Position of Women and Children under Zambia's Customary Laws*, in *Women's Rights in Zambia*, Mindolo Ecumenical Foundation (cicl.) 20-24 November 1974. Also see G. Zulu, J. Mfula, *Changing Patterns of Marriage in Zambia*, in *Women's Rights in Zambia*, op.cit.
49. The Christian marriage does not actually differ from an ordinary marriage. In fact the Code of Criminal Procedure defines the former as a 'voluntary union between a woman and a man to the exclusion of everybody else'. Lombe Chibesakunda, *The Rights of Married Women Under Statutory Law*, in *Women's Rights in Zambia*, op.cit.
50. See the politico-jural magazine *Indépendence et Coopération*, Institut International de Droit d'Expression Francaise (IDEF), Oct.-Dec. 1974, an issue devoted to the Tunisi Conference on the woman condition, showing a complete table of the jural status of the African woman.
51. H.J. Simons, *Women in a Changing Society*, in *Women's Rights in Zambia*, op.cit.
52. The *High Court* of Zambia and the Lower Courts only have jurisdiction over the ordinance marriage, the *Local Courts* over the customary marriage, in the matter say of divorce, minors' custody, etc. The High Court may grant a divorce on the same grounds as a British court might. In case of desertion, a woman must prove that she had never encouraged or accepted her husband's attitude. A detailed scrutiny of the situation will be found in Lombe Chibesakunda, *The Rights of Divorcees Under Statutory Law*, in *Women's Rights in Zambia*, op.cit.
53. Mambou Aimée Gnali, a former MP of the Popular Republic of the Congo, thus comments on the situation: 'In Africa, more than elsewhere, the authority of the law is just not adequate. There is some form of justice in "developed" countries, but in Africa men may resort to the foreign civil code as well as to the customary law, depending on

which suits them best. So, they will pay alimony only if they so choose, and nothing can force them into it, for they can always play smart with their options.' Gnali reaches the conclusion that 'in the present social texture, granting political equality to women, as the majority of countries have done, is just not enough.' (From an interview given to *Mwasi*, No.25, January 1975.
54. W.T. McClain, *The Legal Position of Women*, op.cit.
55. A.J. Hanna, *Storia delle Rhodesie* . . . , op.cit.
56. *Ibid*.
57. J.F. Thiel, *L'Image Statistique d'un Paroisse de Brousse (Manzasay Diocèse Kenge)*, in various authors, *L'Organisation Sociale et Politique* . . . , op.cit.
58. Kanika Mwana Ngombo, *La Polygamie – de la Légitimité a la Légalité*, in 'Zaire', 13 October 1975.
59. Assiatou Diallo, *Recrudescence de la Polygamie*, op.cit.
60. C. Diop, 'Gardienne de la Tradition, Pionnière du Progrès', in *Elima*, 11 May 1975.
61. Church marriage is instead very expensive, and only few outside the élite can afford it. However, it is usually preceded by the customary ceremonial, which is what really counts.
62. H.J. Simons, *Women in a Changing Society*, in *Women's Rights in Zambia*, op.cit.
63. W.T.McClain, 'The Rights of Widows under Customary Law', in *Women's Rights in Zambia*, op.cit.
64. L. Chibesakunda, 'The Rights of Widows under Customary Law', in *Women's Rights in Zambia*, op.cit.
65. *Ibid*.
66. Mpase Nselenge Mpeti, *L'Évolution de la Solidarité Traditionnelle en Milieu Rural et Urbain du Zaïre*, Kinshasa Presses Universitaires du Zaïre, 1974.
67. B. Kilolo, 'Le Droit Coutumier des Successions de la Ville de Kinshasa', in *Cahiers Zaïrois de la Recherche et du Développement*, XVII, 1971.
68. Mpase Nselenge Mpeti, *L'Évolution de la Solidarité*, op.cit.
69. E.A. Hoebel, *Il Diritto nelle Società Primitive*, Bologna, Il Mulino, 1973.
70. *Ibid*.
71. *Ibid*.
72. In all the (patrilineal) tribes of Uganda women were legally 'minors': as girls, they were under their father's authority and custody: as married women, under their husband's. Never, in the eyes of the law, were they regarded as responsible adults. C. White, 'The Politico-legal Status of Women in Uganda', in *Presence*, VI, No.1, 1973.
73. Even though the Ashanti have organized society along bilineal lines, the matrilineal principle is still supreme in political and juridical terms.
74. J.W. Tufuo, C.E. Donkor, *Ashanti of Ghana*, Accra, Anowuo Educational Publications, 1969.
75. Calling a man an idiot was once considered a most serious crime. Hoebel comments: 'Neither Rattray nor Busia nor any other researcher on the Ashanti has, as far as I know, shown the logical basis of this fine

example of male egotism. It is possible though that the Ashanti word translated as "idiot" really meant "someone inadequate to live and stay in charge". Furthermore, the context in which the offence is uttered may well involve some allusion to the incompetence of the ancestor in delivering such a specimen to the world. Male competence seems to mean to the Ashanti a good deal more than female competence.' E.A. Hoebel, *Il Diritto nelle Societa' Primitive*, op.cit.

76. J.W. Tufuo, C.E. Donkor, *Ashantis of Ghana*, op.cit.
77. No doubt polygamy is encouraged by the fact that over the menstrual period women are not to be touched and, even more, not allowed to cook for the man: no wonder if, under the circumstances, the man takes a second wife.
78. Towards the end of the 15th Century, some kings of the Congo had themselves christened: 'Catholic religion supported private property', MPLA, *Storia dell'Angola*, Roma, Lerici, 1968. In this paper by a MPLA militant group from the schools of free Angola, the struggle between matrilineal and patrilineal law is analysed and considered as a struggle between the aristocracy and 'the people'.
79. 'Women's rights have been put in grave jeopardy by the resettlement of the valley: the women have lost their ancient rights without being given any opportunity to obtain new rights forthwith.' E. Colson, 'Land Rights and Land Use among the Valley Tonga of the Rhodesian Federation: The Background to the Kariba Resettlement Program', in various authors, *African Agrarian Systems*, London, International African Institute, 1963.
80. A.A.R. Turkson, *Ghanaian Wit in Song*, Accra-Tema, Ghana Information Services Department.
81. *Ibid.*
82. *Ibid.*
83. From an interview released to *Mwasi*, No.25, January 1975.
84. From a speech published in *Women's Rights in Zambia*, op.cit. See my rendering of it in *Terzo Mondo*, VIII, No.27, January-March 1975.
85. Assiatou Diallo, 'Le Célibat des Jeunes Filles en Afrique', *Amina*, No.39, September 1975.
86. From *Women's Rights in Zambia*, op.cit.
87. J. Vignes, *Sguardo sull'Africa*, Milano, Feltrinelli, 1968.
88. H. Hochegger, *Femme, Pourquoi Pleures-tu? — Mythes Buma*, Bandundu, 1972. The Boma live in a region lying between the Kwilu and the Lower Kasai.

3. The Function of Women's Labour in Less Developed Countries

Womens' Participation: General Data

'In Africa of old everybody used to work', President Nyerere once said. In other words, in Africa of old everybody had their own social function and a source of income.

As a part of a family enterprise, everybody worked according to their capacity and education, though not necessarily full-time. There was usually time for family engagements, for learning or for community obligations. Unemployment was non-existent.

An awareness of the fact of unemployment came with the alarming proliferation of shanty-towns on the city outskirts where people were flocking in search of wage labour. (See Table 9)

At the same time, the decline of rural living standards accelerated the flight to urban areas, which soon involved new strata of the population. If forced labour, the migrations of adult males, and the segregational policy of the colonial administration had penned women in the rural economy, now they too went *en masse* into the towns thus exacerbating the problem of unemployment.

It would be difficult to calculate the degree of women's participation in economic activities, since the conventional notions of employment, underemployment and unemployment are hardly applicable to the African context, characterized as this is by modes of production which, though non-capitalistic, are yet governed by the capitalist principle.[1] For all this, conventional definitions of unemployment such as zero working hours and zero income have been applied, say, to the Kenyan case,[2] and estimates projected that by 1970 the level of urban unemployment in that country would be between 11 and 12% for males and considerably higher for females. (See Table 10) Yet, such a conventional starting point was not conducive to a positive conclusion on the number of unemployed women: on that score, the ordinary methods of assessing the labour force participation rate were found to be inadequate.

Furthermore, although the unemployment rate as worked out by our experts appears to be disturbingly high, it is only the tip of the iceberg. In reality, the 'poor labourers' made up a much larger slice of the urban

Table 9
Productive Population: 1960

Country/Region	Total ('000)	Distribution by Age Group %			Activity Rate %			Females %
		10-14	15-64	65+	MF	M	F	
Africa	**108,826**	**7.5**	**89.3**	**3.2**	**40.4**	**55.5**	**25.4**	**31.5**
West Africa	35,790	7.5	89.6	2.9	45.0	54.3	35.6	39.4
East Africa	34,246	8.9	87.8	3.3	49.4	58.2	31.0	35.4
Central Africa	13,085	7.4	89.4	3.2	44.5	56.0	33.6	38.7
North Africa	18,882	6.5	90.1	3.4	28.9	53.5	3.9	6.7
South Africa	6,822	2.5	94.1	3.4	37.6	55.5	19.6	26.1

Source: Extracted from ILO Labour Force Projections, part II: Africa

Table 10
Forecast of Productive Population: 1970 and 1980

Country/Region	1970				1980			
	Total ('000)	Estimated Activity Rate (%)	Annual Growth Rate 1969-70 (%)	Women (%)	Total ('000)	Estimated Activity Rate (%)	Annual Growth Rate 1970-80 (%)	Women (%)
Africa	**132,479**	**38.5**	**1.99**	**31.1**	**165,379**	**36.2**	**2.24**	**30.7**
West Africa	43,450	42.9	1.96	38.9	53,613	40.2	2.12	38.7
East Africa	41,975	42.9	2.06	35.1	52,688	40.9	2.30	34.8
Central Africa	15,257	42.5	1.55	37.9	18,114	39.6	1.73	36.9
North Africa	23,601	27.3	2.26	7.1	30,969	25.9	2.75	7.4
South Africa	8,197	35.9	1.85	26.5	9,994	34.0	2.00	27.4

Source: Extracted from ILO, Labour Force Projection part II: Africa

population than the estimated 15% (between males and females) officially unemployed. Experts thought it better not to label this slice as 'under employed', since it did include workers doing a hard job for long periods every day. Besides, labourers in this category were engaged in occupations which could hardly be defined as 'marginal' or 'parasitic'.

All this placed the eventual emphasis on the intrinsic value and vitality of a great many activities within the private sector to which many of the 'poor labourers' belonged. It proved to be justifiable, particularly with regard to women, as soon as the artificial division between 'economic activities' and 'other activities' was disregarded. (See Table 11)

Table 11
Unemployed and Low-Paid Labourers by Sex and Status in Nairobi: 1970
(% of the adult population)

	M		F	
	Family Heads	Family Members	Family Heads	Family Members
Unemployed*	4.9	10.0	10.8	22.8
Low-paid workers	13.8	13.6	40.7	31.8
Total	*18.7*	*23.6*	*51.5*	*54.6*

*Persons with zero income and in search of work

Source: H. Singer, R. Jolly, *Unemployment in an African Setting*, op.cit.

The conventional methods of assessing the participation rate of the urban labour force appear to be even more inadequate if applied to rural areas, notably to female labour in these areas. It has been reckoned that in the midsixties one-quarter of African women were economically active (see Tables 12 & 13), mostly as farm labourers (see Tables 14 and 15).

Table 12
Percentage of Female Labour Force as against Total Labour Force by Economic Sector and Region: 1960

	All Sectors	Agriculture	Industry	Tertiary
Africa	**32**	**34**	**15**	**30**
West Africa	39	40	25	46
East Africa	35	37	16	24
Central Africa	39	44	5	14
North Africa	7	5	9	11
South Africa	26	24	7	44

Source: Adapted from Ettore Denti, Africa's Labour Force 1960 in ILO *Employment in Africa*, Geneva, 1973.

Table 13
Regional Distribution of Total Population and
Productive Population: 1960 (%)

	Total Population			Productive Population		
Region	MF	M	F	MF	M	F
Africa	**100.0**	**100.0**	**100.0**	**100.0**	**100.0**	**100.0**
West Africa	29.5	29.7	29.3	32.9	29.1	41.0
East Africa	28.6	28.3	28.9	31.5	29.7	35.3
Central Africa	10.9	10.7	11.1	12.0	10.8	14.8
North Africa	24.3	24.5	24.0	17.3	23.6	3.7
South Africa	6.7	6.8	6.7	6.3	6.8	5.2

Source: Ettore Denti, op.cit.

Table 14
Distribution of Productive Population by Region and Sector: 1960 (%)

		M			F		
Region	Total	Agri-culture	Indus-try	Ter-tiary	Total	Agri-culture	Indus-try	Ter-tiary
Africa	**100.0**	**100.0**	**100.0**	**100.0**	**100.0**	**100.0**	**100.0**	**100.0**
West Africa	29.1	29.6	29.2	26.1	41.0	38.7	56.6	51.8
East Africa	29.7	33.9	16.2	19.5	35.3	39.0	18.3	14.2
Central Africa	10.8	11.0	11.1	9.0	14.8	17.5	3.3	3.5
North Africa	23.6	21.6	24.3	34.0	3.7	2.4	13.4	10.1
South Africa	6.8	3.9	20.2	11.4	5.2	2.4	8.4	20.4

Source: Ettore Denti, op.cit.

The limitations of statistical data which underrate the scope of female labour especially in rural areas has already been noted: here more than elsewhere the demarcation line between 'economic' and 'non-economic' activities, respectively carried out by units within the labour force and units without it, is statistically arbitrary and does not make sense if related to standards of living.[3] An overall picture of the extent, importance and weight of rural women's labour in African countries was provided by Ghana's female representatives at the 1974 Congress of African and Arab women in Cairo.

Quoting the conclusions based on a questionnaire on female labour in Africa set by ECA,[4] Dr Evelyn Amarteifio said:

> On average, a woman spends daily 15 hours working, 1 hour eating and 8 hours sleeping. This study has confirmed the common male habit of letting women do the bulk of the work in the home as in the fields.

Table 15
Distribution of Population by Economic Activity: 1960 (approx. %)

	Agriculture	Industry	Services
Men and Women:			
Africa:	75	10	15
East	87	5	8
Central	84	8	8
West	76	9	15
North	65	11	24
South	42	23	35
Men:			
Africa:	72	12	16
East	82	7	11
Central	76	10	14
West	76	9	15
North	66	12	22
South	43	30	27
Women:			
Africa:	81	10	9
East	92	2	6
Central	95	1	4
West	75	7	18
North	48	15	37
South	37	7	66

Source: *Adapted from* Ettore Denti, op.cit.

Something in the region of 60% to 80%, 70% in some places, of the traditional agricultural work is carried out by females. They clean the fields or prepare the soil for the sowing and the reaping. Rain or sunshine, twice or thrice a day they walk for miles to fetch water, at times carrying their little ones on their backs; they fetch firewood and see to the needs of the children, the old and the adult males of the family. They clean, cook, conserve the produce, and sometimes they look after the domestic animals . . . .

They are expected to perform all this without proper training. In comparison, the man spends less time in the fields, less on housework and has less onerous duties. And he has the training leverage, too. Any monies women may earn from selling farm produce is customarily handed over to the men: should they then need some extra cash to spend on the families needs or on food, as often as not they have to fight for it with the husband or head of family.[5]

With due reservations vis-à-vis statistical evidence when applied to a social fabric as varied as Africa's it is interesting briefly to note the percentage of women's activity in the regions of Africa. Central regions show a constant growth of economic activity within the 10-54 age group and a gradual decline around ages 55-64, followed by a sharp decline for the over-65s.

North Africa is characterized by a very low rate of economic activity for all age groups, typical of Muslim countries and of African territories formerly under Spanish or Portuguese administration. The low proportion for agricultural labour (see Table 15) is due to the number of women engaged in such work as 'family labourers'; by the same token, there is an over-rated proportion of women engaged in the industrial and service sectors. South Africa — and this may also apply to Namibia — is characterized by economic activity in two distinct age groups — the 20-24 and the 45-54 age groups. A situation bearing a striking resemblance to that of most European countries and of the United States.

Women in Industry

As a rule, women in industrial employment make up a tiny contingent of the African labour force, the only notable exception being the West African group.

Political independence has no doubt brought an increase in the number of women workers everywhere; not so much in industry as in the so-called 'modern sector' of the economy: in other words, today more women work for a wage or salary. This increase has, however, taken place almost exclusively in big towns and has so far been confined to women with a high degree of education or good professional qualifications. In the Ivory Coast, in 1965, the number of women working in the 'modern sector' was not more than 6,000 out of 180,000 wage-earners, i.e., just over 3% of the total.[6] Between 1955 and 1963 the rate of female participation in the capital city grew from 6% to 13%, while by 1965, in Accra (Ghana) it had grown to 55%.

In Zambia, in 1963 only 7,000 African females were earning a wage; in 1969, 30,187 were doing so, while 178,504 women were still looking for waged work. This means that of all the women over 14 years old, 18% wished to be involved in the capitalist economy, albeit without leaving the land and, correspondingly, 19% sought to earn a living in town. These figures are somewhat misleading: on the whole, the percentage of female wage-earners increases slowly and in some cases it even tends to decrease.

This trend is probably related to the conflict between domestic and extra-domestic work, unknown in traditional rural society. In African cities, family life puts on a new look and takes on a new quality: as a result, domestic work undergoes a qualitative and quantitative transformation. Tasks such as childcare, formerly collectively carried out by women in the extended family, are now becoming increasingly individualized.[7]

By interviewing more than 1,400 workers from 16 Ghanaian factories (8 in

Accra, 2 in Tema, the others at Kumasi, Zakoradi and in some villages near Accra), Margaret Peil found that women were not attracted by factory work, mainly because it involved regular working hours, which would make it difficult for them to perform their home duties. Women were much keener than men on independent work such as trade, because it fitted in better with marriage and child-rearing.

One feature of the International Year of the Woman was the CADICEC Congress on female wage labour, held in Kinshasa on the 5 and 17 June in the course of which participants emphasized how beneficial it would be if they had half-day a week off duty for shopping.[8]

Thus, wage labour, particularly factory labour, conflicts with domestic work, and yet the wife's wage has become increasingly necessary to the average urban family facing new and considerable expenses. All this is confirmed by Peil's research, which proves that female factory workers are not less 'stable' than male workers. For example, in Tema women have only recently started working in factories, yet the turnover and absenteeism of female workers appear not to be especially high, though they do tend to stay away from work more frequently than men. In Accra, there is no significant difference between the performance of males and females. The majority of women are married and, as far as absenteeism is concerned, their age and marital status seem to be more important than their sex. (See Table 16).

Older married women are more willing to remain as factory workers, obviously because they feel more firmly bound to their place of work than younger women, who can easily find other means of sustenance.

Factory work is likewise favoured by single women such as widows, divorcées, or unmarried mothers. In the Maridadi handicraft factory in Nairobi, most of the 80 females employed are either widows or unmarried mothers.

There is a tendency to utilize women in seasonal or temporary jobs: the Gambia Fisheries Ltd. for example were giving work to 1,080 women in 1973, mostly as occasional workers; 986 women are currently employed by Gambia Produce Marketing Board as seasonal labourers hand-husking nuts for export; also in Gambia, Chellerams Shoe Factory make candles, plastic shoes, woollies and so forth, employing over 1,000 women, most of them on a casual basis — later, we shall see how this applies to farming wage labour.

By far more appreciable seems to be women's participation in small industries and handicrafts in general, although it is by no means easy to assess it accurately owing to the familial or underhand nature of such enterprises, a fact which adds to the difficulties of a more general kind. It is nevertheless safe to say that often 'rural economy depends on products manufactured by women through the use of locally available material'.[9] About half of the handicraft in the Ivory Coast, Upper Volta, Togo and Benin is women's work. Women make up 60% of the labour force in the craft centres of Lesotho (each of them having an occupational capacity of 150-200 units) as knitters, weavers, designers, cloth-dyers and so on.

In Swaziland a whole department of the Ministry of Mining Industry and

Table 16
Factory Absenteeism in Accra-Tema: (Workers Still on the Job 15 Months After the First Interview): by Occupation, Sex and Region of Origin

	Accra %	Accra No.	Tema %	Tema No.
Occupation				
Unskilled	64	(102)	82	(28)
Semi-skilled	74	(180)	71	(160)
Skilled	74	(291)	69	(13)
Clerks	85	(60)	71	(31)
Male	74	(600)	71	(212)
Female	83	(75)	68	(38)
Region of origin				
Accra East District	68	(175)	70	(100)
Accra Central and West District	72	(190)	68	(62)
Volta	79	(81)	62	(32)
Ashanti, Brong/Ahafo	66	(44)	78	(41)
North, Upper Volta	53	(32)	100	(5)
Aliens	73	(153)	70	(10)
Total	75	(675)	70	(250)

Source: M. Peil, *The Ghanaian Factory Worker: The Industrial Man in Africa*, Cambridge University Press, 1972.

Tourism is dedicated to the purchase of all the handicraft coming from the rural areas, where marketing is not really possible. Young or middle-aged women are engaged in the production of carpets or mats made of pliant grass-plants from the Swaziland mountains, sisal saucers, seed necklaces, baskets and dried flowers.

There are three Swazi Flower Centres in the country: these flowers, which are on sale everywhere in South Africa, were being imported by America in the early months of 1975 and Europe also planned to import them. '... I discovered that Swazi women were more active than men .... After long hours of field work, you might still find women manufacturing seed pearls or some other handmade item such as dried flowers and the like for ornamental purposes.'[10]

Women use Swazi Craft warehouses as stores for their products or as hand transaction offices whenever a buyer is around. Most handicraft retail stalls are in Mbabane, a major town of Swaziland. There are about 60 stalls in the country, only six of which are owned by men. Women stall owners buy handicraft items straight from rural women producers, who nevertheless are often left with unsold goods. As far as handicraft is concerned, in many African countries and especially in West Africa, the local market is dominated by women. Women may also own small factories, even though this happens only in countries such as Gambia, where tradition and society permit them to do so.

In Kenya too, women have made the first move towards the promotion of handicraft and the opening of craft shops or stalls in Nairobi: in June 1972, the National Women's Handicraft Co-operative Society entered the record at the Ministry of Co-operation and Social Services. It later became *Maendeleo ya Wanawake* (Women's Progressive Organization) and expanded to over 5,000 clubs and 80,000 members. It principally aims at promoting domestic industry, improving the quality of the produce, unifying prices, creating job opportunities (especially in rural areas) making sale agreements and so forth.[11]

An attempt has been made in many African countries to organize co-operatives for craft production, but in only a few of these countries have co-operatives merged to become strong movements. Some co-operatives have continued for quite a while, but good progress has been made only by those operating in countries where independence has generated a drive towards self-help.[12] Women make up the bulk of the co-op workers, yet in few countries have they been given at least equal managerial and organizational opportunities inside the co-op framework.

In the course of a women's congress in Zambia, the Secretary of the International Co-operative Alliance for women's and youth activities said:

> From experiences I've had for the last two or three years I am personally convinced that the African woman is more eager for learning and social opportunities than it is commonly thought. It surprised me in 1972 to see Nigerian women walking up to hundreds of miles and certainly not in comfort, carrying their children pickaback, to take part in a seven-day seminar on co-operatives. Keeping all of them, and keeping them interested at that, in assembly from 8.30 in the morning till 6 or 7 in the evening proved to be no problem, and at the end of the week the most common regret was that time had just not been enough. So much so that a few of those women were apparently willing to join an extra course, if there was one.
>
> The heart of the matter was, I believe, that, being aware of their limitations, those women were looking for ways and means to use their abilities in such a manner as to expand and strengthen their economic position, without at the same time upsetting the ties and responsibilities toward their families, as would be the case if they were to spend some extra time on formal schooling. This is what co-operation can primarily do to benefit women, whether they are involved in a consumer, agricultural or producer society . . . .
>
> To be successful, a handicraft co-op requires: a) a good standard quality of the end-product; b) the collaboration with a sales organization.

Now, after witnessing women's brave efforts in five or six African countries, I have reluctantly reached the conclusion that both the above requisites have been hard to fulfil probably because they have not been adequately promoted. Thus, a few women have flagged when, after putting up with uncomfortable places making baskets, vases and so on, they have in the end seen their products remain for ever on the shelves of the centres which self-help organizations and groups had started with the best of intentions. I'm glad to say though that a remarkable exception is the Lesotho Co-operative Handicraft Society, which has now a retail unit of its own . . . .

I've been asked many times if I am for societies of 'only women'. Well, I do believe that on the whole the future of co-ops rests on the full participation of both sexes. Nevertheless, for the time being, as women are endeavouring to find the most suitable way to gain economic independence as well as confidence in their abilities, it is only proper that they should be on their own, especially as regards those co-operatives they have started by themselves and where production fits in well with their work. Without men, women must stand on their feet and by so standing they will eventually acquire the necessary managerial expertize.[13]

The Rights of Working Women

In principle, governments issue official statements in favour of female labourers; women's right to equal pay or to maternity leave find ample recognition on paper.

According to para. 42 of the Labour Decree, industrial, commercial or rural employers must grant those women workers who produce a certificate issued by a doctor or a midwife six weeks ante-natal maternity leave as from the certificate date and a minimum of six weeks post-natal leave, or up to eight weeks in the case of an abnormal, twin or multiple birth. The maternity leave must not affect her recreational holiday rights; also, a woman is not to be moved from her home after the fourth month of pregnancy if the doctor or the midwife declare that moving out might be prejudicial to her. A woman worker with child, or the mother of an under eight-year-old child is not eligible for overtime, but still qualifies for full pay. A nursing mother is entitled to an half-hour feeding period twice a day during working hours.[14]

In fact a great deal of collective bargaining contains measures which are in flagrant contrast with the rights as stated by the Labour Decree. Under some agreements, for example, a woman worker will have no maternity leave rights until she has been working for six or sometimes twelve months. In a factory the motion was put forward that a woman with child within her first year of employment should be dismissed: when the women protested, management replied that they were in no position to pay yearly maternity leave to a great number of workers.

In her book, Margaret Peil exposes the recent attempt made by two public corporations and some private firms to abolish the maternity leave, 'which makes Ghanaian women expensive indeed', or to allow it, duly paid, only twice regardless of the duration of employment.

The recent Code of Labour Law in the Republic of Cameroon comprises some very interesting norms for female wage-labourers, mainly concerning maternity; old norms have been reinforced with new ones officially purposing to 'ensure the full development of the woman as a mother and as a worker'. The Code sanctions the right to maternity leave for 14 weeks (eight before childbirth and six after it), full pay over the leave period and the right to one nursing hour off daily for 15 months. Yet, we also find two 'revealing' norms in the Code:

a) A woman whose pregnancy has been certified by a doctor may rescind her work contract without notice and without having to pay the relevant indemnity.

b) During the breast-feeding period, a woman may rescind the contract without notice on the same conditions that apply to a pregnant woman. Thus, there is on the one side an attempt to abolish or restrict the woman's benefits during gestation — such being, as we have seen, the case with Ghana — and on the other a blatant attempt in countries such as Cameroon, to facilitate the interruption of the contract during gestation. The probable result of all this is to discourage women from seeking or keeping waged work and to make them fall back on some 'marginal' activity or on what in West Africa is *the* job for a woman, namely commerce.

Business Women in West Africa

In the majority of West African states, trade or — as Meillassoux put it — market trade is by tradition an essentially female activity.

African market places have always been important transactional centres under the control of women: 'Their stalls spread out for hundreds and hundreds of yards. They sell all sorts of things, such as farm produce ... manufactured or handicraft items ... in places like Malanville ... every Sunday morning turns into an international event.'[15] At Lomé and Cotonou markets the space reserved for cloth-selling is almost entirely occupied by women, the so-called 'cloth-retailers'. At Cotonou the Chamber of Commerce has released up to 275 licences, 225 of them to women. On the whole the distribution system is almost exclusively controlled by thousands of female retailers.

Over 25,000 traders turn up at the various Accra markets daily: 85% of whom are women, many of whom start business with a less than twenty-pound capital. Only about 5,500 of these traders have a regularly rented stall.[16] 60% of the traders deal in local food and fuel; 15% are artisans, say, tailors, and only 25% deal in imported goods.

Ghanaian markets are organized and ruled by a 'Queen Mother'; she has many tasks on her hands, which are not necessarily the same at every mart.

The Queen Mother of a town market is the elected representative of all the retailers selling the same goods: there will be one for the yam sellers, one for the cassava sellers and so on. Her chief task is to protect the sectorial interests of the retailers she represents. Should she fail to do so or should she take advantage of her position for her own benefit, she will be removed in the Ghanaian way, which is customarily a democratic one.

In the rural areas, where market dealings are to a great extent about collecting food produced on the spot and wholesaling it to the retailers who come to them, the Queen Mother is the elected representative of the supplying and the trading farmers. But in towns and large villages with only a limited space for a market place and consequently a restricted number of regular traders, a Queen Mother has the important function of ensuring that retailers have a fair share of space and supplies. Her function is particularly important when supplies are scarce; such 'regulating' function was of paramount importance in 1965, when there was not much food in store.

A Queen Mother may also be called upon to ensure the highest selling price possible or to act as a guarantor for retailers: whenever a lorry load of food comes to the market, she guarantees payment to the wholesaler and the lorry-driver, who may be the same person.

Lastly, besides guarding sectorial interests by securing supplies at a reasonable price and negotiating sale prices, a Queen Mother arbitrates in disputes between traders belonging to her own group or represents them in agreements or disputes with other market traders or a wholesaler.

The economic activities of women traders clearly affects some other sectors of society. Margaret Peil's study[17] on the occupation of fathers of students entering the University of Legon in 1963 as compared with the 1951-53 data, when that university was the University College of the Ivory Coast, led to surprising results.

Over the 1951-53 period, parents of the majority of the students were plantation owners or fishing dealers; 15% were lesser professional people and 14.4% were petty traders. By 1963, the latter were in second place: 'These traders are mostly women who, according to the 1960 census, make up 84% of the traders throughout the country . . . . These women are now playing a role in social change, manifested in social mobility, second only to the plantation owners.'[18]

The commercial activity of women also has a direct influence over the family organization. A woman may contribute to marital stability by contributing to the economic well-being of the family, but she may also be the main cause of marital instability whenever she raises the question of a woman's role within the family structure. Through their commercial activities a few women do manage to shirk their domestic duties and by-pass the authority of the man as the head of the family. Additionally, they have better opportunities to engage in extra-marital relations, ultimately violating the unfaithfulness taboo. 'Many women take shelter from their domestic duties or the unbearable psychological pressure at home by spending more than 12 hours a day, six or seven days a week, at the mart or in travels.'[19]

Tradeswomen's influence makes itself felt not only economically and socially, but also politically. Ghanaian Queen Mothers were frequently supported by the Convention People's Party in their efforts to gain some political control over influential tradeswomen.

Gisèle Ligan explains that the Lomé Women Cloth-Retailers Union

> is the largest professional group in the capital. It makes its voice heard in the running of the country because of its undeniable political influence. It is a social force which has a say in the social, economic and political decisions of the government because of the big role played by the women of Togo in the conquest of independence. It was also due to their considerable financial support in the 1968 free parliamentary election under the UN supervision, when Sylvanus Olympio became the first president of the Republic. Again, it is a common belief in Lomé that it was largely because the Union withdrew its support that President Grunitsky fell. And President Eyadema is well conscious of their influence.[20]

These retailers (easily distinguishable thanks to their corpulence, which is a sign of wealth in Africa)[21] have their own representatives in the political office of the Togolese People's Rally, the only party in Togo, and take part in many projects of the community, among which was the building of the Lomé stadium — giving their financial contributions they have decided upon during their weekly conference.

At times, these women have succeeded in setting up a concern of their own; some of them have inherited the necessary capital through their extended families, some have married businessmen by whom they have been settled in small commercial firms, which usually prosper. In Ghana, these firms are supported by financial institutions among which the Office of Business Promotion, which gives aid particularly to petty traders, retailers, hawkers, stall vendors, etc. Ghanaian business people may receive financial assistance from commercial banks or, if they are not in the 'bank stream' yet, they may still operate on a small scale under a government-sponsored Small Business Credit Scheme. (See Table 17)

To all appearances, it is not difficult for women to get a bank loan, and not only in Ghana. The Lomé cloth-retailers as a rule enjoy the trust of the local banks as 'they pay back their loans regularly and can mortgage their houses'. The ten women or so who import directly from the franc, dollar and pound areas receive credit certificates. 'This enhances their current accounts and increases their profit margins.'[22]

Yet, many of these women have no schooling and are therefore unable to assess their turnover. Fearing tax control, they prefer not to keep a detailed account of their business and rather go by a rough estimate based on common sense. In this way they make their management easier, but also they can keep their concerns going only by virtue of their specialized business, usually confined to one kind of goods.

Table 17
Borrowers Under the Small Business Credit Scheme: Ghana

Region	F	MF	F(%)
Ashanti	697	1,179	59.1
Brong Ahafo	445	807	55.1
Eastern Region	718	989	72.6
Central Region	528	1,144	46.2
Accra Suburbs	406	861	47.2
Northern Region	81	254	31.9
Upper Region	184	432	42.6
Volta Region	148	238	62.2
Western Region	447	758	59.0
Total	*3,654*	*6,662*	*54.8*

Source: B. Asirifi, 'Handicraft and Small Industry Policy in Ghana' in ILO ECA, YWCA *African Workshop on Participation of Women in Handicraft and Other Small Industries*, Kitwe (Zambia), December 1974.

> No doubt the bankers' help plus the legendary insight and common sense characteristic of women keep the ball rolling; yet commonsense has, alas, its own limitations, and so women usually expand only up to a point. In order to develop, a commercial activity must be well structured and well organized.[23]

The only way to keep track of the evolution of a business is book-keeping. In Lomé, more and more cloth-retailers have realized the necessity of organizing their business on a solid base and have consequently abandoned their customary ways. Now they often have the assistance of an employee who, without being a chartered accountant, is nevertheless quite capable of recording the ups and downs of their business; some retailers take great pains to attend literacy courses: 'so that', they say, 'we will be in a position to deal directly with our customers, European and African alike.'[24] In the Ivory Coast, businesswomen take advice from specialized organizations on how to vitalize their concerns. One such organization, the OPEI, has been promoting business since 1969 by looking into applications for credit and finding the necessary funds. Many firms recently set up in Abidjan have been given the go-ahead by the OPEI, which follows their progress and sends out its own experts or provides permanent technical assistance, giving information and sponsoring managerial courses. In the face of all this, trade is in recession, which means that it is becoming more difficult for businesswomen to maintain their traditional position of economic and social privilege.

Bohannan and Curtin thus sum up the present-day position of businesswomen in West Africa:

Women used to handle most of the buying and selling in West Africa and in the Congo . . . . Since the second and third decade of the 20th century, if not earlier, the bulk of the internal trade of subsistence goods throughout the Western African area has been safely in the hands of women. Their wealth and activities may have been over-estimated by travellers, but it would be hard to deny that some women, mostly from the Yoruba and Dahomey areas, built vast commercial empires and even came to be the main outlets for European import-export companies. Things are changing now. Men are now competing with them and are enjoying better and better trading facilities as the market expands and, in economic terms, moves from the periphery to the centre.[25]

Recession has not hit women's commerce solely, for it has crippled trade as a whole, and the reason is probably to be found in the dependence of African commerce on international capitalism, which thwarts the investment potential of the local bourgeoisie primarily 'in such strategic sectors as banks, air or maritime transport, where foreign capital reigns supreme.'[26] The crux of the matter is that, as modern commerce increasingly competes with traditional commerce, the importance of women's trade gradually declines, as it becomes more and more confined to the gathering and reselling of food crop surplus in local and above all in town markets. 'In the market of today two types of exchange co-exist and overlie each other. Food crops are still largely handled by females, whereas import goods are falling into the domain of male traders.'[27]

Food markets have a crucial importance for the suburban survival, even though, mainly because of the diminished production in rural areas, they are far from being adequate; yet it is their very function and basic poverty that makes it impossible for women not only to attain wealth but to expand their trade significantly.

The function of women's trade in towns will be analysed in detail later. Let it suffice here to notice its relevance to the subsistence and the survival of the urban masses as well as its basic economic negativeness. G. Althabe explains:

> The question is brutal: how can these urban masses *survive*? There are indeed the local agricultural activities in towns and in the suburbs, primarily carried out by women, and there is as well food sent by village relatives; yet, the principal process remains the redistribution inside the town of the amount of money circulating as wages. Two main forms of redistribution come to the fore: a) one taking place within the framework of the family solidarity . . . and b) one occurring through the middlemen mushrooming in the urban quarters of the populace. This microtrade mainly relates to foodstuffs, which thus reach exorbitant prices only badly disguised by the small amounts at issue. These exorbitant prices connected with the middlemen's minimal profits, allow a redistribution of the money circulating in town: it is

a way of sharing poverty and its increase.[28]

Urbanization and Womens' Work

It has been said that the modern city is the place where the change in status of African women can be best observed.[29] A statement that in part stems from underrating the importance of women's work in rural areas and its implications for the family structure. Nevertheless, it could hardly be denied that urbanization brings in new societal structures and causes perceptible and immediate conflict between traditional structures and the novel, economic phenomena: hence the cultural (in the anthropological sense) and economic uncertainty as well as the ambiguity of values as peculiarities of urban life which significantly affect the status of women.

First, we should clearly distinguish between colonial and post-colonial urban conditions, bearing in mind that in Africa the degree of urbanization depends above all on the stabilization of the urban labour force and in particular on the percentage of family nuclei – women and children – who live in town.[30] At the turn of the century, when, as we have seen, urbanization had made little headway and the male presence in towns was preponderant, 'the extreme competitiveness women are thrown into . . . no doubt produces pathological effects, which range from a widespread commercialization of sexual relations to a general attitude of aggressive anti-feminism.'[31]

In such conditions, far from 'being able to reverse her conventional position of inferiority', as Baladier maintains,[32] the urban woman experienced a novel brand of violence which deprived her of her own identity; little wonder that psychoses and mental illnesses were soon to appear. Lanternari quotes various studies on mental disorders among the Tallensi people in Northern Ghana, covering the years from 1934 to 1937 to 1963. Over such periods the Tallensi underwent a notable change and experienced a massive even though temporary migration to the urban south of the country. To all appearances, the psychoses of male migrants did not originate in particular traumas, but in the malaise related to the new social environment.

But the contrary applied in 10 out of 17 cases concerning women, whose psychotic crisis was precipitated by some significant incident: perhaps soon after a first journey to the South or during their stay there in the aftermath of traumatic circumstances such as their husband's death, the loss of one or more children, barrenness and so forth. Such traumas had obviously operated on a psychosis-prone terrain, following the stress caused by the environmental alienation (which might anyway occur even in their native environment). Thirty years ago, i.e., at the time of the first investigation, a psychotic crisis would not erupt so easily even in the wake of such personal traumas mentioned above.[33] Thus, the urban woman finds herself in a condition of personal and social insecurity which, in the light of her greater economic dependence is far more dramatic than that affecting men.

'At the village it was she that, even though exploited by the man, produced, sold and exchanged the products. In town, as a wage-earning female labourer, she finds herself begging morning after morning: instead of decreasing, her dependence grows.'[34]

The problem of integrating urban women in society did not fail to invite the concerned if somewhat peculiar attention of the colonial power, which at times set up social security services with a view to having these women under control. The first of such services, around 1911, was entrusted to the Benedictine Mission operating in the copperbelt of Shaba, better known as Katanga, in co-operation with the big companies which had installed themselves in the area. As from 1934, following the arrival in Zaire of social workers recruited by the mission on behalf of the mining companies, 'educational centres' for women and in particular 'training centres' for the younger ones were formed, with a view to ideological conditioning rather than offering the women real solutions to their predicament. A similar social security function was fulfilled by the Protestant missions.

The process of urbanization began during the colonial period, but soon after independence it rose to an unprecedented level: a yearly increase of 7% to 10% was common all over the African continent.

As has already been pointed out, women who have just arrived in town can barely look after themselves. Often they cannot find work even as domestics, given the colonial habit, still very much alive, of using male help both in public places and in private houses. Also, working as a maid, particularly in public places, is deemed a 'dirty job', bound to lead to prostitution and suitable only for unschooled women who have to keep themselves and their children after being deserted by their husbands or lovers.[35] Even educated women, aspiring to office work, which is the most popular female occupation, in towns, often have to face blackmail from their employers, only too ready to claim sexual favours in return for providing work.[36]

Clearly migrant women find themselves tackling urban labour from a position of extreme social weakness. True, in the traditional society, as a field labourer on behalf of her husband, she would necessarily combine work and sexual services; nevertheless, she had greater social strength and security and some bargaining power.

The spectre of prostitution and the fear of loss of the head-of-the-family prestige makes urban males unreservedly hostile to any extra-domestic occupation of their wives:
'If my wife earns some money, then she becomes too independent and does whatever she likes. And I won't be able to control her any more.'
'A married woman who accepts employment of any sort becomes brazen and disobedient to her husband.'
'My wife works as a cook, a washer and a childminder entirely against my will ... I am quite satisfied that a married woman ought to be utterly dependent on her husband.'
'My wife drinks, and no matter if it is beer or brandy; I believe she does so because she's working.'[37]

According to a workman from the Ivory Coast, a woman in employment 'only thinks of the pay to come at the end of the month; thus, she no longer behaves as her mother would. She gradually loses the good old habits of faithfulness to the husband, respect toward the parents.'[38] This hostile attitude toward female extra-domestic work often goes hand in hand with a refusal to allow daughters to receive any education, which is seen as tantamount to allowing them the opportunity to find paid work.

Yet, beside this widespread opposition we find that female work is recognized as a 'necessity': several studies concerning low-income areas of African towns have revealed that men do declare for some extra-domestic activity of their wives as long as this helps to increase the family income.[39]

Far from passively suffering this attitude on the part of men, women have endeavoured to organize themselves for survival as autonomous beings in the urban situation: thus, traditional women's associations have become friendly societies for financial and psychological assistance. Among them is the *muziki* organization in Kinshasa.

The name of this organization means 'not older than the oldest man or woman in Kinshasa'.[40] Before it existed — up to 1960 — the word simply meant 'the bosom friend' and was used by men to refer to the woman they most fancied. The early *muziki* associations, made up of single women, sprang up around 1968. These women formed groups of three to six members linked by obligations of mutual solidarity; they would meet at one of their homes at least once a month to celebrate and strengthen their bonds of friendship. The men were immediately opposed to such associations, which were 'too feminist' in their eyes. Though initially unmarried women constituted the bulk of the *muziki*, as emphasis was gradually placed on the economic character of the organization, change was under way.

One of the earliest *muzikis* (its members took an oath of loyalty on 15 July 1962) has recently revealed itself an ensemble of 'respectable and respected wives of teachers or workers'[41] each of them engaged in some small but lucrative business. They had their own articles of association, a *mère-chef*, a sort of vice-president and a secretary who also kept the members' register.

> 'We are a friendly society rather than a society of friends', [the *mère-chef* said to the interviewer]. We meet twice a month or whenever one of us is in need of help or there is occasion for a family celebration such as a birth or an anniversary. We are organized in such a way as to make our members feel that they are part of one family and should consequently help one another. On the occasion of our fortnightly meetings, each *muziki* offers the host a certain amount of money, which may be anything between 10 and 20 zairis, depending on her means. A round of visits is then fixed: all the members are in fact visited at agreed times.[42]

Ultimately, the urban woman is generally in a weaker position when compared with the urban male. She enjoys only such general benefits as being near the centres of power or of a better opportunity to educate herself, or other benefits she may earn for herself together with other women.

Urban Petty Tradeswomen

The typical work conditions of the urban woman will be considered here, with Kinshasa as our focal point.

Kinshasa, until 1953, could be described as an area of 'male demographic dominance'. Throughout this time the women, particularly the rural women, were subject to more and more arduous labour conditions, because far from enabling the worker to provide for his family, his wages had been devised in such a way as to maintain his dependence on his family, or at least partially so.[43] In 1922, a decree which determined the minimum wage for Kinshasa labourers was reckoned would cover the bare necessities of a bachelor's life. It was made up of three parts: a daily minimum wage, a food allowance, and a housing allowance.

The daily minimum wage was based on a standard estimate which included household items, clothing, luxuries, and 5% savings overall. (See Table 18)

The standard estimate was liable to an increase or to a decrease of 10% according to the nature of the work. Likewise, the food allowance was more or less according to the type of work: it was estimated to supply the labourer with 2,250 calories per day for light work, 2,855 calories for average work and 3,350 calories for heavy work. (See Table 19)

In 1953, for the first time, women migrants outnumbered men in Kinshasa: the 'demographic recovery' was under way. The bachelor's standard estimate was slightly increased and thus became the family standard budget. Since the single labourer's food allotment would actually contribute to support the entire family, family allowances were linked to the single allotment, so that the sum paid for one child corresponded to one-quarter of the man's food allowance, while that paid to his wife was half, providing she lived in the urban area and had at least one child. In the traditional milieu she had no right to the allowance unless she had three children to support. As a result, a wife joining her husband in town could not afford to stay at home, for the man's wage was insufficient to cover consumption. Thus, petty trade soon became the typical occupation of the urban wage-earner's wife.

A survey conducted in Kinshasa during the 1970s revealed that 35.2% of wage-earners' wives were in trade on a regular basis.[44] This is how it went: the man would give his wife 2 to 10 zairis out of his wages, which she would use to buy goods to sell. 'With the pittance they give me at the end of the month, my wife buys a basketful of smoked fish which she then resells. It's on this money that we live.' (*Boy*, a domestic labourer and a father of five, earning a monthly wage of 15 zairis.)[45]

Thus, the woman used the money she earned to feed her family. This marginal sum was crucial for the family survival, since it would bridge the long gap between wage-days. The money invested by the wife was retrieved only little by little according to the progress of selling, and usually the money

Table 18
Standard Estimate for the Determination of the Daily Minimum Wage: 1954

	No.	Duration (years)		No.	Duration (years)
Household items			Jackets	1	1
Pans	1	1	Raincoats	1	1
Plates	1	2	Shoes	1	1
Basins	1	2	*Miscellaneous*		
Buckets	1	1	Trunks	1	10
Demijohns	1	1	Soap (bars)	52	1
Glasses	1	1	Thread (reels)	2	1
Knives	1	1	Needles (packets)	1	1
Cups	1	1	Lamps	1	1
Bedding items			Fuel oil (litres)	12	1
Mattresses	1	3	Matches (packets)	6	1
Mosquito-nets	1	3	Hand towels	3	1
Luxuries			Machetes	1	1
Cigarettes (packets)	52	1	Hoes	1	1
Various: 50 francs per annum or 100 francs in case of residence in a major locality			Wood (pieces)	12	1
Clothing			*Savings*: 5% of the total		
Shirts	2	1	*Taxes* plus additional hundredths		
Suits	3	1	*Bicycles* (if any) 1-5 years		
Belts	1	1	*Total p.a.* divided by 300 = daily wage		

Source: Ordinance No. 22/408, 12 December 1954.

Table 19
Daily Food Allowance in Léopoldville: 1959

	Ordinary work (grs.)	Light work (grs.)	Heavy work (grs.)
Rice	286	215	357
Fresh fish	33	33	33
Dried fish	43	43	43
Beans	86	86	86
Chikwanga (manioc bread)	264	264	264
Palm oil	42	42	42
Salt	15	15	25
Manioc starch	142	–	286
Husked goobers	30	30	73
Sugar	20	20	20
White bread	13	13	13
Vegetables	38	38	38
Manioc leaves	286	286	286
Bananas	75	75	75
Fresh meat	13	13	13

Source: *Rapport sur les Salaires dans la République du Congo*, 1960.

would last until the following payday. Women constantly tried to set aside a small fund for the purchase of goods at any time, yet the poverty of most families often forced them into disrupting their activities for a while, as they lacked goods and money.

> There was a sorry scene at the bus stop for Ruashi the other day. A few women around here sell pancakes, groundnuts, bananas and the like there. The other morning at about eleven o'clock some policemen turned up at the bus stop for Ruashi. As soon as the women saw them, they tried to get away with their merchandise. On impulse, the cops tried to snatch it from the women. Confusion and stampede ensued.... It would certainly be better for the women to sell their goods at the mart, as other women do. But they have explained to us why they do not do so. Big markets being fiercely competitive, the women prefer to go to places where they may have an easier access to customers: a bus stop is one of them. Some of the pedlars who had just suffered the onslaught were weeping at the thought that their trading was over, now that the only goods they could rely on had been ruined.[46]

The survey on Kinshasa trade revealed four basic types: the so-called 'manoeuvre' trade, the on-the-premises trade, the inland trade, and the market trade.

In African quarter jargon, 'to manoeuvre' means to receive and collect the goods from the interior, and carry them to the various markets for the sale to retailers. Quite a few women are involved in this 'manoeuvring', which requires a sizeable capital but at the same time brings large and immediate profits. The transport of the goods usually takes place early in the morning by bus or taxi-bus or even on foot.

Many women exhibit their merchandise in front of their houses, on stones, barrels or a trestle table: this is 'on-the-premises' trade. Cigarettes, matches, canned food and soap are the best-selling items. This kind of trade leaves the wife some time for her domestic occupations, and customers may be served by other members of the family.

The inland market, an increasingly male domain, presupposes great financial means: understandably, it is usually the privilege of rather wealthy families. Women travel by boat to the most distant villages in order to buy foodstuffs for the town markets.

> Fish is the staple diet of most if not all Kinshasa families. Fresh or smoked (*mbisi ya kokauka*) fish comes from the interior mainly through the urban tradeswomen unceasingly plying between Kinshasa and the coastal fishing villages. Our *mamans* in trade make their voyages along the Zaire river on Onatra boats or on private whaleboats.... The fare and the length of the voyage depend on the distance, but on average, trip and stay will not last longer than ten days.... On the spot, these tradeswomen usually spend their nights at the place of some fisherman they chance to have made friends with. In time, they usually become good friends of the fisherman's whole family. After receiving the fish supplies and selling their merchandise — mainly cigarettes, soap, sugar, salt, milk — our *mamans* wait for the boat that will take them back to Kinshasa.[47]

These women have priority on any boat sailing on the river or any of its tributaries: because 'without them the city would starve to death'.[48] They lead a hectic life.

> Although as a rule they know the boat timetable, it may well happen that they arrive at the pier only to find that the boat has gone. Having a ticket and their goods already on the boat, they won't give up; this means flinging themselves into a taxi and rushing to Ndolo harbour, Kauka in fact. There, they can hire a pirogue which will take them to Malaku, and there yet another pirogue which will closely follow the boat in spite of all the whirlpools and the big waves she is making. Needless to say, going aboard is no easy achievement and then, once one of these brave women has made it, she is in for quite a welcome from her tradesmates or the Onatra police who are only too prompt in punishing such a way of boarding.[49]

In fact these women must put up with a good deal of harassment on the part of the river police as well as with some act of banditry likely to take place when the boat is well down the river.

Lastly, market trade is indeed the most popular of the four basic commercial pursuits in Kinshasa. At the market, women sell foodstuffs, and in order to do so, they take their children along and stay away from home for long spells. This causes more than one war of words with their men: 'My wife used to sell rice at the market. One fine day I caught her in the bar all set for a drink with a fellow: since then, I've forbidden her to go to the market. However, I still intend to let her have another go at her business, but if she plays the fool again, I'll send her back to her parents at the village.'[50]

A kind of mafia is now springing up and by degrees enmeshing these women; public officers and 'private citizens' are doing their best to extort money from them in exchange for 'protection' and 'advice'.[51] It is not by chance that central market inspectors at the Kinshasa market have been dubbed by the populace the 'barons of the market'.

Urbanized Women 'Return to the Soil'

A return of women to the land is now in progress in every African urban area; women also do some food crop farming in towns, on the plots at the back of their houses or in suburban bush. The man's wage itself is usually calculated on the assumption that he may live 'on his wife's farming' after all.[52] Therefore, for many labourers who are classified as urban dwellers a combined subsistence and cash income is still of some consequence.

From Houyoux's survey on Kinshasa it emerged that 42 wives (4.1% of the wage-earning families) were keeping up their agricultural pursuits in town: 'Seven days a week, Mrs X goes to the fields. She fetches firewood, *saka-saka* (wild spinach) and manioc. Back home, she makes manioc loaves for resale. Her husband, a hospital washerman, earns 12.88 zairis a month. Truly, this family could not survive without this woman.' A woman tells how: 'I've made up a plot out of my piece of land; also, I've started some rearing which I've now put at my elder brother's disposal. If he drops in and I have nothing to give to him, I send a chap for one of my beasts. This is how I cope with my large family.'[53]

The survey has also revealed that many heads of families draw a supplementary income from their women's farming or rearing: what is not consumed by the family goes to the market, as already shown, and the proceeds will go to satisfy the exigencies of the extended or the conjugal family. Betty Preston Thomson has carried out a similar investigation in the Main Town Location and the Chilenjie Suburb in Lusaka.

At the time, the Chilenjie Suburb, on the eastern outskirts of the city, was largely inhabited by civil servants, the ratio being of 40.3% to the whole population. The houses, built with government aid, consisted of two rooms plus a kitchen and toilet. The whole lot occupied less than one-eighth of an acre, so that there was enough space for an orchard or garden. Vegetables and various crops, such as peanuts and gourds, were widely cultivated and flowers were grown in front of more than one house; there were also many trees.

The Main Location, where 33.2% of the population were employed as domestic servants was a much less attractive area, with its narrow rows of huts all alike. It had been constructed 'on the cheap' by the Town Management Board as a settlement for rural migrants. In the old part of the suburb there were 800 one-room shacks, either rectangular and covered with corrugated iron, or round and covered with straw. Every eight shacks were served by two latrine blocks, one water pump and one washing slab. In the middle, a small brick building was divided in four sections: those were the kitchens. There was little or no cultivation around the shacks because of shortage of water and space: some of the huts were hedged in by euphorbias and, here and there, a few pumpkin-vines were being grown. Orchards were few, nevertheless 56% of the families in the sample would have one in the bush, where maize, groundnuts and gourds were the main crops.

At Chilenjie, no maize was grown in the vicinity of the houses, yet each family was entitled to a plot of 100 x 50 feet. 71% of the families would put this to good use, while 7% would grow nothing at all. (See Table 20)

Table 20
Garden Produce
(% on the total of gardens)

Produce	Main Location 104 kitchen gardens (%)	Chilenjie Township Gardens Urban	Chilenjie Township Gardens Extra-urban
Maize	92.2	–	72.3
Groundnuts	55.7	77.8	66.1
Gourds	60.5	48.7	15.4
Beans	24.0	19.5	13.8
Tomatoes	–	16.7	–
Sweet potatoes	9.6	9.7	11.8
Lettuce	–	5.6	–
Cabbages	–	4.2	–
Potatoes	–	2.8	1.5
Spinach	–	–	1.5
Peas	–	1.4	–
Egg-plants	–	1.4	–
Cucumbers	1.0	–	–
African maize	1.0	–	–

Source: B. Preston Thomson, 'Two Studies in African Nutrition — An Urban and Rural Community in Northern Rhodesia', in *Rhodes-Livingstone Papers*, No. 24, Manchester University Press, 1968 (1st Edition 1954).

Maize fields are liable to become infested with snakes, mosquitos and suchlike, so the municipal authorities have by decree tried to have them located not too close to residential areas. The edict is, however, often ignored, but since they are in no position to prevent or restrict maize growing, the authorities never go beyond sending warnings and circulars.

Women labourers, nevertheless, usually have a long walk to reach their urban fields. As a rule they do not avail themselves of proper facilities: for example, very few of them 'use fertilizers and, more often than not, the outcome will be far from gratifying. Yet, it is their claim that they cannot afford to buy fertilizers and are therefore happy to use their village methods.'[54]

As in the village, women here carry on a system of communal work: 'Two or three of them work one field together and then they move on to the next field; the most laborious among them even have three different fields each, for different types of cultivation.'[55] In brief, female labour, albeit precarious and technologically backward, is indispensable to the daily survival of the family. Nevertheless, the hyper-exploitation of women and the decline in the social value of their labour — which is still unpaid in a society increasingly dominated by cash economy — have negative repercussions which ultimately affect the cost of the male labour force as well.

Domestic Labour

> I'm pounding the millet for John
> As he sits
> Lounging over his big stomach
> (Song of Lozi women)
>
> Pounding the millet is tiring
> I wish I was eating
> Instead of pounding
> (Song of Tumbuka women)

Traditional domestic occupations such as cooking, cleaning or attending to the basic needs of the family for water and warmth are no doubt more energy and time consuming tasks in rural than in urban areas.

> African women start carrying loads when they are very young; they are still carrying them when they are old. Young girls carry bucketfuls of water on their heads for miles and miles, old women bear huge faggots of firewood.... In a letter to the *East African Standard* a woman figured out that she had been carrying 8,000 bucketfuls of water in 20 years.[56]

In the traditional environment domestic labour remains a largely communal occupation and as such, it does not isolate the woman from the rest of her community, which does appreciate the significance of her daily work. Women often share the food preparation, and thus combine the economic and the social side of their lives. Food preparation, in particular, involves considerable and elaborate effort, so much so that in some traditional areas the first meal prepared by the wife has been ritualized. Thus, among the Ngoni of Zambia,

> At the beginning of marital life at her husband's village, a woman is not permitted to cook until she is expressly invited to do so by her parents-in-law. Until then, she receives cooked food from the co-wives or from her mother-in-law or the latter's mother. Such a state of affairs may last one month or one year and ends on the *mphekiso* (cooking) ceremony.
>
> They say that the bridegroom's parents would feel ashamed if they did not treat the bride as a guest until time comes for her to share the running of the house. Then the man's parents fix the day of the ceremony. On that day, sisters, mother and grandmother of the husband prepare flour, porridge pats and set out the plates . . . . One of the man's sisters takes the bride into the mother-in-law's hut where, following the instructions of the women who have gathered in there for the occasion, she sets about cooking. Actually people say it's the bride who does the cooking, but all she really does is to look on as her sister-in-law cooks. Under the mother-in-law's direction, the porridge is apportioned into the plates . . . . One dish is sent to the man's father, one to the husband who eats it together with his brothers, and one to the most notable woman in the village; the women in the kitchen have some dishes for themselves. The father-in-law is expected to say if the porridge is well done, and he may well say that it is underdone and his daughter-in-law has still a long way to go. Such a remark would be tantamount to a rebuke but, whatever the father may say, the ceremony will not be repeated and from now onwards the bride starts cooking regularly for her man. If the man's parents are well-off, they may slaughter a goat or a sheep for the occasion, but these may also be sent for the purpose by the woman's parents. The latter, however, are not allowed to witness the ceremony.[57]

Food preparation is so long that some help on the part of other women is necessary. For instance, the flour is never prepared more than 24 hours in advance and a woman who has been in the fields all day will be too tired for millet-grinding or bread-making in the evening.[58]

It is an even longer and a more elaborate procedure to prepare cassava, which in colonial times replaced millet almost everywhere. The plant roots are peeled, wrapped in leaves, then kept underwater for two or three days in the hot season and six or more in the wet season. The roots are then dried on tables in the sun in the hot season, and cut, laid on mats and frequently moved for the best use of the short sunny spells in the wet season; they may also be dried over a slow fire. Many other foods are dried in the sun or on the fire to preserve them for prolonged use.

Making allowances for the time spent in fieldwork and food preparation, it is not surprising that not more than one cooked dish is prepared per day, generally late in the afternoon. In some seasons, the women stay late in the fields, and the feeding of the whole village is consequently affected.

In sum, traditional domestic work fits in with the greater part of the current self-supporting activities, which do not yet reflect the traditional sexual division of labour. The division of labour inside a rural village has been studied by G. Kay by taking a Bemba-speaking Ushi village as a sample.[59]

The typical dwelling is virtually nothing more than one sleeping room. Except in case of rain, all the household activities take place in the open or on the verandah, or in some cases in a separate kitchen. The meals are generally taken out of doors, either in the verandah shade or in other places outside the house. 88.5% of the food (mainly insects, of which 19 edible varieties are known) is gathered by women both young or old.

Many more activities take place in the village and generally take up as much time as that needed for gathering food. These may be divided into four main groups: household work (27.50% of the total working hours); food preparation (51.50%); craft work (4.50%); construction work (16.50%). Women are engaged in over 80% of these activities ('which', Kay notes, 'have so far drawn comparatively little attention on the part of the observers') which occupy up to 53% of their working time.

Their main chores are the fetching of water and firewood, cleaning the house and its surroundings, spreading mud on the floors, cleansing kitchenware, bowls and the like, and washing clothes and bedding. In January and February, women make fuel, since it is difficult to get dry wood during the rainy season; finally, they keep the grass around the house tidy.

Kay also reckons that 15,018 meals are served in a year, and in the same year a woman spends over 1,000 hours performing her chores; or, more precisely, 1,732 hours if she is over 45 and 1,416 hours if she is under 45.

In the Ushi village under scrutiny, women constitute 60% of the adult population, thus outnumbering men who frequently migrate in search of wage labour. Yet, it is not on the strength of their number that local women work more than their local male counterparts do, as the survey seems to suggest — the fact is that men contribute less to the village economy in sheer terms of working hours per capita.[60] None of them work longer than eight hours per day, the average being 6.6 hours for the young and 5.7 for the old. And as for the young men, even when they stay at the village, they unquestionably have a much easier life than the girls have. We should, however, think twice before ascribing the whole affair to the 'nature' of the African male, for this would be an easy way of indulging in racism. The decline of crafts and increase of manufactured utensils and clothes, the prohibition of hunting (traditionally a man's pursuit) as well as the unceasing quest for waged work entailing only temporary residence in the village, have all contributed much to bring about the present situation. Nonetheless, all this does not deprive the woman of one single penny's worth of her labour.

In the final analysis, the characteristically rural situation in the village studied by Kay appears to be as follows: the young males, who made up 28% of the sample, did only 13% of the work whilst the old males, 17.5% of the sample, did 15%; the young females, 35% of the sample, carry out 42.9% of the work, and the old ones, 19.5% of the sample, did 28.4%. In short women work on average over eight hours per day, in fact 9.2 hours if they are young and 9.3 if they are old; a working day of 12 or even 14 hours is not unusual.

In towns too, housework is very little eased by such facilities as women usually benefit from in industrialized countries. The majority of the urban population lives in conditions which are far from easy.

Suffice it to mention here the hideous mushrooming of houses or the conditions in the suburbs, where illegal settlements have already reached alarming proportions. Lusaka, for example, is hemmed in by illegal immigrant quarters. Here, there are no streets worthy of the name, no waterpipes, no garbage collection, cesspools or electric lights. Over 35 shanty-towns are to be seen in the industrial area of Kitwe, and in some of them over 1,000 people live.[61] Only a tiny minority of African women are currently enjoying the pleasure of a modern house well equipped with electric appliances, and it is in this respect that the class gap becomes most wide and significant. 'The multi-class system, well known to industrialized countries, is even better known to us . . . . Where, say, some women are already using a geyser, a washing machine or an electric or gas cooker and up-to-date utensils, many of their fellow-countrywomen are still washing themselves and their linen in a river, deep in the bush.'[62]

The housewife, as a social figure, has already made her first timid appearance in Africa, though only within the new bourgeoisie. Still, the full participation of urban populations in the cash economy has upset traditional housework patterns. All the women, even in the shanty-towns, now find themselves facing new tasks, which more and more resemble those of a typical Western homemaker. On that score, it would be useful if advice on food purchase, general expenditure or modern methods of childrearing appeared in the local press. If things are not as they should be, if the money is not enough for two meals a day, this is due not to the meagre wages or the lack of services and so on; the fault lies rather with the woman, who is unable to perform her new duties in a satisfactory or sensible way.

> Some homemakers are utterly reckless. As soon as they have some cash, they spend it without first doing their sums; naturally, only days later they find that not a penny is left to see them through the month. Borrowing will be the next logical step, and step by step they become perennial debtors and beggars . . . . Citizens, to remedy this evil, it is essential for you to know in advance what your family needs are or, in a word, to manage your budgets wisely. It is in co-operation with your husbands and even more in accordance with them that your budgets must be made. And always remember, citizens, that your budgets

should be put down in writing, for thus you'll be able to check them properly and see that they do not contain any surplus.[63]

Work in Rural Areas

Agricultural production, by far the most important sector in the economy of most African countries, has dropped to a low level of late.

According to FAO data (which should perhaps be taken with reservations) the 1973 overall production was down by 3%, the fall per capita being 6%, while in 22 countries food production per capita was below the 1961-65 level. In 1973, the output of basic food, such as sorghum and millet, unexpectedly fell by 17%, against an ever increasing population growth rate. (See Table 21)

Table 21
Overall Food Production in Africa: 1960-72 (in tons)

Staple diet	1960	1969	1970	1971	1972
Wheat	5.5	5.8	6.6	7.4	8.2
Rice	4.6	7.1	7.2	7.3	7.7
Maize	8.9	12.0	11.5	11.9	12.3
Sorghum and millet	15.1	18.1	17.5	18.8	18.3
Sweet potatoes	19.7	21.4	23.2	22.7	23.0
Cassava	26.8	34.3	37.9	39.4	39.0
Total growth rate (%)	*1960-70*	*1969-70*	*1970-71*	*1971-72*	
	2.5	4.3	3.7	1.2	
Produce for partial export:					
Sugar	0.9	2.1	2.2	2.4	2.5
Palm oil	0.9	0.9	1.0	1.0	1.0
Meat	16.7	19.7	20.1	20.7	21.2
Overall agricultural produce	117.0	145.2	149.5	155.1	157.5
Total growth rate (%)	*1960-70*	*1969-70*	*1970-71*	*1971-72*	
	2.5	3.0	3.7	1.5	

Source: A. Rake, 'Collapse of African Agriculture', in *African Development*, February, 1975.

Rather than linking the decline in output to the demographic factor, we prefer to associate it with rural transformations imposed by the capitalist penetration, such as the forced monoculture confined to export produce, the consequent increasing dependence on foreign markets, and also the division between traditional agriculture and modern agriculture. The latter factor in particular has substantially complicated the issues of labour in rural areas through the creation of novel stratifications and social classes.

We believe that Seidman is right in arguing that the emphasis on the 'urban-rural gap' tends to overshadow the inner income gap, consequently, disguising the class difference which undoubtedly exists in urban as well as in rural areas. In real terms, the income gap either within an urban area or a rural area is wider than that between an urban and a rural area. (See Table 22)

Table 22
Family Incomes: Southern Province of Zambia: 1970 (in Kwacha)

Income source	Low-income Group Total income	Per capita	High-income Group Total income	Per capita
Proceeds	56.85	5.9	783.70	59.01
Farm expenditure*	53.08	5.51	28.67	2.16
Rural money income	3.76	0.39	755.03	56.85
Family consumption value	85.02	8.83	149.74	11.27
Rural total income	88.78	9.22	904.49	68.12
Non-rural income**	141.20	14.66	82.72	6.23
Total income	229.28	23.88	987.49	74.35
Family consumption value	85.02	8.83	149.74	11.27
Total money income	*144.96*	*15.05*	*837.75*	*63.08*

*Wealthy farmers bear a lower expenditure if compared with the less wealthy ones: the former tend to hire their own mechanized machinery, mainly tractors, to the latter, thus lowering their costs.
**The lower income group usually gets more out of their wages than does the higher income group, primarily because low-income farmers often work also as day labourers.

Source: A. Seidman, 'Urban Wages Tempt Zambians into the Cities', in *African Development*, October 1974.

The greater part of agricultural export produce comes not from the traditional agricultural sector but rather from modern capitalist plantations or, in other words, from 'high productivity modern sectors of the economy'.[64] It is, nevertheless, true to say that the division between the modern agricultural sector and traditional agricultural sector does not necessarily tally with reality: farmers may produce both food and cash crops, the latter mainly going to satisfy the local urban demand. It is a fact though, that

> the marketing of the produce is chiefly dependent on the foreign demand, the export demand, that is — and only secondarily on the urban, or local, demand. Furthermore, this agriculture is not modern enough and does not make use of industrial products, such as fertilizers and machines, for all its working for the market.[65]

It is in this sector most of all that female labour force is used.

All the data we have been able to collect has fully confirmed the utilization of female labour in the backward sector of the national economies, principally in subsistence farming. The majority of rural female labourers may be labelled 'unpaid family labourers': in Zambia, for example, the lucky ones who manage to secure a remunerated job make up a bare 14% of the rural labour force.

A higher productivity in traditional farming is commonly acknowledged as indispensable to prevent African farming from collapsing. Yet, a) it is out of reach in an economy dependent on international capitalism, and b) it 'implies profound technological transformations, which are difficult to achieve because of their questioning of established social structures as well as ways of life and cultures linked to old-fashioned primitive techniques.'[66] In other words, a higher productivity would involve a diverse utilization of the female labour force as well as its proper qualification, which would inevitably have an immediate and far-reaching effect on the social and political role of the woman.

Agricultural Work and Traditional Society

We have already stressed the husband's customary right to use the labour of his wives in so far as they are bound to till the fields he keeps for his own use, in addition and prior to tilling the fields designed for their children's and their own sustenance. But when it comes to consumption, the wives' fields have an unexpected priority over the man's. Thus, the man becomes the owner of the 'surplus produce'; and this, coupled with his economic strength, paves the way to the rise of private property.[67]

In more recent times, such peculiar as well as traditional brand of female rural labour has often laid the cornerstone of financial success for a few small planters of West Africa.

With reference to the Nzima of Ghana, Lanternari has observed how the manager and aspiring owner of an industrial plantation, being hardly in a position to clear and adapt a largish piece of land without labour force, must rely on an initial capital, and this he obtains from the market sale of the products exceeding the needs of his family.

> It can be seen, [Lanternari concludes] that there is an operational continuity between the traditional and the modern system. The farmer draws enough strength and money from the old system to gain access to the new one.[68]

The truth is, he draws the 'strength and money' he needs from the unpaid work of the women in his family.

Yet it is an old custom among the Nzima that women may freely dispose of any surplus product of their fields. The sale of any surplus is the only source of monetary returns for rural women: only rarely do they work for a wage and have only a marginal share in the circulation of bridewealth, which instead is an important source of income for men. This independent

Women of Africa

income women have may, at times, assume substantial proportions, even though it often happens that it is not even considered when the crop sale income is evaluated.

On analysing the rural economy of the Luvale people, White has collected data which also refers to the women's incomes. (See Table 23)

Table 23
Luvale: Rural Income According to Sex (in £.s.d. & translated to £ & p. approx.)

	M £	s	d		F £	s	d	
Cassava	1	12	8	[£2.52p]	1	9	9	[£2.17p]
Groundnuts		17	3	[£1.86p]	1	8	10	[£2.06p]
Other products		7	0	[84p]		7	0	[84p]
Perennial crops		12	3	[£1.47p]		4	0	[48p]
Total	*3*	*9*	*2*	[£4.10p]	*3*	*9*	*7*	[£4.17p]

Source: C.M.N. White, 'A Preliminary Survey of Luvale Rural Economy', *Rhodes-Livingstone Papers*, No.29, Manchester University Press, 1968.

These data clearly show that women's main income (50% or more in the sample) accrues from farming, followed by beer selling. White also wonders why 'in debating income from the export and sale of products, women, who still had some part in it, have not been taken into account: in other words, the estimated income deriving from the known agricultural sales, represents only half of the relevant real income.' White concludes: 'my figures confirm that agricultural output for sale is twice as important for the local economy as assumed before.'[69]

Cash crops were introduced not only in large plantations, for they have been replacing traditional food crops everywhere. Unfortunately, the modernization of agriculture has adversely affected the customary rights of women: the man has been keeping the proceeds from cash-crop sales for himself, regardless of whether the crop has been grown on the women's field or on his, and he has only permitted the women to sell the food crop surplus. Consequently, women have resisted the substitution of cash crop for food crop (which causes an impoverishment of traditional food cultures) both because it is their duty to feed their families by farming and because they do derive a personal income by this means. In the absence of any relevant benefit they have refused to convert some of their fields to cash-cropping; they have also been reluctant to spend their time and energies in their husbands' fields. Never mind tradition.

> It is only the monies from the sale of such established cash crops as coffee and tobacco, grown on lands not allotted to the wives, that the husband claims for himself. In 1957 it was decreed that wives should

not be allowed to plant cash crops autonomously. In fact wives did not show any particular concern in doing so; on the contrary, they objected to the planting of cash crop even in their husbands' fields, since this would reduce the amount of food crop land. All this puts to the test the man's authority over the woman, given the man's frequent attempts at winning the woman over to his cash crops. There is no guideline in customary farming for this activity, and nearly all women oppose it. Then the husband sticks to his right to be obeyed, and I must say that in a good many of the cases I've observed, the man proved that he was able to get some help from the woman; it seems that despite all her complaints, only rarely will she openly defy her man's authority.[70]

It is nevertheless, on record that in 1964, Kenyan women's anti-cash crop stance prevented the success of the tea-growing project on the part of small landowners. Farmers' wives found that it was better for them if they harvested the tea-shrubs themselves and dried and sold the leaves on their own behalf. When tea was picked and sent regularly to the factory for curing, the profit was higher but it was the husband's exclusive privilege.

This of course does not mean that local women are by nature or mentality tied to tradition and traditional farming systems. On the contrary, where women, either widows or wives in the absence of their husbands, have managed the farm alone, they have been quite willing to try new techniques in so far as their farms have often been referred to as 'paragons of progress'. Why? Simply because in some cases women have been allowed to retain the full profit, which they have endeavoured to maximize by putting government experts' advice to good use.

It should also be borne in mind that the introduction of the cash crop has contributed a great deal to lowering the wife's status within the polygamous family:

> In thriving areas, polygamy has become a peculiarly economic issue, following the introduction of commercial crops such as coffee and tobacco .... There is the shrewd big planter who invests his returns in bridewealth in order to increase the number of his wives (labourers, that is) and turns a blind eye to their behaviour, since they supply him with extra labour force he might easily lose if he was too strict .... Some of these women, well treated by the planter who approaches them as a bride would be approached in her own tribe, settle down in their new family comfortably enough. But many others complain that their husband is not treating them either as wives — they rarely see him and never receive a gift from him — or as labourers, as they are not being given any wage. In 1946, when forced labour was abolished in the French colonies, quite a few of these women went to town while others returned to their native clan, which saw to their remarriage. Nowadays, women who feel unhappy about their enforced jobs usually resort to a common tactic: they quit at coffee weeding or picking time,

and no other time could be psychologically more effective than that. Then, the husband sues them on the grounds of desertion.[71]

Such attempt to utilize women in the modern agricultural sector while keeping them tied down to traditional production relations, demonstrates once more the close interdependence between the feminine condition inside the family structures and the utilization of feminine labour.

Modernization of Agricultural Work, and the Woman

'A common platitude of African life is that women do all or most of the rural work while, by comparison, men are a slothful lot .... Yet there is some truth in it.'[72] The truth is that men work comparatively little in the subsistence farming sector since they mostly seek wage employment in the modern farming sector. Even when they are not employed as rural wage labourers, they are, much more than women, in some sort of remunerated employment. Kay, for instance, has noted that in the village of Kalaba the young men are the ones who share least in the activities of their family groups, simply because they spend a relatively high portion of their working time (15%) in the so-called 'beer parties', namely on jobs done on behalf of third parties in exchange for beer, salt or other commodities — positions that otherwise would probably stay unfilled. Conversely, women, even when they are engaged in cash-crop farming, are still doing primarily precarious jobs. In Ghana, for example, four types of rural labour may be distinguished in addition to the farmer's and his family's: permanent wage labour, annual labour, crop-sharing and casual labour. Three of these four are covered by comparatively long-term contracts between the farmer and the labourer; the fourth is characteristically seasonal work, precarious and consequently 'feminine'.

Thus, we will find housewives working as part-timers, particularly in the rice plantations of Tamale and in the sugar-cane plantations of Akuse. Yet it has emerged from field research, that these women do aspire to a permanent employment in the plantations,[73] in a word, to a steady waged job. Research has also revealed that the educated men working in the sugar-cane plantations of the Akuse area tend to view rural work as a makeshift, while the educated women express little distaste for such work, albeit they find it quite heavy and thus are inclined to throw it in.

Mechanization of agriculture has variously affected African women's labour, and not necessarily for the better. First it should be noted that only men have benefited from training in mechanical matters and ways to use the new machines. But the introduction of private property and consequent allotment of the land, by forcing women to spend more time in moving from one field to another and often far-away field, have made it impossible for them to attend literacy or refresher courses on farming.[74]

Second, traditionally male tasks, such as hoeing and ploughing, have been given the highest priority as far as mechanization is concerned. When traditionally female tasks such as sowing, harvesting and produce conversion were mechanized, women found themselves jobless or, as a UN bulletin put it, 'free

to devote themselves to their other tasks, namely, to the family.'[75]
In reality,

> women have frequently found themselves dispossessed of their former income sources: it so happened, for instance, that in the framework of the Niger rural project women could no longer, for lack of raw materials, attend to their customary occupations, i.e., spinning, cloth-dyeing and palmoil making.[76]

The modernization of the traditional rural sector is, therefore, a most pressing problem for governments, and any project tackling such issue will have in the foreground the peasant woman inviting the general attention to the quantity and the quality of her work in the fields. In a recent interview, Mrs Manima, Minister for Social Affairs of the Democratic Republic of the Congo, has declared: 'In the rural environment, the question of the peasant female is basically a question of extremely vestigial tools of production, which entail overwork for a mere pittance. Moreover, the fact that there is no regular outlet for the produce causes a considerable waste and eventually disheartens women.'[77]

Women's and girl's overwork was the topic of a conference in Lomé in 1972, which saw the participation of eight African countries: Cameroons, the Ivory Coast, Gabon, Mali, Mauritania, Niger, Chad and Togo. On that occasion it was said:

> In most of our regions the rural woman is overburdened with work, and usually she is in her prime. It is for the woman to play a major part in the agricultural production. In many regions she does 50% of the work in the family fields and nearly all the work in her own fields whose yield gives sustenance to her family and to her children. On top of this there are chores and *corvées*, plus the conveying and the marketing of the crops within the village. The eight countries are very concerned about the effects that present circumstances may have on the wellbeing of women and children and more in general on the progress of the rural world.[78]

The Commission specifically dealing with female labour as related to planning schemes submitted the following report:

> In most cases the improvement of food output depends on our girls and our mothers. There must then be a priority target in any:
> — mass information campaign;
> — land allocation, in particular of irrigational areas for vegetables and fruit growing;
> — supply of equipment and chemicals for the treatment and preservation of food;
> — loans for sowing, small-scale rearing, gardening, fish production, etc.

Some male resistance to this female-led action is to be anticipated. It is therefore necessary to take steps towards:
— women's grouping;
— women's participation in intermediate structures such as co-operatives;
— a more favourable attitude on the part of men (through a pedagogic and political approach).

Women's participation in co-operation is no doubt an important starting point for the analysis and solution of many rural questions. Rural co-operation on the other hand is no novelty to African women. Among the Ntomba and Basengele of Zaire, for instance, co-operation within the economic and agricultural field is referred to as *ntikiano*, and has a good potential: 'Albeit practised by females, *ntikiano* may give rise to a middle class in every place or community.'[79] Basically, it relates to the assistance women give one another in the preparation of a large groundnut or manioc, or some other field. All the participants accept the principle of mutual help and each beneficiary is bound to supply all the others with food and beverages.

Such tradition of communal work could be put to profitable use for the setting up of co-operatives if the customary privileges of the household heads did not represent a stumbling block to the development of modern co-operation.

Working in the fields is carried out communally by women, but the sale of the most important products — those for commercial use — as we have seen, takes place in a quite different socio-economic context:

> The household head alone can join the commercial circuit with his goods, and there he finds himself competing with other household heads and is consequently induced to take up an individualistic attitude. Consequently, the co-operative approach is bound to disappear.[80]

The question is not ignored however; on the contrary, we find that it is often the core of some relevant political debate.

In a seminar on female labour at the Mindolo Ecumenical Centre of Kitwe, Muriel Russel observed:

> Many African countries are still so basically rural that it comes as no surprise that rural co-operation has expanded remarkably, in particular where governments have given a substantial technical aid and some financial support.
>
> Unfortunately, in building the basic co-operative structures women have largely been left behind, partly because of the common assumption that they are nothing more than a supplementary labour force and partly because of the obstacles raised by national laws as well as by the very regulations of a few co-operatives.
>
> Where property is a man's privilege, women will have no access to a

co-operative as fully-fledged members. Besides being unfair to women, this no doubt comes as no boon to urban male labourers forced into entrusting their wives with the management of their farms: in fact this entails that they are provisionally divested of their co-operative rights, since women are not entitled to act as their deputies on that score. Yet, not everything is lost, and there are even signs of activities aiming at solving the problems caused by these restrictions.[81]

At this stage, there can be little doubt that a serious programme of rural development must go hand in hand with the transformation of traditional family structures. Otherwise, a heavier exploitation of women is the only alternative, without even the counterbalance of a higher productivity.

Diet Taboos: The Nutritional Problem

In the rural setting, low incomes and inadequate distribution bring diet into close association with the standard of rural production rather than with the standard of living. Hence, the decline of subsistence farming is the main cause of malnutrition.

Millet, for example, has been generally supplanted by cassava: this perennial plant is probably today's commonest staple diet, while millet is now primarily used to make beer and is a staple ingredient only in those ritual foods where cassava is not used. The nutritional value of cassava has been the subject of more than one debate: it has been established that it is exceedingly poor in proteins and in the long run has a detrimental effect, probably due to its prussic acid.[82] In Zambia, Kay has noted that the popularity of cassava is mainly due to the policy of colonial administrators who tended to introduce or promote its growing everywhere as a 'spare crop' in case of famine.

It was, however, chiefly where Africans were divested of their best lands by their white masters and penned in reserves that cassava became an essential crop

> thanks to its resistance in the event of drought, its capacity for growing luxuriantly even in poor or indifferent soil without exhausting it, and finally it requires relatively little work and space; cassava allows a stable settlement, and even where primitive farming methods are used, it can feed more mouths than any other crop on any other soil.[83]

It should also be said that in some rural areas the only proteins to be consumed are those provided by insects such as locusts and the like: according to FAO experts, more than 25% of the African population suffer from insufficient supply of proteins.

The urban environment, in full demographic expansion, enjoys infinitely higher financial returns than the rural, as it can avail itself of a manifold and dense commercial network: here, it is the economic standard that determines the diet. Obviously, the greater the means, the better the ability to consume food and to satisfy needs. According to a recent interview,[84] in Kinshasa, only families with a monthly income of more than 60 zairis can afford an overall adequate diet, even though not even that appears to be good enough to cover the individual calorific requirements. If undernourishment is the word for the 71% belonging to families whose monthly food expenditure ranges between 15 and 60 zairis, total malnutrition is positively the case with families below the 15-zairi level, who make up 15.3% of the consumer units. The situation is little better in the large towns of Africa.

At the time of Thomson's survey, in Lusaka Main Location, 30% of the families could not afford the minimum requirement of 3,000 calories per head during the weeks of highest expenditure, and 80% could not do so during the last week of the month, when money was scarce. 10% of the families (20% on the basis of a calculation by units) could *never* afford the vital protein foods.

Various and strange have been the investigators' comments on these data. Thomson, for one, goes so far as to say:

> The figures seem to indicate a tendency to eat more than necessary at the beginning of the month [sic!], especially as regards meat and fish. The average African seems unable to make suitable plans for himself or to put aside a small sum for expenses other than alimentary.... [And again] instead of spreading their wages over the month, African women devour large slices of it [sic!] in a matter of days.[85]

Another researcher is censorious of the inclination of 'Lubumbashi people to undernourish themselves in order to have some monies left for a booze-up or a spree'[86] as everybody knows, the poor are not entitled to the luxury of having fun.

Houyoux, for his part, views as a 'nutritional error' what is in reality nothing but a fatal issue of poverty: 'Forced by her limited budget to a choice, the housewife will opt for the cheaper and unfortunately less proteinaceous foodstuffs, in a word, for quantity rather than for quality'.[87] Deep down, the whole issue may well be a matter of 'diet taboos'; if it is so, it certainly deserves a special consideration.

Diet taboos do exist, and at times constitute a serious handicap to diet improvement. In effect, man being a social entity, his very 'biological hunger' is moulded by his cultural environment: 'each human group proceeds, according to its cultural level, to an original division by which what falls into its social domain is deemed edible and what does not non-edible.'[88] Diet taboos affecting women can be solely explained in terms of dire social poverty coupled with the priority accorded to the man's feeding needs (which cannot be justified by his heavier workload but finds ample justification in his greater social power): by this token, in the Equatorial region of Zaire, women are not allowed to eat certain kinds of fish, under penalty of obscure diseases;

in the Kwango area of Zaire, they are forbidden to eat snakes, wildcats, pangolins, monkeys, buffaloes, antelopes, in fact meat of any sort; in Kasai, women may not take part in parties in honour of their forefathers where meat is the staple diet; in some Lala villages of Zambia, women and girls are prohibited from eating eggs, as these are supposedly conducive to barrenness. All these beliefs are not so much founded on superstition as precise and carefully justified social priorities.

Thomson's study of three Lala villages shows the men as being properly fed at the expense of the women and children: 'Probably, the women are the ones who suffer most (although the trial bites they pick up out of the pans may be sizeable indeed) and with them the children aged about four, who usually eat with their mothers.'[89] (See Table 24)

Table 24
Calories by Age Group and Sex in Three Sample Villages in Serenje District, Zambia (average)

	Calorie requirements by group			Calorie intake by group			Ratio of calorie intake to requirement		
	A	B	C	A	B	C	A	B	C
Whole village	2,298	2,212	2,268	1,392	1,650	1,269	61	75	56
Men	3,030	3,202	3,025	3,506	3,542	2,709	116	111	90
Women and children	2,205	2,020	2,131	1,160	1,300	1,012	55	65	48

Source: B. Preston Thomson, *Two Studies* ..., op.cit.

A FAO study confirms:

> In tropical Africa, children's and adolescents' food is often not adequate to cover the energy they need for their development, and as a result their growth rate is rather slow. This seems to be connected with the fact that the adult males of the family as a rule have priority when food is shared out.[90]

It has been frequently stressed that children, particularly in their early age, are most liable to be affected by malnutrition. Yet, caring about the child's nutrition presupposes improving that of the mother during gestation and breastfeeding.[91] The woman's undernourishment may seriously damage the future child and may also provoke a miscarriage or premature birth.

Breastfeeding — primarily in rural areas — may continue one or two years longer than is considered usual, and if this is exhausting for the mother, it will nevertheless usually shield the baby from the gravest symptoms of malnutrition, even though it delays its growth because of the want of complementary food.[92]

In towns, the feeding-bottle is an ever more frequent substitute for the mother's breast. There is little doubt that this represents a serious danger for the baby, both because it is not always possible to secure the necessary health conditions, such as the sterilization of the feeding bottle, and because women, mostly illiterate, don't know how to measure out the powdered milk. A few experts have forcefully pointed out the hazards of bottle-feeding in Third World countries, as well as the commercial speculation it has given rise to — but so far nobody has much concern for the well-being of the mother, whose breast is often turned into a sore by the baby's milk-teeth.[93] The only remedies available to suckling mothers are the traditional ones — which are difficult to practise in towns and are growing rarer in villages.[94]

In sum, comparative studies on the growth rate of the African and the European baby have revealed that at birth the former usually weighs 250 to 500 grams less than its European or North American counterpart. Luckily, its mother's milk not only helps to make up for this handicap, but even puts it ahead until the sixth month. From then onwards breastfeeding is no longer appropriate, particularly because such vital factors as iron and vitamins C and D are no longer adequately provided by the mother's milk, and the baby's growth decreases against a European baby. By the time the African child is two years old, it will usually be one or two kilos underweight, and it will also have a swollen abdomen and appear to lose its vivacity. But it is when the baby has become a weanling — and this may not happen before it is three years old — that the real danger starts. The term *kwashiorkor* stands for a syndrome of an infant deficiency disease whose main cause is dearth of proteins. Literally, in the Ga language of West Africa (Ghana), the word means the 'first-second', namely the disease the first-born may develop when its mother is expecting a second baby, since it generally only occurs in children between the weaning age and the age of five. A *kwashiorkor* child puts on no weight, looks sad and loses its appetite. In case of an acute form, if not properly treated it will die, and even when the form is not so acute, the child may be easy prey to other diseases or become permanently mentally and physically retarded. Undernourished or malnourished children generally live in communities affected by infectious and parasitic diseases, whose evil scope it would be difficult to define, although it may be safely said that deficiency diseases usually appear in the aftermath of seasonal dysentry or diarrhoea epidemics.

Almost every child living in tropical regions is a victim of intestinal parasites. Part of the food taken by the children goes to feed their intestinal worms, part is evacuated through diarrhoea and the remainder is badly absorbed because of other chronic infections: it is generally acknowledged that malnutrition predisposes children to infection, and infection exacerbates the effects of malnutrition.

Diarrhoea, dysentry and other infantile diseases due to unhealthy conditions of life are the most frequent causes of infant mortality. In Africa, drinking water is a most precious commodity: in some regions, water reservoirs are entirely polluted by bilharzia worms, a parasitical disease which comes second only to malaria as a world disease.

> Drinking unpolluted water is commonplace in developed countries, but it is far from being so in developing countries, where — to go by OMS statistics — 5 million or so children are nowadays dying from diseases from polluted water. Every year, a total of nearly 500 million people fall victim to water-caused typhoid or paratyphoid fever or some other sort of fever, as well as water-caused dysentry and cholera.[95]

Such a dramatic state of affairs cannot be remedied, as FAO and a few African governments seem to believe, simply by some form of 'nutritional education' imparted to families and in particular to mothers. Before this can be effective, there are many and diverse problems to be solved.

Notes

1. Some scholars have suggested new and interesting 'definitions': 'In a recent analysis of the concepts of employment, underemployment and unemployment, Mouly defines "employment" as a situation in which some money is received in return for a direct personal participation in the productive process. Also, he suggests that such fundamental relationship should be formulated at diverse levels, namely the individual or familial level, or the level of a social group forming a production and consumption unit, such as a co-operative or a self-sufficing village, in which any decision aims at the maximum advantage of the community.
   The good point of such a definition is that it goes closely enough to the social function to which the term "employment" is related.' P. Ndegwa, J.P. Powelson, Introduction to *Employment in Africa*, op.cit.
2. H. Singer, R. Jolly, 'Unemployment in an African Setting', in *Employment in Africa*, op.cit.
3. H. Singer, R. Jolly, op.cit.
4. Economic Commission for Africa, UNO.
5. As reported in *The Ghanaian Woman*, July-September 1974.
6. They were 10,000 in 1970 and 30,000 were expected by 1980. See L. Roussell, 'Employment Problems and Policies in the Ivory Coast', in *Employment in Africa*, op.cit.
7. ECA, 'Women: The Neglected Human Resources for African Development', in *Presence*, VI, No.1, 1973.
8. Some participants reported the deplorable fact that some employers refused to grant any accommodation or family allowance to single mothers: also a married woman labourer was bound to avail herself of the medical assistance provided by her husband's employer even when her own employer could supply her with a better doctor. Mutaba Ka-Manji, 'La Maman Zaïroise et le Travail Salarié', in *Salongo*, 20 June 1975.
9. Jasleen Dhamija, 'Potential Role of Handicrafts and Small Industries

in Economic Development', in ILO, ECA, YWCA, *African Workshop on Participation of Women in Handicrafts and Other Small Industries*, Kitwe-Zambia, 9-20 December 1974.
10. T.D. Lamini, 'Handicrafts and Small Industries Policy in Swaziland', in ILO, ECA, YWCA, op.cit.
11. A.B.N. Wandera, 'Handicrafts and Small Industries Policy in Kenya', in ILO, ECA, YWCA, op.cit.
12. The Nuoboa Co-operative Organization is currently being formed in Ghana. A novelty in the Ghanaian co-operative system, it will include *inter alia* a powerful female organization to arrange women in groups designed to accelerate economic and social development through a co-operative action. Nuoboa literally means: 'You aid me and I aid you in a collective form.'
13. M.J. Russel, 'Women's Participation in Co-operatives', in ILO, ECA, YWCA, op.cit.
14. Dr Seth Twum, *The Worker, the Employer and the Law — A Comprehensive Study of Ghana Labour Law*, Teller International Publications 1973.
15. G. Ligan, 'Women in Business' (an investigation carried out in the Ivory Coast, Upper Volta, Togo and Dahomey), in *Entente Africaine*, 9 March 1972.
16. R.M. Lawson, 'The Markets for Foods in Ghana', in various authors, *Readings in the Applied Economics of Africa*, Cambridge University Press, 1967, Vol.1.
17. M. Peil, 'Ghanaian Students: The Broadening Base', in *British Journal of Sociology*, March 1965.
18. C.A. Ackah, 'Social Stratification in Ghana', in *Insight and Opinion*, VI, No.2.
19. A. Brunger, 'Women in Dahomey', in *Women in the Struggle for Liberation*, World Student Christian Federation, III, No.2-3, 1973.
20. G. Ligan, op.cit.
21. *Ibid*.
22. *Ibid*. But in Niger, e.g., small shopkeepers have no credit facilities. The woman owner of a fashion shop thus voiced her complaints to Ligan: 'The Chamber of Commerce only deals with Europeans . . . . There are no brave women in Niger. When I say what is going wrong, I don't mean to attack the regime. I am a nationalist and indeed love my country and the People's Rally which I do not intend to leave. I'm only remonstrating against injustices and abuses. It's my great hope that things will be different when women enter the National Assembly.'
23. *Ibid*.
24. *Ibid*.
25. P. Bohannan, P. Curtin, *Africa and Africans*, New York, 1971. In addition, 'The majority of Western African markets are showing signs of radical changes. Although markets in West Africa have the same function as shops have in Europe, the trend points to change. Indigenous shops are growing in number and importance, particularly on the outskirts of the larger daily markets in the main towns.'
B.W. Hodder, *Economic Development in the Tropics*, London, 1968. The shopowners are mostly men.

26. C. Meillassoux, op.cit. An exhaustive analysis of the 'dependence' of African commerce can be found in Samir Amin's works: *Trois Experiences Africaines de Développement: le Mali, la Guinée et le Ghana*, Paris, Presses Universitaires de France, 1965; *Le Développement du Capitalisme en Côte d'Ivoire*, Paris, Minuit, 1968; *Le Monde des Affaires Sénégalais*, Paris, Minuit, 1969. *L'Accumulazione su Scala Mondiale*, Jaca Book, Milano, 1971.
27. C. Meillassoux, op.cit.
28. G. Althabe, op.cit.
29. K. Little, *African Women in Towns*, Cambridge University Press, 1973.
30. 'With reference to Black Africa, it has been observed that the degree of urbanization of any local population was contingent not only upon the ratio of the urban population to the overall population but also upon the average length of stay in towns, upon the ratio of the families dwelling in town to the number of men working there, and also upon the degree of mutual economic dependence between urban and rural population, on the urban stabilization, and so on and so forth.' R. Stavenhagen, *Le Classi Sociali nelle Societa' Agrarie*, Feltrinelli, Milano, 1971.
31. G. Balandier, *Le Societa' Comunicanti*, Laterza, Bari, 1973. 'This reversal of situation, which serves as a prelude to the recognition of the new woman status, is by no means a pathological phenomenon, albeit certainly a source of temporary disorder.'
32. *Ibid*.
33. V. Lanternari, *Occidente e Terzo Mondo*, Dedalo, Bari, 1972.
34. 'La Donna in Africa', in *Terzo Mondo Informazioni*, March 1974.
35. D. Chishiba, 'The Plight of Bar Waitresses', in *Zambia Daily Mail*, 6 December 1974.
36. ' "Sex-first" Bosses under Fire', in *Times of Zambia*, 13 February 1975. On the occasion of a seminar in Lusaka on the role of women in Zambia, Christine Mulundika urged the women to denounce anybody promising work in return for sex.
37. P. Mayer, *Townsmen or Tribesmen*, Oxford University Press, Cape Town, 1971.
38. R. Deniel, 'Images de la Famille en Côte d'Ivoire', in *Jeune Afrique*, 18 April 1975.
39. Fatoumata-Agnès Diarra, *Femmes Africaines en Devenir – Les Femmes Zarma du Niger*, Paris, Anthropos, 1971; M. Westergaard, *Women and Work in Dar es Salaam*, University of Dar es Salaam, 1970; M. Byangwa, 'The Muganda Woman's Attitude Towards Work Outside the Home – A Study on the Economic Status of the Married Woman', in *Sociology Paper*, No.53, Makerere University.
40. 'Les Mamans Muziki', in *Horizons 80*, 5-12 July 1975.
41. *Ibid*. Gatto Trocchi quotes another women's association 'popular in Kinshasa . . . known as *likelemba*. It consisted of a group of women who paid a given sum at specified times. Each time the total was in turn paid to one of the members, according to an order fixed beforehand: after the last member had received the sum, the association would dissolve'. C. Gatto Trocchi, *Le Giumente degli Dei*, Bulzoni, Roma, 1975.

42. *Ibid.*
43. 'André Boloko, a trade-unionist, has given us a disturbing portrait of this almost uniquely ruthless system of exploitation. As an object-lesson, he has singled out the town of Nioke, with a population of about 10,000. The biggest employer in town was FORESCOM, a subsidiary plant of FORMINIÈRE (Sociéte' Internationale Forestière et Minière du Congo), in its turn a subsidiary plant of the Societe Generale.

    In 1956, most FORESCOM labourers were receiving 0.30 dollars per day plus free lodging. About 80% of the married workers owned cassava fields cultivated by their wives, and about 67% supplemented their incomes with some weekend fishing. Rather surprisingly, *most unskilled labourers were highly dependent on their own families at the village.* 70% or so of them would receive parcels from home two or three times a month. None of the workers under scrutiny appeared to be remitting money to their villages.' Various authors, *Patrice Lumumba*, Panaf, London, 1973.
44. J. Houyoux, op.cit.
45. *Ibid.*
46. K. Mwepu, 'Un Peu d'Égards pour la Femme Commerçante!', in *Taifa* (a Shaban daily), 27 December 1974.
47. 'Bateau et Loisirs', in *Salongo*, 12 May 1975 (a dossier on the women traders of Kinshasa).
48. 'Voyager, que de Soucis!', in *Salongo*, 12 May 1975.
49. *Ibid.*
50. J. Houyoux, op.cit.
51. 'Assez d'Exactions contre les Vendeuses', in *Zaire*, 6 October 1975.
52. J. Segers, A. Habiyambere, 'Les Conditions de la Croissance', op.cit.
53. J. Houyoux, op.cit.
54. C. Sikaneta, 'It's Back to the Land for Urban Women', in *Zambia Daily Mail*, 2 May 1975.
55. *Ibid.*
56. A. Wipper, 'Equal Rights for Women in Kenya?', in *The Journal of Modern African Studies*, IX, No.3, October 1971.
57. J.A. Barnes, 'Marriage in a Changing Society', op.cit., Ethnologic Appendix No.2.
58. 'From dawn to sunset the most characteristic sound of tropical and sub-tropical villages from the Gulf of Guinea to the Indian Ocean is not the exotic rhythm of tamtams but the sound of the big pestles with which women beat and grind the grain to make flour.' C. Gatto Trocchi, op.cit.
59. G. Kay, 'Chief Kalaba's Village — A Preliminary Survey of Economic Life in an Ushi Village, Northern Rhodesia', in *The Rhodes-Livingstone Papers*, No.35, Manchester University Press, 1964.
60. 'Here, we have not examined the political and social tasks which pertain almost exclusively to a man as his contribution to the life of the village.' G. Kay, op.cit.
61. 'The village sanitation was somehow guaranteed by the fact that the house clusters were few and far between and the several cesspools or wood facilities permitted an amount of hygiene that would be

adequate by Western standards. In towns, the lack of sewage and drinking water has dramatic effects: women have to face difficulties not unlike those at the village, such as the water *corvée* and the elaborate food preparation, without, alas, the balancing support of their extended families.' C. Gatto Trocchi, op.cit.

62. Baleka Bamba Nzuji, 'Que signifie au juste la libération feminine?', in *Cultures au Zaire et en Afrique*, No.1, 1973.
63. P. Kalala, 'Le Budget Familial: Un Problème?', in *Zaire*, 7 July 1975.
64. A. Amin, *L'Accumulazione su Scala Mondiale*, Jaca Book, Milano, 1971.
65. *Ibid.*
66. *Ibid.*
67. See *Storia dell'Angola*, edited by MPLA, op.cit.
68. V. Lanternari, *Antropologia e Imperialismo*, Einaudi, Torino, 1974.
69. C.M.N. White, 'A Preliminary Survey of Luvale Rural Economy', in *Rhodes-Livingstone Papers*, No.29, Manchester University Press, 1968, (1st Edition 1959).
70. E.V. Winans, 'The Shambola Family', in various authors, *The Family Estate in Africa*, London, 1964. Also see A.M. Kamark, *The Economics of African Development*, New York, 1967.
71. Sr. Marie-André du Sacre Coeur, op.cit.
72. G. Kay, 'Chief Kalaba's Village', op.cit.
73. B.E. Rourke, F.A. Obeng, 'Seasonality in the Employment of Casual Agricultural Labour in Ghana', in *The Economic Bulletin of Ghana*, No.3, 1973.
74. Such situation has been exposed in 'Women: The Neglected Human Resources for African Development', op.cit.
75. *Femmes Africaines*, CEA, Bulletin des Programmes en Faveur de la Femme.
76. *Ibid.*
77. From an interview granted to *Amina*, June 1975.
78. UNICEF, Conférence de Lomé: Enfance, Jeunesse, Femmes et Plans de Développement, Lomé, 1972.
79. Mpase Nselenge Mpeti, 'L'Évolution de la Solidarité', op.cit.
80. C. Meillassoux, 'L'Economia della Savana', op.cit.
81. M.J. Russel, 'Women's Participation in Co-operatives', op.cit.
82. It has been maintained by many dieticians that cassava, being a quasi-pure starch, has no real nutritional qualities. Additionally it is basically poisonous; therefore, it must be cooked before eating. As for millet, it is less valuable than wheat, since it has a 8-9% content of proteins as against the 11-12% proteinic content of wheat. When very refined, millet flour has a proteinous content of 4-6% and lacks tryptophan, which is an amino acid essential for the maintenance of good health.
83. G. Kay, *A Social Geography of Zambia*, London, 1967.
84. J. Houyoux, 'Budgets Ménagers . . .', op.cit.
85. B. Preston Thomson, 'Two Studies . . .', op.cit.
86. F. Grevisse, *Le Centre Extra-coutumier de Lubumbashi*, 1951.
87. C. & J. Houyoux, *Conditions de Vie dans 60 Familles à Kinshasa*, 1970.
88. Tchamala Mulembwe, 'L'Alimentation Zairoise', in *Horizons 80*,

17-24 May 1975.
89. B. Preston Thomson, op.cit.
90. FAO, *Africa Survey — Report on the Possibilities of African Rural Development in Relation to Economic and Social Growth*, Rome, 1962.
91. See UNICEF, *L'Enfant dans le Tiers-Monde*, Paris, Presses Universitaires de France, 1965.
92. 'Unfortunately, in areas of great hunger, a mother may well feed her children longer than she is due, at times up to three years. Often she has nothing but her own milk to give to them. An urge to secure life for them prompts her to snatch it from herself. And so, she passes on to them all the energies she gets from her meagre diet, only too willing to be stripped by her needy little ones. For them, her sacrifice is the only chance of survival. Yet, if life is thus secured, neither health nor a regular development is. After five months, the mother's milk will no longer suffice.' B. Bellonzi, 'Anche il Seno Materno Puo' Essere piu' Povero', in *Noi Donne*, No.47, 1 December 1974.
93. Dr Adewale Omolulu has stressed the hazards of bottle-feeding, particularly in rural areas and indicated as the three main reasons for its popularity a) the growing number of women who work in an office or in a shop; b) the persuasiveness of sales techniques used by food factories, and c) bottle-feeding as a symbol of social mobility (being fashionable with the élites) and the feeding bottle as a symbol of Western civilization.
94. One of such remedies is a decoction from liana leaves of which part is drunk and part massaged over the breast and the back, or the leaves are ground and added to the food. The most popular remedy is papaya, which is either used for massages and steam baths or broken up between two stones when it is still green and pounded in a pestle. Part of the pulp is used for breast massage, and the remainder is diluted with water and kept on the boil for some time, while the patient exposes herself to the exhalations from the hot steam. Once cold, the decoction is taken in doses during the day.

'If we consider the two-year breast-feeding a young mother is forced into, we can easily imagine the care and the concern that go with the breast and its precious content. The early post-natal months as a rule go pretty smoothly, and the mother does little more than undergoing a "keep fit" treatment usually consisting in daily light massages with pulverised leaves of *Paullinia pinnata*. Later on, her milk becomes scarce and she must then resort to the whole range of presumably galactopoietic drugs.' J. Kerharo, A. Bouquet, *Sorciers, Féticheurs et Guerisseurs*, Paris, 1950.
95. UNICEF, 'L'Enfant dans le Tiers-monde', op.cit.

4. Demographic Control: Tradition and Innovation

> Look, woman, at the barren woman
> Alas, alas!
> The childless woman
> Look, oh, look
> At the childless woman
> He who knew you once
> No longer knows you
> You, a barren woman
> Look, oh, look
> At the childless woman
>
> Ah, this womb of mine
> Is the cause of my fall
> And brought dishonour on me
> Yes, this womb of mine
> Is the cause of my fall
>
> *Two Popular Songs from Ghana*

Traditional Control of Reproduction and Motherhood

Most agricultural countries have their own good traditional reasons for desiring a high female fertility rate: suffice it to quote here the importance of 'human capital' along with the mechanism of 'social security' which rests on kinship in such countries. The motives behind the desire for a large family have been institutionalized through various and complex rites, taboos, social behaviour and beliefs.

The Akan of Ghana, for example, believe that their ancestors still exist in some land of the dead from where they can influence life on earth. The Akan consequently maintain that reproduction as a means of replacing the ancestors is a man's primary function: a man dying without issue is a taboo man.

During the first eight days after birth, a child, the new-born baby, who is perceived as a reincarnation of its forefathers, remains a spirit, after which it becomes a human being and takes the family and ancestral name. A child is believed to possess two inner factors: the spirit, i.e. the personality, which it receives from its father, and the blood, i.e. the material part, which it receives from its mother.

There are fertility rites invoking blessings and protection for women so that they may be abundantly fertile. The Akan pour wine on to the soil as they pray: 'Long live this town, long live our chief, long live our families, may our harvest be prosperous and our women be fertile.'[1]

During the rite of the bride's commitment to her bridegroom, the officiant prays thus: 'May all our Gods bless them and grant them good health, and may the woman bear twelve children so that she may sleep in twelve beds.'[2] Rattray relates that one of the prayers in the puberty rite goes like this: 'May the elephant give you her womb, so that you may bear ten children.' And when the tenth child is born, the multiparous woman is acclaimed through an elaborate ceremony and the sacrifice of a sheep for the soul (*kra*) of her mother. The seventh or eighth child is given a special name to mark the fortunate event. In brief, the social system of values 'tends by means of proper gratifications to stimulate the "zeal" for maternity.'[3] Additionally, there is an equally strong pressure in the many tribes where a woman has no social status until she becomes a mother. It is a Babembe custom that only a four-time mother will cease to be a *ms'ea* (girl) and become a *mwamba* (woman). In the eyes of the Kabi and the Hausa, a woman is a minor until she is delivered of her first-born. Should she be barren, she will be socially mature only after her parents have found a foster child for her.

A childless couple will explore every avenue in their search for the causes of their sterility and a remedy to it. Among the Lobi, for example, childless couples undergo biological tests in order to ascertain which partner is the culprit.

Usually though, sterility is deemed an essentially feminine 'attribute'. The well-known Akan ritual of the fertility doll (*Akuaba*) is a remarkable example of a psychotherapeutic treatment of sterility. The doll is made by the husband of the barren woman who carries it on her back, plays with it during the day and at night takes it to her bed, until she bears a child. Better known and more popular are the various anti-abortion and anti-sterility treatments, which make use of customary drugs:

> Before returning the sterile woman to her kin, her master and lord will have her examined by the most distinguished healers in the region or in the neighbouring districts. In a Kru tribe living near Grabo we have actually met two Liberian 'gynaecologists' or witchdoctors, who had been summoned there by the locals because a few of their women were barren.... Several indigenous 'doctors' have mentioned cures for a self-inflicted abortion or a multi-miscarriage (mostly due to blennorrhea or syphilis), reportedly capable of securing a successful pregnancy.
>
> In Upper Volta, Mossi females use a blend of *Banhinia reticulata* and *Sarcocephalus esculentus* leaves. They drink part of the decoction and rub their bodies with the rest of it. Guro and Gagon women extol the properties of the *Ricinodendrum africanum* bark or of the

degrékwo pulp if mixed with pepper. The Kru prescribe a decoction made from *boa-holi* bark or from *trichoscypha* to be taken as a potion, as well as a decoction made from *maweson* or *touklébo* leaves for ablutions, while *boaga* or *kado* root-powder are usually mixed with food.[4]

Praise of motherhood and a real desire for it do not exclude some forms, at times elaborate, of birth control. The notion of spacing out births is not foreign. Policies exist aiming at preventing too close pregnancies, such as sending away an expectant mother living in a polygamous family. The woman stays with her parents until her child is able to walk, which may be a few years — while the co-wives run the conjugal home. The pregnancy and departure of another wife usually coincides with the return of the first.

In many societies, a nursing mother will not have intercourse, in order to avoid pregnancies in such a delicate time for her and her baby. Leaving aside ritual abstinence and abortion — which is much commoner than it is generally thought — there are many more customary methods of birth control.

Romaniuk's careful investigation indicates as a practice in many regions of Zaire 'the expulsion of sperm by means of a post-coital scouring of the vagina'; women of the Kindu and Kasongo territories use a lotion made from a decoction of tobacco leaves; Bakusu women resort to a blend of pineapple juice, while frangipani juice is the favourite thing among the Lusambo. While we cannot deny any spermicidal virtue to all these concoctions, yet it is a fact that no relevant test has been carried out so far.

In some regions, the semen is ejected by some sort of manipulation: the Azande of Bondo, for example, crouch down, sprawl their legs and rhythmically beat their backs until the sperm is ejected, while the neuro-muscular technique constitutes a most cherished sperm-ejective practice among Kisangani women, particularly if they are engaged in prostitution. Occlusion is not unknown: among the Budja, the only contraceptives in use are cloth or cotton tampons, which are placed over the mouth of the uterine cervix to hinder sperm from entering. The Azande of Dungu instead insert a rolled up *nongo* leaf into the vagina.

Romaniuk notes that

> among the oldest examples of occlusal practices in Africa, the most revealing are those reported by Walter Master, a medical officer who, as he worked among the Bapinde and the Bambunda, had the opportunity to examine several cases of occlusion of the uterine mouth, two of which were indeed fatal. Since these cases date from the years prior to World War I, when European influence was hardly noticeable, we may assume that they were part of a customary practice.[5]

Romaniuk has also noted the remarkable method, employed by the Langelimia (Banalia), of introducing a vegetable product — apt to provoke total amenorrhoea — beneath the skin by making a cut on both sides of the renal region: as soon as the substance exhausted its virtues, menstruation would occur again. There are reports of the existence of medicaments capable of stopping menstruation among other African peoples.

Contraceptives introduced by the colonizers do not appear to be very popular, arguably because they are expensive and, besides, dramatically reduce sexual enjoyment. Likewise, *coitus interruptus*, which is undoubtedly the most ancient and widespread contraceptive method on earth, does not seem to be much practised: the fact is that it requires the co-operation of the couple or at least the consent of the man, and it may well be that a man is willing to resort to it only during the breast-feeding period.

We may ultimately assume that the rejection of withdrawal and the customary connection between family organization and family planning demonstrate that the social control over women as a reproduction control is, in traditional societies, of more consequence than any contraceptive practice.

Yet, as we have seen, such practices are far from being unknown; thus, it seems reasonable to infer that their relative marginality is related to their being too 'individual' as well as too 'feminine': their use would in fact imply a positive control over reproduction on the part of women. This is precisely what — in the eyes of our rulers — should never be allowed to happen.

The Cliteridectomy 'Mystery'[6]

Cliteridectomy, also known under the euphemistic name of 'female circumcision', serves a purpose described by an anthropologist as 'highly problematic' and even 'mysterious'. Yet, 'whatever its transcendent significance', it is unquestionably related to 'the process of oppression and marginalization the woman is subject to.'[7]

Alex Zanotelli, a Combonian Father, carried out interesting research on this mutilation of the female genitalia and produced a detailed account of the various types known in Sudan.

The most extreme consists in the removal of the clitoris and the labia minora; a second type involves the removal of the labia minora and part of the clitoris, and the vagina is partially sewn with three stitches; also, part of the clitoris and either of the labia minora may be removed, while the other labium is sewn on the opposite side leaving only a small orifice; a fourth type is represented by the excision of the clitoris, and a fifth by the partial excision of the clitoris.

> Dr Sayyd Abd al Hadi, an eminent Muslim from Sudan, has censured this rite as a crime against the dignity of the person. Only few, I believe, have a notion of how painful and humiliating cliteridectomy may be .... From my research it has emerged as a plain truth to me that the sole aim of female circumcision is to afford the greatest sexual gratification to the male. For, it is he that is entitled to have full

enjoyment; as to the female, she doesn't count much: she is mainly instrumental to the pleasure of the male . . . .

Female circumcision is a serious mutilation, which affects vital and delicate organs . . . . In all the five types I've mentioned, the clitoris is wholly or partially excised. Everybody knows how important a sexual organ this is for the female, given the fact that its function is not unlike that of the penis in the male body. A hot debate is currently going on among experts to establish whether the vagina or the clitoris is the seat of female sexual gratification. In either case, both are necessary for a normal and healthy sexual relation. I must confess that I was disturbed when a woman confided to me: 'To me, it doesn't make much difference if my husband hits me on the face or has sex with me'.[8]

Thus, the excision of the clitoris is a horrible mutilation which prevents the sexual satisfaction of the female, whereas it enhances the sexual (or is it sadistic?) pleasure of the male. Not only this, for it is also a counter-productive practice as regards fertility: this is the actual 'mystery' about the whole affair. In the course of excision, the whole reproductive system is seriously jeopardized and may even incur atrophy. Sterility is commonplace among circumcised females, and hospitals certify that some babies are dead at birth due to the badly damaged genitals of the circumcised female.

It would appear then, that in societies practising cliteridectomy, women's unconditional docility and subordination, rather than their fertility, are the main concern. In order to achieve this, they callously resort to practices which humiliate and destroy women's resistance through pain.

It seems to me that cliteridectomy should be associated with the issue of the social control over the woman as a 'reproducer of producers' rather than male sexual behaviour. What is at stake here is not so much the assertion of male sexuality, as Zanotelli suggests — as the repression of female sexuality and consequently of any free pre- or extra-marital liaison the woman may set up: brutally maimed, she is bound to keep her sexual behaviour well within the marital institution, as a strict duty she may in no way shirk.

When cliteridectomy is carried out on a very young woman, it is bound to have a profound effect on her psychological attitude toward sex. The young woman embarks on her mature life loathing her own sex and every activity related to it. Her first traumatic experience has left a deep scar on her. Naturally enough, she is afraid of sex including of course marital sex, even though she will eventually accept the latter, knowing that there is no way out for her: it would be shame to rebel, a weakness not to bear the consequences of pregnancy and childbirth, painful as the latter may be after circumcision.

'What has been wrongly defined as the insensitivity of the black woman is in reality her stiffening in face of pain, the pain she has learned to conquer and scorn since when, as a pubescent girl, she was confronted with excision.'[9]

In Alex Zanotelli's opinion, the responsibility for the persistence of such custom lies mostly with all those men, educated or not, who refuse to take an uncircumcised female as a bride. It also lies with those parents, primarily mothers and grandmothers, who are determined to persuade, if not force, their daughters and granddaughters to submit to tradition from fear of never getting married. Doctors and civil authorities as well as with teachers, catechists and priests instead of stubbornly ignoring the rite — as they do — should provide proper sex education to the young and bring to light the rights of women. Anti-abortion laws should also be issued and enforced. Above all, women themselves should take courage and rise in defence of their dignity and freedom.[10]

Such dignity and such freedom was not upheld by Jomo Kenyatta, who supported cliteridectomy as an 'authentic custom' of Africa, even though the women of Kenya constantly declared against it: 'Despite tradition, this operation is utterly useless and likely to be in the long run extremely dangerous to the woman.'[11] There are also people who, like certain 'intellectual' supporters of Mobutu's regime, regret that such practice is no longer so popular as it used to be. 'Unfortunately, good old habits such as this one are now being relinquished in favour of practices and techniques which come to us from foreign customs.'[12]

The 'Demographic' Problem in Colonial Times

The low birthrate in many African regions soon affected the recruitment of labour power and thus caused some understandable concern among the colonial authorities. This was in turn put down to the climate or to the primitive conditions of life of the Africans, and diverse and bizarre theories were formulated over the issue, while anthropologists complained about the lack of medical studies on sterility and its causes.

Various political measures were taken in order to overcome this hindrance to a rapid and intense exploitation of African resources. Thus, the *Commission for the Protection of the Natives* in the ex-Belgian Congo suggested a tax allowance and a reward to prolific fathers. Moreover, on the assumption that polygamy was detrimental to procreation, the Commission imposed a special tax on polygamists for each extra wife and, to prevent the spread of contagious diseases, it required that any person leaving its traditional setting for a town should be provided with a *passeport de mutation*, which could be obtained only after a medical check-up. In fact the earliest and most probable cause of the massive depopulation of vast areas of Africa was slave trade.

About Zaire, Romaniuk wrote:

> We can see that sterility zones tend to coincide with the territories where, during the second half of the 19th Century, slave traders played havoc with natives. Slave traders were active mostly in the east of the country, i.e., in Maniema and in North Katanga starting from Zanzibar, and in the North starting from Khartoum. The devastating effects of manhunts in these regions are probably still felt today in the form of a

low birthrate following social disorganization and the propagation of venereal diseases.[13]

Colonial wars followed by the bloody quenching of riots have accomplished the task. According to statistics, throughout the colonial period and down to the First World War there was a constant decrease of the birthrate. There are no reliable data for the inter-war period, and it is, therefore, hard to pinpoint a clear trend, nevertheless it can be said that generally it was toward a stabilization of the birthrate. On the contrary, during the last decade of the colonial period there was a sharp rise in fertility; a logical outcome of the wedding boom around the 1950s, when women had free access to towns. Yet, at the time of Romaniuk's investigation in the former Belgian Congo '20% of the females over the reproductive age have never given birth to a live child.'[14]

White's research among the Luvale in 1959 confirms that

> the Luvale birthrate is low . . . . The census figures collected by the provincial administration point to a stationary population, but at the time of the census an immigratory flow from Angola was in progress, and so the stationary level may well be only a flight of fancy.[15]

Among the causes of the Luvale low birthrate, infant mortality ranks prominently, but a sharp fall in fertility was the main reason.

The high sterility rate, particularly among females, has to date been a characteristic of many African populations. Unfortunately, it seems that the issue will not be successfully tackled inside the present structures, for all the initiatives that may be taken by the various governments, economic dependence, zero growth and the spread of poverty and endemic diseases are the real determinants of the phenomenon.

Abortion

Abortion has often been referred to as a cause of falling birthrate, primarily in Central Africa.

When the Commission for the Protection of the Natives of the former Belgian Congo met for the first time in Banana in 1912, the question of a falling birthrate was well on the agenda, and on the assumption that it was basically due to abortifacient practices, the participants unanimously agreed that the police should chase and punish any woman committing the 'crime of abortion'.

Several investigators have now concluded that over the colonial period there was a far from negligible number of self-inflicted abortions: some of them have attached this to loose morals and even to some psychic alteration ultimately engendering 'dread of motherhood' in African women shocked by European 'civilization'.

We believe that self-inflicted abortion is on the one hand a response to the insecurity of life and society during the colonial occupation and on the other a deliberate act of rebellion against a certain shape of family structure, and in particular of conjugal relationships. When asked, women have often said that revenge against their husbands was their reason for aborting.

An informant from Ponthierville said that 'abortion is only performed by women who married unwillingly and now refuse to produce children to the benefit of their husbands or their families'.

In the words of another informant from the region of Basankusu,

> Abortion is a common event indeed, and it is almost always devised and carried out without the husband's knowledge. The woman often manages to keep it secret, aided by the solidarity of the neighbourhood. The motives for aborting may be as various as family quarrelling, the failure to pay part of the dowry, or a serious offence. Also, a woman may be induced to abort by a desire for revenge against her husband.[16]

Such statements call for a cautious assessment, for men are very often only too ready to accuse women of self-inflicted abortion when it may be a miscarriage which the woman wishes to conceal, as it might be taken as an evidence of failure: there is no need to underline here, the significance of such climate of suspicion towards the woman. It seems that the refusal to procreate, manifested by abortion, is common in patrilineal societies; and, says Romaniuk, it is no mere coincidence.[17]

Azande women, for instance, say they are

> utterly fed up with the idea of having to bring children into this world and nurture them, only to come up against the ultimate fact that once they have grown up, the father and his family will reap all the benefits while they, the mothers, have no say in their children's marriage and no participation in the bridewealth.[18]

It seems that it is not the violence produced by the colonizing process, but the very structures of traditional societies that drive women to refuse motherhood by way of abortion.

In polygamous tribes, the woman is often goaded into a 'back street' abortion by her jealousy towards the co-wives as she fears being separated from her husband on the strength of some religious or social dictate, such as the prohibition of copulation during gestation and breastfeeding. The mother of a child conceived in adultery will also resort to abortion in anticipation of some serious conjugal conflict or a criminal action; as will an unmarried woman living in a society which harshly condemns any 'unorthodox' birth. Yet, in spite of the frequent abortions, single mothers are numerous. Once virtually non-existent or, at least in matrilineal societies, tolerated, single mothers have now become a real problem for society. The relevant figures are appalling, and notably in big towns.[19]

In Kinshasa, illegitimate children — known as *ba mbotela*, which means children generated in a disorderly manner — are often the target of open contempt, to the extent that calling somebody *mbotela* would be tantamount to a serious insult. Nonetheless, a survey in 30 Yansi villages in 1967 revealed that single mothers made up a good 47.43% of the whole local motherhood. A major cause is no doubt the difficulty in contracting a regular marriage because of the high bride-price.

Thus, abortion is the 'contraceptive' method most in demand among the women of traditional societies. The probable reasons are that: a) It is technically simpler than any chemical or mechanical contraception; b) Unlike such contraceptive methods as the *coitus interruptus*, it does not require the co-operation of the couple; c) It may be carried out at any time during gestation. This is important because, although at first the child may be wanted, subsequent events may induce the woman to change her mind and opt for abortion. In practice, only abortion seems to allow a woman in traditional society a real choice, even though she is likely to pay a very high price for it.

Among methods of abortion in traditional societies, foremost are decoctions from various plants such as manioc, tobacco, yam, papaya, mango, frangipani — all of which may be either taken by mouth or through the vagina. A decoction extracted from a strong variety of pepper known as *pili-pili* has been reported as being used in Zaire, primarily in the Equator province: it is so strong that, in large doses, it may cause internal burns, and in fact many ovaries were found to have been literally burnt following a *pili-pili* washing.

The Babindji of Kazumba take a potion made by cooking *babou* roots (which are also used in fishing), which is expected to bring on abortion within 12 hours. The Batshok know a substance they call *mutshatsha* which, in large doses, may be lethal.

Less popular seem to be mechanical abortifacients, which rely on recently introduced procedures such as the insertion of sharp sticks and stalks in the vaginal canal in order to 'kill the foetus' or the use of quinine, obviously after the European fashion, which has been repeatedly reported to Romaniuk.

The Bufalero of Uvira have a different way. In the words of an informant, 'To prevent dishonour, they put the pregnant girl in a sealed hut and let a peculiar substance burn in there: the girl will lapse into a state of semi-consciousness, during which abortion occurs.'[20] Whether this practice is by itself conducive to abortion or only to a lethargic condition highly suitable for manipulation, our informant does not say.

Romaniuk finally comments:

> We do not know how effective these procedures are. No analysis has ever been carried out to establish the chemical structure of the ingredients used in them and to test their abortifacient power. We are nonetheless impressed by the variety of the procedures. No doubt a

few of them are nothing more than magic practices and therefore hardly effectual; yet, it would be indeed surprising if none of the items in such a vast assortment had efficacy of some sort. Still, any of these effective procedures would in all likelihood be dangerous.[21]

In the Ivory Coast *Mareya spicata* is one of the plants most frequently used. It is highly purgative, in fact so forcefully that, albeit the foetus is as a rule correctly expelled, still the mother's life is exposed to serious danger. Elsewhere in the same region, women use *Turraeanthus africana*, better known as *avodire'*, and *Trichilia heudelotii*, another drastic though a less dangerous cathartic, whose bark powder they mix with food.[22]

In Ghana, it is a common practice in most rural areas and in some urban communities to tie a piece of string to a twig of *Jatropha* which is placed in the womb and then pulled out by means of the string as soon as the woman starts bleeding. Many 'spontaneous' miscarriages treated in hospital are probably induced in this manner.

> Abortion is a most common surgical operation to be performed in the principal hospitals of Ghana. It is estimated that in the Korle Bu Teaching Hospital of Accra over 4,000 cases are being dealt with every year — most of them, it is also estimated, are self-produced abortions.... Yet, this is perhaps just a small portion of the abortions which occur in the community. In fact, if we take into account all the cases that never end up in hospital, the overall figure in a big city like Accra may well be in the region of 10,000.[23]

In a seminar on family planning, Dr Lucia Pobee from the Korle Bu hospital pointed out that in Ghana, now, 'out of 330 cases of abortion, five are lethal: three of them from haemorrhage, one from kidney infection, and one from tetanus'.[24]

Hospitalization, most frequent in case of haemorrhage, does help calculate the extent of the phenomenon in the urban setting: by estimate, one-third of the blood bank store in Ghana goes to save women from the consequences of abortions, most of which are clandestine. Officially, abortion is a crime, and thus is concealed. This is so even in the newly independent states, where the official attitude towards it is rather censorious. As a result, any serious research on the subject is bound to run into difficulties, as Caldwell's experience in Ghana demonstrates:

> It had been hoped that our investigation would provide some positive indications on the abortion rate, but just before our tests began, the government announced that the death penalty for this practice was to be enforced. The announcement did not make clear enough whether the penalty would be inflicted on the patient or on the author of the operation. Therefore, we had to turn all our questions about personal experiences into generic ones.... Our impression is that the relatively

high number of women refusing to give an answer betokens a personal experience.[25]

Significant, though, was the answer given by a woman telephonist: 'It occurred very frequently before the government made it illegal.'

Naturally, the 'severity' of the law leaves much room for the illicit profits of more or less 'back street' abortionists. By Ghanaian law, abortion is permitted only if it is essential for the life or wellbeing of the pregnant woman, and a judgement to this effect is made by the medical officer who, in legal terms, 'is acting in *bona fide*'. But of course, 'in hospitals where a qualified doctor is permitted by the law to perform a "*bona fide*" abortion, a great number of such operations are carried out not for the sake of the patient in dire peril, but rather for the sake of money.'[26]

There are other justifications for an abortion, mainly social, even in a non-traditional environment, such as the desire to attend some schooling or training, or fear of losing a job or even of getting the sack. And then there is always the unwanted pregnancy, or the pregnancy following the previous one too closely; finally, comparatively few women resort to abortion for 'health reasons'. Even in avowedly socialist countries, abortion is prosecuted as an 'attack on race'.

On the occasion of a radio debate in Zaire, the Minister of Health and Social Security and the Director of the National Health Service condemned any premature termination of pregnancy. The latter revealed that in 1972 some 729 abortion cases related to schoolgirls had been on record, 20 of which had been fatal; according to Dr Ondaye, 50% to 75% of pregnant schoolgirls resort to abortion, 80% to 95% of them to back street abortion. The Minister ended by saying that

> we should not forget that ours is a developing country . . . . We cannot build our nation if our young women are killed by clandestine abortion in the face of the laws for the protection of life. It would be a shame if, after we have gone . . . there should be nobody else around.[27]

Yet, in Africa too, the debate on abortion as a question closely related to the more general issue of the position of women has finally begun. At last, in spite of great difficulties and blatant contradictions, the voice of women is being heard. In *Ideal Woman*, the only magazine for women in Ghana, we can read:

> Abortion is now a problem for the law, and the law cannot put an end to it. Abortion is now a problem for our society, and we must find a solution to it . . . . We must prevent our young women from committing themselves into the hands of quacks . . . . Society must change its stance towards abortion and the women who resort to it.[28]

In December 1973, there was a six-day seminar at the University of Accra,

Legon, on abortion; the general theme was *Medical and Social Aspects of Abortion in Africa*. In the course of the seminar, Professor Ndeti of the University of Nairobi submitted his study on 'Abortion in Traditional Societies: a Sociological Review of Abortion in Six Countries of East Africa'. On the strength of statistics then available to him, he demonstrated how abortion was on the increase everywhere and asked for African governments to critically reconsider their hopelessly repressive law and change it. During another conference on abortion in Accra in 1974, out of 250 participants, mostly women, 128 declared for the legalization of abortion and only 82 against it.

The Family Planning Controversy

The question of abortion is closely linked to the demographic question in general and to the so-called 'family planning' issue in particular, which, through the spread of modern contraceptive methods, is expected to cure the 'social sore' caused by abortion. Indeed, the point at issue appears to be fairly complex. It is a fact that African states 'are on the whole showing scarce enthusiasm for a low birthrate policy'.[29] This is understandable if we consider that Africa accounts for one-quarter of the globe and one-tenth of its population. Africa is not Asia: its problem is not over-population but depopulation. It is also a fact, nevertheless, that the urban population of Africa is growing at a fearful rate, and an increase of the urban young population means an increase of dependent population, a phenomenon destined to retard economic development.

Yet, despite the 'scarce enthusiasm', various African nations, including Kenya, Ghana, Nigeria, already have a demographic policy supported by their governments and often integrated into the national development schemes.

Kenya was the first African country to start a national family planning scheme at the beginning of the 1960s. Also, family planning associations are now privately operating in Zambia,[30] Madagascar and in most francophone countries.

It should be stressed at this stage that capitalist birth control certainly never aims at solving the problems of the masses and also that the ambiguity of the official demographic policies of economically and politically dependent countries stems from their very lack of autonomy. In its modern form, birth control is not prompted by local exigencies but by well defined external pressures. For the International Bank of Reconstruction and Development, for instance, it is a prerequisite for a loan that the country applying for it should be committed to partially invest it in a family limitation programme. The World Bank, for its part, has openly threatened to withdraw its credits from those countries which will not pledge themselves to embark on a birth control policy.

The International Planned Parenthood Federation, very active in imposing birth control measures including sterilization, is intimately associated with some American and multinational monopolies. On the other hand, it was under the direct pressure of the World Bank in 1972 that Mauritius transformed the Catholic Action Familiale and the Mauritius Family Planning Association into government organizations.

Thus, a correct solution of the demographic question and a correct approach to birth control as part of the development process can only be envisaged within the framework of development plans in countries which do not depend on international capitalism.

Nonetheless, even those African countries which at the NU-sponsored Bucharest Conference on population in 1974 declared against family limitation, did not do so in a consistently anti-imperialist and revolutionary perspective[31] but rather against the background of the cult and myth of the 'number-means-power' concept, fostered by the dreams and nationalistic hopes of the new African ruling classes. And the students of the university of Kumasi stated in their newpaper: 'Population ties in with political power: a people great in number will always be listened to . . . .'[32] Yet, political power *for whom*? The very term 'people' is really a nondescript one, when we start from the premise — misleading and biased — that there are no classes in Africa.[33] This flat rejection of any form of birth control on the part of students and national bourgeoisies seems to be a provocative statement rather than the enunciation of a real need. It will appear even more so if we can ascertain the real target of African family planning schemes.

The demographic project of Ghana, formerly privately launched by the Christian Council of Ghana and the Family Planning Association, is now a public project co-ordinated by the Ministry of Economic Planning as a factor in the strategy for national development. The appropriation for the family planning budget increased from 0.5 million cedis in 1971 to a minimum of 1.0 million cedis in 1973. Further, family planning is now one of the regular services to the mother and the child provided by the Ministry of Health. The first family planning volunteer groups were formed in Ghana around 1957, and about ten years later the Planned Parenthood Association of Ghana, a general association for family planning, was formed.

It was by heeding the advice and expertize of the people actively involved in this organization that the Ministry of Economic Planning launched a national demographic policy scheme, which gave large scope to voluntary organizations. The Ghana Population Policy Manifesto, issued in 1969, stated: 'The government's demographic programme involves a close connection with the national health programme. The government will therefore support PPAG's voluntary activities and will give the agreed assistance.' The government's plan included the training of doctors, health personnel, social workers and family planning experts. Eight centres in the country cover nearly every regional capital: the main hospital in Accra dispenses about 900 intra-uterine contraceptives and 700 oral contraceptives every year. Although at the Ministry of Information an official has been assigned to deal with family planning information in rural areas, the strange phenomenon may be observed that it is the urban populations and notably the higher social classes that largely benefit from the government's programmes and the availability of contraceptives. 'The modern form of the family planning movement originated as an individual effort in families where the need for modernization was being felt: in other words, the contraceptive practice was often a privilege of the urban élites within the high income bracket.'[34] (See Table 25)

Table 25
Family Planning Clinics: 1970: Beneficiaries by Region

Region	Number of beneficiaries	Total distribution of beneficiaries (%)
Accra	1,029	61.76
West Accra	268	16.09
Ashanti	181	10.86
East Accra	89	5.34
Central Accra	68	4.08
Volta	31	1.86
Brong-Ahafo	–	–
Northern Volta	–	–
Upper Volta	–	–

	Staff providing the service	
Capacity	Number of beneficiaries	Beneficiaries (%)
Doctor	1,099	65.97
F.P. Nurse	382	22.93
F.P. Ancillary staff	9	0.54
Others	53	3.18
Not specified	123	7.38

Source: D.A. Ampofo, *The Family Planning Movement in Ghana*, Accra, 1971.

Truly enough, at the time of Caldwell's investigation, the urban élite was already making ample use of contraceptives.[35]

In brief, family planning appeared to favour the rise of the new urban bourgeoisie while practically ignoring the rest of the population.[36]

In the final analysis it most significantly led to giving life and shape within the urban élite to the 'modern' family with a restricted and properly planned number of children, for whom it is easier to provide adequate schooling and upbringing. It has become manifest by now that not only does the demographic policy of these countries only look after the interests and needs of international capitalism, but also the interests and needs of the local ruling classes. If birth control has been welcomed by the bourgeoisie (and also by some sectors of the proletariat), still it has not necessarily been understood to be a 'rejection of motherhood'.

In Kinshasa, the Wanted Motherhood Service is now operational with reference to the issues of sterility and family planning. Although contraceptives are freely available at this centre, its aim, duly underlined by the staff on several interviews, is not to limit the number of births but solely to help parents to pre-arrange the number of their children and space out pregnancies; in other words, to better foresee and regulate the population increase without actually preventing it. It is easy to infer from the above that primarily the women of the new middle classes (and, in part, of the wage-earning class too) will benefit from the modern contraceptive techniques. Significantly these women are at the receiving end of the advocacy of the 'worth' of procreation and the acceptance of motherhood, providing it is well regulated and planned. Only these women are in fact in a position to carry on the issues concerning the meaning and worth of motherhood from a woman's standpoint.

> The liberated woman ... should not reject marriage but freely accept the man who suits her, so that she may find her own worth in his company. No longer should she evade motherhood but instead restrict it with reason, and space out births in accordance with her husband for a greater freedom.... Never shall the liberated woman repress her femininity.[37]

We are confronted here with diversified forms of family planning according to social classes, along with a general and extremely high praise of motherhood: the African woman, any African woman, is in the first place a mother, and her social 'worth' is linked to her fertility. Undeniably, 'forcing birth control on women who are out of work and so financially dependent upon their husbands, for all this unable to play a significant role in the social and political life of their countries'[38] brings no emancipation and no happiness.

On the other hand, the myth of the Mother and its implied motherhood at all costs, especially in fascist countries such as Zaire, certainly does not betoken respect of the traditions and the exigencies, whether material or not, of the people and in particular of women. The exaltation of maternity, which conceals the coercion of maternity, lends itself nicely to a better social and political control of females as reproducers of labour force. The more or less blatant imposition of motherhood, or rather of it as a woman's inborn attribute, does not render a country any freer or its economic future any brighter. Rather, the contradiction between the necessity of reproduction and the exigencies or aspirations of the masses of women may well engender an unbridgeable gap.

Planned Motherhood?

It seems safe to assume that a woman who expects good progress and a successful outcome of her gestation will choose to be a mother.

It is all the more significant then that such an issue seems to be scarcely felt by the very governments which commend maternity so highly. Little is said about the usual conditions of childbirth which, because of general hardships, is far more hazardous for African women — and even more so for those who live in rural areas — than for their Western counterparts.

> Childbearing, they say, is particularly easy among the 'primitives': indeed, it would be no nine days' wonder to see a young mother grind millet in the wood or fetch water from a river only hours after delivering. Yet, according to what women say, an awkward and laborious parturition is a rather frequent event.[39]

Undernourishment, so characteristic of a pregnant woman in rural areas, is made even worse by the inadequate protection of her peculiar state: still, she must go on making bodily efforts and travelling to and from work until the day she is delivered.

> The Mbiem of Zaire are certainly keen on maternity, and yet this does not come to their females without danger: various complications often go with it. The birth-registers of the Banza-Lute show that out of 379 births 166 were accompanied by some difficulty or other; it is on the Beno maternity hospital record that out of 2,192 births, 77 were miscarriages (2.64%), 83 were still births (2.85%), and 86 were premature (2.95%): such figures probably do not cover even half of all the parish births, since many women take themselves to hospital only if they anticipate an awkward delivery.[40]

In traditional societies, the mother-to-be would be presented with a remarkable display of solidarity.[41] She would be exempted from work and for three months or so assisted by her mother or an elder sister, who would stay constantly at her side even when they lived far away. Alternatively, the woman could stay with her family, and if so, her husband was expected to pay regular visits to mother and child. Nowadays, this token of solidarity often takes place only just before or after parturition.

According to calculations concerning West Africa, a considerable proportion of women (43% on average, 95% in the worst cases) give birth in the conventional manner, that is to say, away from a health centre and with the single assistance of a woman belonging to the family or of a 'traditional midwife'. The latter will often resort to customary treatment throughout gestation.

> In order to have fine children, a woman must make herself washings of various kinds during the whole gestation period: *Momordica charentia, Euadenia trifoliata, Fagara Xanthoxyloides, Physalis angulata* are the staple ingredients.... Vomiting, oedemas, gastro-enteritis, piles and varicose veins receive a particular treatment..., local or internal,

based on some decoction . . . . A healer even boasted of a water-breaking method for difficult cases, which by all means brutal, must nevertheless bring some result: a banana bloom would be filled with palm oil and introduced as deep as possible in the parturient's mouth; she would consequently experience vomit spasms which, acting upon the intestinal peristalsis, would cause the breaking of the waters. A few vegetal species employed in aid of child-bearing are actually known for their cleansing and diuretic virtues supposedly acting on the abdominal organs.[42]

'Traditional midwives' know of some efficacious drugs, which may be administered orally or rectally to induce labour; besides, they massage the parturient's abdomen or renal region with medicamental liquids such as *Fleurya aestuans* or *Aframonum juice*. In order to obtain the expulsion of the placenta, a decoction of *Oxyanthus tubiliflorus* may be drunk. *Elaeis guineensis* will also serve: after its root has been carbonized and pulverized, salt and palm oil is added, the drug is then swallowed with some water: the effect will be immediate. Young mothers-to-be, if they can, generally adhere to particular diets and foodstuffs seasoned with 'magic' plants or some other specific seasoning.[43]

Most women are still bound to resort to these customary methods, which were once functional and probably effective enough but are now inadequate and bound to be discarded, following the negative campaign for so long conducted by the 'white science'.

The 1972 Lomé conference stressed the inadequacy of such methods and blamed them for the increase in such childbirth diseases as umbilical tetanus, puerperal infections and various relevant complications; the same methods were considered to be responsible for the rise in childbirth mortality. On that occasion it was also pointed out that in rural areas only the populations living near to the dispensaries and maternity hospitals of the main localities could benefit from their services.

Other factors contributing to the underuse of maternity hospitals and dispensaries in rural areas are the distance from health centres (many women give birth on the way), the lack of facilities for the collecting of parturients, the cost of living in a strange place and, finally, a sense of displacement.

> In Zaire, often for lack of transportation, the parturient women of Mbaya Larme cannot take themselves to the Bagata hospital, which is 40 kilometres away, too great a distance for them to cope with. Besides, they find the charge for childbearing assistance too high. Therefore, they are left with the only option of paying the fine imposed on the parturients who do not go to hospital.[44]

Moreover, in rural areas only wage-earning women (in West Africa, for example, they make up 1% to 3% of the total wage-earning population) are entitled to maternity leave; all the others must keep working till they give birth and must resume work soon after.

In urban areas, the conditions are decidedly better for women in wage employment or wives of wage-earners, quite indifferent for the others. In fact, it is the wage-earning sector that turns to the maternity services or to the medical officer for help; and this is the *sine qua non* for benefiting from the pre-natal allowance and the family allowance reserved for the wage-earning sector, public and private alike. Unfortunately, clinics and maternity wards are only too few for the exigencies of the population; also, they are often in a poor state and have scanty facilities; besides, the doctors' and nurses' attitude tends to follow notorious Western models, as is well shown by the following investigation conducted by a national newspaper.

> When the [birth] throes started and uncontrolled cries for help came out of Mary, the nurses scolded and mocked her. They said that 'it would teach her to stay out of an extra-marital pregnancy in the future.' Mary is not married: she had to bring forth her baby without any assistance. The degradation inflicted on her by the nurses is with her to this very day, even in her dreams ....

Sister Bessie Nyirenda, of the paediatric section at the University Teaching Hospital of Lusaka, says: 'It is true that at times a nurse may have to rebuke the mother-to-be for not following the instructions. Some women are lazy, some coward'.

Yet another woman, a married one, claims that the treatment she received at the hospital as she was about to be delivered of her third child, was 'unbelievable'.

> While I was in travail I would call for help every now and then. I was told that the hospital was not my home and I was making too much fuss. Also, I was reminded that I had already had two babies and so why was I so nervous, they wondered. Besides, my time was not up yet. It was only when they saw the baby coming out that a nurse came to help. Honest to God, it was a nightmare.[45]

Notes

1. A. Ampofo, *The Family Planning Movement in Ghana*, Accra, Ghana Universities Press, 1971.
2. *Ibid.*
3. A. Romaniuk, op.cit. Among the Tutshokwe of West Kasai, upon childbirth both father and mother change their names. They will be called by the baby's name plus *Sha* as a prefix for the father, and *Na* as a prefix for the mother, both meaning 'of'. Thus ShaMubi means Mubi's father and NaKawelo means Kawelo's mother. Anyone who still called them by their previous names would insult them and in the same

breath imply failure to acknowledge their social status. Of course father's and mother's status are equal; still, if motherhood is an end in itself, fatherhood is a source of social and political power.
4. J. Kerharo, A. Bouquet, op.cit.
5. Contrary to what some say, this is by no means a general desire, as demonstrated by the frequent self-inflicted abortions. In the course of a consultation organized in Zaire for the benefit of the sterile Befale females (a largely sterile race, in fact) Dr Van Riel and Dr Allard were amazed at the poor interest that the initiative had aroused among the young women in comparison with the elder ones. 'The general trend here', they wrote, 'seems to be a poor concern with motherhood and a late desire for children on the part of the young women. Yet, in 1956, during a visit in Boende territory, we were literally pestered with young women's requests for drugs against sterility.' A. Romaniuk, op.cit.
6. A. Romaniuk, op.cit.
7. I. Magli, op.cit.
8. A. Zanotelli, 'Female Circumcision: a 'barbarous' and immoral rite', in *Insight and Opinion*, VI, No.1, Accra-Tema, n.d.
9. J. Kerharo, A. Bouquet, op.cit.
10. A. Zanotelli, op.cit.
11. A statement by Margaret Koinange, as reported in A. Wipper, op.cit.
12. MNT, 'La Circoncision: un Rite?', in *Zaire*, 12 May 1975. 'It has been our constant assumption that preparation for marital life is a bilateral affair. It is *with a view to securing conjugal harmony* that a girl undergoes excision of the clitoris' or some other sort of manipulation of her genital organs such as the elongation of the labia minora, for example, in Ruanda. In the opinion of our 'intellectual' commentator, 'this practice does not alter in the least the meaning of the rite, which the Banya-Ruanda and the Burundi call *Gukuna* and usually perform at the oncoming of puberty, announced by the blooming and hardening of the breast. If untimely performed, *Gukuna* may cause kidney trouble to the girl and thus imperil her health. The most immediate purpose of this multi-purposed operation is to elongate the organ and by this extend the erogenous zone thus making the midwife's task by far easier. Once again, marital life is the issue. Elongated labia minora act as a *cache-sex* in the interest of hygiene and out of shame.

Last and perhaps most important of all, comes the aim to put more joy into sexual intercourse on the grounds that marital dissatisfaction may well be conducive to unfaithfulness. It has been observed that sexually unsatisfied men and women look fretful and nervous. The final role of the rite is to prevent to the utmost those petty tiffs which are so likely to break out in the course of marital life.'
13. A. Romaniuk, op.cit.
14. *Ibid*.
15. C.M.N. White, op.cit.
16. A. Romaniuk, op.cit.
17. In his oft-quoted book, Romaniuk relates a dramatic incident of refusal of forced maternity: 'We chanced to receive the confessions of a Mbole (Mongo) female about her secret practices. She was a young woman aged 27. After becoming a widow, she had been unwillingly

married to the brother of her late husband. From her previous union she had had five children at regular intervals. She was quite prepared to have more children, albeit not with her new husband, a lame man she was not in love with, she said. When asked what she would do to prevent pregnancy, she replied that she would do some washings after copulation, and in the morning she would cleanse herself with a decoction based on papaya or banana leaves. Also she would refrain from sex for three or four weeks.' A. Romaniuk, op.cit.

18. *Ibid.*
19. Illegitimate births in Pretoria: 1933-34: 40%; 1934-35: 59%. In a Johannesburg suburb, in June-September 1940, out of 15,000 inhabitants 65% were single mothers. In L. Mair, op.cit.
20. A. Romaniuk, op.cit.
21. *Ibid.*
22. Kru women prefer *Cissampelos owariensis*: its thick fleshy leaves go into the making of a paste, half of which is taken orally, whereas the other half, diluted with water, is used for washings. In the Sudanese zone, the most sought-after abortifacients are without doubt *Kail cédra* bark and a decoction of *Entada sudanica* leaves, the latter being usually blended with local soap.
23. From the column 'Talk to our Doctor: Abortion', in *Ideal Woman*, July 1974.
24. 'Quand les Femmes de la Banque Commerciale du Ghana s'occupent du Planning Familial' in *Amina*, No.39, September 1975.
25. J.C. Caldwell, op.cit.
26. T.G.K. Owens-Dey, 'The Right to be Born', in *Ideal Woman*, June 1974.
27. As reported in *Mwasi*, No.23, November 1974.
28. T.G.K. Owens-Dey, op.cit.
29. Derek Llewellyn-Jones, 'Human Reproduction and Society', reviewed in *West Africa*, 2 June 1974.
30. From the *Times of Zambia*, 4 February 1975: 'The Zambian Association for planning and family well-being will take its programme to the people by means of an advertising campaign, seminars and the opening of new offices within the current year. In line with the 1975 association schedule, which was authorized by the executive manager Mrs Mella Chibumba at Ndola yesterday, four seminars on family planning for women, men, youths and secondary school students will be held. Furthermore, a professional commission composed of doctors, health assistants and teachers is due to be formed. It will meet four times a year in order to be informed about any new methods of contraception or new publications on birth control. Also, a commission of journalists has been scheduled for the broadcasting and advertising on the Radio and TV of family planning news.

The University of Zambia and the Ministry of Education are expected to arrange the speakers while the regional and the central offices of the International Planned Parenthood Federation will produce the pamphlets, studies and various other materials. The seminars will serve the students as an introduction to family planning and other aspects of family health, nutrition, education and hygiene. The activities of the

association, once extended to a large number of influential people, will be a valid support for the success of the family planning enterprise in the community.'
31. Some African nations believed to have found a way out by claiming that they needed social and economic development and also, even though only in a subordinate way, limitation of childbirth. Such approach is in reality too vague to be satisfactory.
32. In the same newspaper, these students offer some suggestive advice to women. After coaching them on such chores as cleaning and cooking (and always on time, please), they go on to say: 'It is good that when the man is back, his woman is there. If he arrives and you are out, and no note is there to tell him where you can be found, suspicion and displeasure are bound to ensue. Be kind to your guests. Do not make up or dress in a way he does not fancy. If you go to a club, make sure first that your man approves of it and don't go out without him too often, anyway.' 'Family Planning? Not for me', in *Focus*, Kumasi, May-August 1974.
33. 'In Africa, even before the colonial period, there were already social classes, albeit not fully developed yet.' MPLA, op.cit.
34. D.A. Ampofo, op.cit.
35. On asking his interviewees how they felt about the proposal to set up family planning hospitals, Caldwell learned that 'more women than men approved of it'.
36. In Mauritius, for example, villagers complained that the government FP hospitals closed at 4 pm and as women usually returned from the fields later, they were given no chance to go there. Clinics were instead open for longer hours!
37. B. Bamba Nzuji, 'Que Signifie au just la Libération Feminine?' in *Cultures au Zaïre et en Afrique*, No.1, 1973.
38. B. Zwane, 'Birth Control or Social Justice?' in *Africa*, December 1974.
39. Kerharo, Bouquet, op.cit.
40. J.F. Thiel, op.cit.
41. The still widespread custom, whereby a husband gives presents to his wife soon after she has given birth is quite significant. Among some ethnic groupings, where paternal authority is not strongly felt, the clan gives presents to the new mother; among the patrilineal Ga, instead, the father receives even more substantial gifts than those offered to the mother.
42. In big towns such as Kinshasa, even women who take advantage of prenatal check-ups try to secure the traditional medicaments to help childbirth, either from the interior or from some other woman.
43. Traditional medicine also treated many feminine troubles, such as vaginal ablutions, basically hygienic but also therapeutic. Amenorrhoea was treated with ablutions based on *Microglossa volubilis* or *Uncaria Talbotii* leaves were recommended. Such ablutions were also popular with women afflicted with venereal diseases, in order to sooth postcoital irritation. Nowadays, traditional medicine appears to be little interested in gynaecological issues, although genital diseases grow more serious and frequent.

'Among the many healers we have questioned, only few indeed

were the "specialists" willing to take menstrual disorders seriously ....
Accidents are often serious, but the local woman is too busy to care.
When in pain, she just goes into the wood in search of soothing plants.
And if she doesn't know of any, she will turn to some knowledgeable
neighbour for aid; a healer is her last resort.' Kerharo and Bouquet,
op.cit. 150 women show up daily at the gynaecological dispensary in
Kinshasa: 'Gynaecological pathology is a most serious problem of our
women.' Mutinga Mutuishayi, 'Morbidite' des Femmes — Une
Experience de l'Hopital Mama Yemo', in *Zaire*, 20 October 1975.

At the Mama Yemo Hospital on average about 900 beds are occupied by women as against 340 by men; of those 900 beds, 560 are taken by parturients and 350 by other patients. 4,500 people turn up daily at the general dispensary; of these, only 350 are males.

44. A. Müller, 'La Structure Sociologique de Mbaya Larme', in various authors, *L'Organisation Sociale et Politique*, op.cit.
45. D. Chishiba, 'Are Nurses Cruel to Expectant Mothers?', in *Zambia Daily Mail*, 31 December 1974.

5. Women, Education and Political Movements

Initiation Rites: The Customary Approach

The initiation ceremonies performed at puberty have often been defined as the 'informal school' of traditional societies. In the past, in some societies these ceremonies would last several months and their primary object was the intellectual, moral and physical training of the initiated. But as formal schooling gains ground, these ceremonies are gradually dwindling to a ritual symbol of the integration of the young in the social life of the group.

Customs vary from tribe to tribe, but generally the purpose of girls' initiation rites is to provide instruction on the conduct of all the important aspects of a woman's life, childbirth, domestic and social duties; in brief the ritual preparation and acceptance of a girl's obligations as wife and mother. 'A female's initiation takes less time than a male's, since the notions a girl has to acquire are usually confined to issues related to conjugal life.'[1]

These rites serve a somewhat conservative function, as the women of Mozambique vehemently pointed out on the occasion of their first conference:

> The rites of initiation may take different forms in different regions, yet they have the common purpose of instilling an attitude of submission to man into women's hearts by making them accustomed to the notion that they were born to take second place in society.
>
> During the ceremony, the girls are told that from now onwards their task is to procreate and attend to their husbands and their homes, and any other task is forbidden to them. These initiatory rites, surrounded as they are by an aura of mystery and religious solemnity, have such a devastating psychological impact on the girls that they are mesmerized into a blind acceptance of the indoctrination through a traumatic experience bound to affect them for the rest of their lives.[2]

During initiation rites girls are taught techniques of coition and erotic dances believed to make them more attractive to their husbands, but this is not part of a boy's initiation, he learns about such matters directly from his elder friends or father.[3]

The focus of female initiation is a preparation for fecundity, the focus of male rites, obviously is quite different. According to Peter Just, who studied *mukanda* (the male initiatory rite of some matrilineal tribes of Zambia), such ceremonies largely serve to initiate the novice into male solidarity and as such they constitute an act against matriarchy. *Mukanda* thus ritually marks the principles on which male/female antagonism rests; above all, it ritualizes the rupture of the mother-child bond — a kind of ceremonial conquest of the Oedipus complex. The mythical origins of *mukanda* illustrate this:

There once lived a woman who had a little son. One day they went together in search of some firegrass. The boy tried to follow his mother who showed the way as she picked the grass.

Suddenly a branch dropped and cut the boy's penis. The boy fell down crying. In anguish his mother took him to the village. There, some men said: 'The boy must be taken away from his mother and any other woman.' Then they took a razor and circumcised the boy. They did so on the boy's father's responsibility. A few weeks later the boy had already recovered, and the men were pleased to see that the wound had healed, and decided to try the same with another boy. It went just as before: after a few weeks the boy was healthy again and looked more beautiful than ever. People began to realize that it was better for all males to be circumcised, and adult men were circumcised as well. They danced and drank beer to celebrate the removal of the foreskin. This is how *mukanda* began.[4]

Peter Just underlines the fact that the boy cuts his penis while trying to follow his mother, and the decision to complete the circumcision is taken collectively by the men of the village. The boy's submissive behaviour towards his mother is seen as responsible for the wound, and it is the collective action of the village males that cures him. It follows that *mukanda* does not help a male to become fertile but it does help 'cure' him of social dependence by growing strong and gaining power thanks to the solidarity of other males.

The Tutshokwe, a matrilineal people now to be found in Angola, Zambia and Zaire, perform a female puberty ritual called *tshikumbi*.[5] This ritual celebrates the transition from girlhood to womanhood and purposes to 'initiate girls to their future functions as brides and mothers.'[6] As soon as a girl experiences her first menses, she informs her mother or some other female next of kin who in turn informs the *tshikholokholo* (the chief initiator of the ceremony — usually the girl's grandmother). It is her duty to attend to the girl's hygiene, ensure that all the initiatory rites are performed correctly and to educate the girl in her new sexual, familial, social and moral life.

On learning of the menses, the *tshikholokholo* and the old women of the village take the girl to a large tree outside the village, and there they are joined by all the initiated women from her village and neighbouring villages uttering shouts of joy.

As the girl receives the initial hygienic treatment and instructions, the magic dances start. A group of women armed with whips and sticks move to the village singing 'songs without shame'. These songs largely describe the male and female sexual organs and stress how important a woman is for a man. They are usually accompanied by *na mwadi*, a lascivious dance mainly designed to produce laughter and entertainment.

Here are two songs performed for such an occasion: in either, a woman sings of the delight she has just experienced in the course of a succesful copulation.

> The stones I relished yesterday
> The stones I relished yesterday
> I've not enjoyed today
> Tomorrow I won't enjoy any more
> The stones I relished yesterday
>
> Na mwadie e e e
> Na mwadie e e e
> She grasps the rod
> And plunges it into her vulva
> As she plunges it into her vulva
> She savours its delight
> Na mwadie e e[7]

Before sunset, the women return to the novice and perform the final dances before they disperse. At nightfall, the *tshikholokholo* and other women take the girl to the hut in which she will stay during the initiation period. Here she is kept on a strict diet: as a staple food she will have to be content with fried manioc tubers. Also, she must always speak under her breath and never lift her eyes to the women who are visiting her. When sitting, she must keep her legs crossed. No complaints are permitted to her. She may drink water once or twice a day but may not wash herself.

The *tshikholokholo*, who stays with her, calls upon the girl's sister-in-law for help, and the latter will teach her *na mwadi* and a few songs. She will also help the *tshikholokholo* to teach the novice *kumenga*, namely the way of taking an active part in coition — as well as different coital positions. The girl is also given lessons in anatomy and physiology along with 'beauty' lessons which are particularly concerned with potion-making.

In addition, the *tshikholokholo* informs the girl about her marital rights and duties and all her moral and social obligations: the girl learns how to run her home properly and how to prepare and present food to her husband and guests. She also learns that she must

> refrain from stealing and insulting, respect her own husband as well as other women's husbands, be always kind and good to children, in sum be a good custodian of tradition by paying homage to the elders and to the customs of her people. To better take in these lessons, the girl is

asked to repeat them and if she fails to do so properly, she is in for a beating.[8]

The girl is then taken to the river for a 'purifying' bath, since menses are undeniably an impurity. Back from the river, the *tshikholokholo* arranges a small ceremony with the participation of all the initiated women of the village, during which the girl is given a new name — although she will change this again after the birth of her first-born. Finally, the novice returns to her father's house if she has not yet been wedded; if she has, a 'transfer' ceremony will take place when she makes an official move to her husband's house.

Tshikumbi, formerly essential in Tshokwe societies, is on the decline and in many places is no longer performed. One reason is that girls can move at ease these days, and school takes her away from maternal tutelage. Thus, first menstruation may occur when she is away from home, maybe at the school which is probably far away from home; hence, she cannot make the customary announcement.

Such ceremonies, nevertheless, are not simply concerned with rites of passage from childhood to adulthood. At one time various kinds of 'initiatory' ceremonies might be performed throughout an individual's lifetime. Some of these ceremonies are of great interest, for example, *tshiwila*, which is the second female initiatory rite among the Tutshokwe.

Tshiwila is only for women with some experience of life; usually only married women, widows or mature unmarried women already initiated into *tshikumbi* are accepted. This rite is for the brave women who are determined to assert their identity and their dignity vis-à-vis men, by facing and overcoming difficulties usually confronting the latter. In its structure, organization and content, *tshiwila* strikingly resembles *mungonge*, the initiation rite for adult men; a woman who has been initiated into *tshiwila* knows almost everything about *mungonge*, the sole, important difference between the two rites is that women are not permitted to resort to *mbongo*, which may be defined as a spirit reverting to life when invoked, and capable of imparting a magic force.

Tshiwila is a short ceremony, lasting only one day. Like *mungonge*, it begins with a challenge by the novices to the initiator. It should be mentioned that the *ngolami* (elderly women who have already undergone the test) incite and mock other women who have not for their lack of experience and courage as apparently they are incapable of going further and are satisfied with *tshikumbi* and thus to be left to the mercy of the man. Sooner or later the women tire of being mocked and the day comes when they decide to become initiated. On that day, they send a normal and unconditional challenge to the initiator, inviting her to initiate them promptly. After undergoing an endurance test followed by a wisdom test, during which they are invited to say if they have ever committed adultery, and if they respect their husbands and care for their children, the time for advice comes: any elder with advice to offer gives it freely. Space does not permit a report of all their recommendations, but it can be said that they rest on the basic idea that a woman must not define herself solely in relation to the man, for she is above all 'a woman among women'.[9]

A woman, it is suggested, must first of all be proud of her own sex and never be ashamed to demonstrate her feminine qualities: she must rid herself of any sense of inferiority she may have vis-à-vis the male. Besides, she must defend the honour of her own sex against the opposite sex, and never, never should she humiliate another woman in front of a man.

When all the advice has been given, the initiates acquaint themselves with *mbongo*. This part of the ritual is largely concerned with the knowledge and power of magic. It seems that *tshiwila* was originally a male initiation rite and *mungonge* a female one; but later, it seems, men took *mungonge* away from women and left them *tshiwila*. One woman gave the following explanation:

> At the beginning, *mungonge* was an initiation for females, and *tshiwila* for males. When the men saw that women knew the mystery of *mbongo*, they felt that their self-respect was at stake; 'What?', they wondered, 'Should we grant women the faculty to perform such extraordinary deeds?' And so, they decided that from then onwards *mungonge* would be for men, *tshiwila* for women. Yet the women claimed a substantial tribute, which men promptly paid.[10]

Tshiwila is now declining, and so is *mungonge*, the former more so than the latter. The reasons for this obviously lie in the evolution of society, and notably in the mobility of young women, who are now usually on the move with their husbands. 'But perhaps there is more to it: the female outlook on life no longer is reflected by an initiation of the *tshiwila* kind.'[11]

What is actually disappearing today is the traditional form of female solidarity, which this ritual expresses so well. This is a pity, as among other things, such solidarity would minimize the rivalry among co-wives or between women from the husband's family and his wife. And it is a fact that tensions due to such rivalry tend to explode more dramatically and more frequently these days.

Schooling

Formal education in Africa discriminated against females from the start; perhaps this is hardly surprising since it was patterned upon the Western model.

When it was introduced, there was some reluctance on the part of families to send their daughters to school, because girls could be put to better use in the home and in the fields. Besides, there was always the suspicion that they might become too independent.

In reporting Busia's study on social transformation in the urban area of Sekondi-Tokoradi in 1950 or so, Caldwell noted:

The criticism of the sexual morals of schoolgirls appears to be well grounded: a few relevant cases have emerged in the course of the investigation. Premarital sex between schoolgirls and labourers or students seems to be a routine affair. Even instances of childbearing or abortion have been reported. For all that, the extent of premarital sex appears to have grown out of all proportions in the popular tales . . . . Parents put the blame for the girls' misbehaviour on teachers, who duly reciprocate, although at times 'misbehaviour' apparently only refers to non-conformity to the customs sanctioned by the community.[12]

The type of education imparted to girls is also of some significance. In Ghana, the first school for girls was opened at Cape Coast in 1821 by Mrs Harriet Jarvis, the widow of a merchant company officer: sewing and home science were the main subjects as the education of wives and housewives for resident merchants was a top priority. Seven years later, the institute was closed. In 1836, still at Cape Coast, another school for girls was opened under the headmistresship of Mrs Wrigley, the wife of a Methodist missionary. The syllabus consisted of reading, sewing and catechism. This school was attended by 30 girls, but by 1840 their number had leapt to 80. In 1874 a 'high' school for girls was inaugurated, with an enrolment of 14. Only lower school girls with an adequate educational history, a good degree of literacy and fluent English were admitted. Among the subjects taught were embroidery, dressmaking, needlework and crochet.

Such a limited outlook on women's education is even less excusable by the consideration that the schools were largely in the hands of missionaries.

Although things have somewhat improved in the wake of political independence, it should still be said that by and large the various governments have shown no real desire to cater for female education. On top of this, there is the only too cautious attitude of international organizations. One FAO report reads as follows:

> Where customary beliefs oppose women's education, it seems only fair to concentrate teaching on those matters which are most obviously characteristic of females. It is certainly better to have a school for sewing and cooking than no school at all. A teacher may well give the girls a smattering of mathematics, science, hygiene etc, as they learn how better to cook, keep the house tidy, mind the children and contribute to rural progress.[13]

In 1960, only one-third of 15 year-old Ghanaian girls had had some schooling, while 66% of them had had none. Against this, more than half of the 15 year-old boys had been at school, whereas 46% had not. The 1970 census showed some improvement, but the gap is still wide for the age group 15 and upwards. (See Table 26)

Table 26
School Attendance in Ghana by Age Groups/Sex: 1970 (%)

	6-14 years			15-24 years			25+		
	None	Past	Present	None	Past	Present	None	Past	Present
T	37.5	4.4	58.1	40.7	33.1	26.2	77.8	21.9	0.3
M	33.5	3.9	62.6	25.9	37.6	36.5	67.0	32.5	0.5
F	41.6	5.0	53.4	54.5	28.9	16.6	88.4	11.6	0.0

Source: 1970 Census

Local surveys in village schools have confirmed that rural Ghana still favours schoolboys over girls.[14]

Yet, Ghana is to all appearances one of the most progressive African countries as far as womens' education is concerned. Elsewhere, figures are lower, and particularly so for women in universities.

In Zaire, for example, according to UNESCO figures, only 95 females, making up 4% of the total, were attending the university in 1965, and by 1971 they had gone up to 561, i.e., 5% of the total. An official report from UNAZA, the National University of Zaire, goes as far as saying that there has been 'a remarkable increase in the number of university female students', as proved by the fact that in 1974 the female/male ratio was 1 to 13, while in 1975 it *appears* to have become 1 to 10. Needless to say, thank Mobutu for that!

> Only a few years ago the education of women stressed to a very large extent their role as procreators and nurturers of children. Also, women were expected to attend to the needs of their families. Such being the prospect, parents had all the reasons in the world to wonder why they should send their daughters to school. As to rights, women had not many: rather, they had a string of obligations, foremost among which an unconditional submission to the husband or to the man *tout court*. Now, times have changed . . . . Thanks to our President, citizen Mobutu Sese Seko, the education of women and the acknowledgement of their rights have become a reality and can surely go down on record as one of the achievements of the Second Republic. Of course, women's evolution is still facing a few difficulties.[15]

In reality, the general trend is towards the establishment of 'women's professional training' centres and courses, which are obviously designed to produce modern and efficient 'housewives' and also to equip women for the usual ghettoes of 'woman work'. A typical specimen is the Mama Mobutu Sese Seko professional training centre for women, which was set up seven years ago and is now running courses for over 1,500 students. The centre is divided in 12 departments, the main ones being the departments of agriculture, sales, commerce, needlework, upholstery, embroidery, crochet and typing. Produce from each section is sold outside and the proceeds go towards the cost of the maintenance of the centre.

Such discrepancy in education between men and women — really extensive in some countries — adversely affects marital relationships: paradoxically, in modern middle-class families, even in monogamous ones, it exacerbates sex division.

Women's Participation in Religious Liberation Movements

'Cultural Backwardness' and Sorcery

Rural society in general and rural women in particular have frequently been accused of being unable to adjust to social change and new social needs — of being backward and conservative.

Certainly, African women have kept their rural ties to a greater degree than have the men. They maintain and pass on the traditional customs and life-styles; yet, this by no means signifies cultural, social and political backwardness — any suggestion that it is may well be a reflection of the chagrin of colonialists and of the social strata enslaved by neo-colonialism when confronted with the unexpected reactions of the female masses.

Opposition to certain modes of industrialization, for instance, does not necessarily betray a conservative attitude of the mind, but rather may be due to the vested interests of some social groups. Thus, the wifely status has often been negatively affected by the introduction of new modes of production which have deprived the woman of her own sources of income and made her more dependent on her husband and thus economically and socially weaker.

Ibo women, for example, rebelled against the introduction of oil-mills and tried with little success to prevent it. Oil-mills did increase the quantity and quality of palm oil and therefore raised the average wage level, but at the same time they deprived women of work and resources of their own and thus increased their dependence on their husbands. Prior to this, women prepared the oil for their husbands to sell, but they would also retain and sell part of it for their own profit.

If the uneasiness of the woman in the face of change has appeared to outsiders as backwardness, to rural eyes such change has rather appeared as witchcraft.

It is neither the purpose nor within the scope of this book to attempt an analysis or interpretation of latter-day witchcraft. Avoiding generalizations on the phenomenon, an attempt will be made to define it particularly as a woman's response (made *by* women but also *against* women) to the cultural impoverishment which is 'among the major causes of modern Africa's crisis'.[16]

It has been said that a belief in sorcery indicates tensions in a social system, also that it has a cathartic quality, since it 'allows people to express feelings of hate which, albeit wrong as a rule, have suddenly become permissible to someone who believes they are suffering from somebody else's unjustified hostility.'[17]

It seems reasonable to suggest that the rise of sorcery is related to the problems of social change, and in particular to the changing role of the woman in the family and society. Like any other irrational belief, it presents contradictory facets and elements and, for women, witchcraft may provoke divisions and quarrels, but also, it may be a source of cohesion and strength.

Among the Luo of Kenya and Tanzania, for instance, a woman's relationship with her husband's family is immensely important, given the fact that she stays permanently with his kin. Until the day she brings forth a child, her loyalty towards her husband's lineage as well as her qualities as a wife are in doubt. Even as a mother, she may find it difficult to obtain land and, more importantly, cattle for the sustenance of her husband and her children, because of the competition from her mother-in-law and other women in the family. Thus, she lives in an atmosphere of insecurity and constant struggle, and every set-back in her role as a bride or a mother may worsen the situation. As soon as the tension reaches flash point, it is transformed into a crisis of possession and mutual accusations of witchcraft.[18]

Witchcraft may also be instrumental in the ejection and demotion of socially weaker females, namely the elderly. Debrunner has gathered some testimonies, for example, the following from a Ghanaian student: 'Since witchcraft is largely put down to old women, any mishap affecting a woman in the family is ascribed to them. If something is not done about it, these old women will eventually have no say whatever in family affairs.'[19]

In the past, women past the procreative age often held an honourable position in society. Now, their status is considerably lower, and certainly unequal educational opportunities are partly responsible for bringing this about. Today, women students are held in higher esteem than their mothers or grandmothers, with the result that old women are resentful, while the young ones have a sense of guilt towards them and in an effort to overcome this accuse the old women of witchcraft. In northern Nigeria, men charge women traders with sorcery; to them, witches' congregations are nothing but a nightly replica of women's merchant corporations.

> Siegfried Nadel . . . discovered that the Nupe of Ilorin had elaborate and detailed ideas about the existence of a witch organization led by the tradeswomen's chief, a real and identifiable person. He explained that belief by assuming that Nupe women are so successful in their trade that their men often depend financially on them and understandably resent this.[20]

Through magic a woman may assert herself and thus convey the message that she is not just a producer of progeny but, apart and beyond this, she is entitled to her own life and to be her own self. In fact many women accuse themselves of casting a magic spell on their children thus causing their death; subconsciously, they associate the death of these children with their own rebellious desire for independence. Naturally, their fantasies of child-murder, or rather about suppressing their maternal role and forced motherhood — engender a sense of guilt and ultimately the self-accusation of witchery. Besides denying motherhood, sorcery often denies sexuality in that as an important factor in the demographic increase it is linked to its reproductive purpose. Far from providing sexual gratification as it did in Medieval Europe, African black magic claims to have the power to destroy sexuality; in some cases, as with the Nzima of Ghana, it 'gives the joy of sexual abstinence',[21] that is to say, it destroys the very sexual potency of the witch.

The snake reputedly lodging in a witch's vagina may well have had a phallic connotation originally, yet it never appears as an object of pleasure; rather, as a thing to be possessed. Some believe that, as long as it stays in the vagina, the woman will not conceive: thus, the snake becomes a symbol of rebellion against sexuality, notably the sexuality indissolubly linked to procreation.

Messianic Movements and Religious Sects

Christian missions contributed significantly to the process of deculturation during the colonial period, not only and perhaps not so much through their campaigns against traditional religions as through their attacks on particular customs and institutions of society such as, especially, polygamy.

Contrary to what might be expected, the crusade against polygamy was not greatly appreciated by the women, mainly because it was conducted with colonialist criteria, methods and aims which took little account of the real and immediate exigencies of women.

> In a recent study, Rev David Barret has called attention to the fact that the missionary assault on the family, that is to say, on the elemental unity of traditional African societies, is among the factors provoking a most strong reaction among the native groups, which then led to the cornucopia of socio-religious separatist or — in Barret's words — independent movements.
>
> The conflict between missions and the polygamous establishment has often assumed a dramatic tone, and the reaction has often been massive. When, in a big town in Nigeria, a minister refused to christen a polygamist, two thirds of the population walked out on their church. It may come as a surprise, although an understandable one, that any countermoves in the struggle against the Christian outlook on polygamy should have been led particularly by native women. In one of the salient points of his analysis, Barret himself makes it clear how the anti-polygamous onset was, in effect, detrimental to women. It upset the woman's position in society by forcing polygamous husbands into dismissing all their wives but one: this deprived the woman of her status, her security, her economic and religious power, and ultimately brought down the very foundation of the social fabric of African tribes. Hence, the predictable reaction of women: they have assumed

a leading role in propagating estrangement from the missions, and in initiating or increasing independent religious movements all over Africa.[22]

The decline of traditional values and religions, along with enmity towards mission Christianity are significant factors contributing to the increase in new syncretic religious movements. An important and even crucial role in these is played by women. Some movements have been founded by women who have abandoned marriage and all sexual relations in order to be free to preach.

The Legio Mariae of Kenya, for example, although founded by a man, was in fact characterized by Gaudencia Aoko, a Luo prophetess who joined the Legio following the death of her two children. In the Ivory Coast, the Deima cult was established in 1942 by Marie Lalu who, albeit a married woman, took a vow of chastity; her mission was carried on by another woman, Princess Geniss, who had also abandoned marital life. Zambia saw the movement of Mai Chaza (Mother Chaza) and that of Alice Lenshina Munlenga Lubusha. In 1953, the latter underwent a religious experience, during which, she related, she had actually died and been taken to the presence of God by whom she had been entrusted with two books and told to return to earth and preach against evil. She had many followers, and eventually founded the Lumpa Church, which between 1955 and 1957 was about 100,000 strong. Its stronghold was the Chinsali Ward and its temple was at Kasomo, Alice's birthplace — but it spread rapidly to neighbouring wards. Various sections were also set up in some towns along the railway line, but they were never to be so strong as the churches of the north, where Alice's followers soon gained some authority and consequently, as we shall see, developed a tense and gradually deteriorating relationship with the government as the political independence of the country drew near.

There are more women than men in the greater part of the 'independent' Christian communities, regardless of their size. Women make up at least two-thirds of the non-missionary church members, and in each of these churches they have their own responsibilities, quite distinct from those of the men. They conduct the choir during a function, organize prayer meetings for the sick, mutual aid and social activities. And it is of course on their efforts that the community rests; celibate priests, for instance, live on the work of the women in their community.

The few men in such organizations fall into three categories: those within the 25-45 age group occupy all the posts of some responsibility, have special powers or fulfil honorary functions; the younger ones attend their sect schools and endeavour to become influential members of the community; the elder ones provide the ordinary congregation. Such division of tasks appears to signify the victory of the young over the old, whom the new cult has divested of their power to communicate with the forefathers.

Many interviews carried out by Marie-France Perrin Jassy, mostly among the Luo of Kenya and Tanzania, have revealed that there is a connection between joining one of these movements and absence of social cohesion.

> A polygamist who is debarred from [Roman Catholic] sacraments, a church follower aspiring to become a catechizer, a catechizer hopelessly aspiring to become a priest, a childless woman, a bachelor without the means to get married, all these people look for compensation of their frustrations. Here, we find once again the twofold problem of the Luo society, i.e., the problem of social cohesion threatened by the insecurity born out of the break-up of societal structures, along with the question of social mobility hindered by the frustration stemming from the dissociation between objectives and means of access to a higher status.[23]

The majority of women in these communities are misfits by definition, since tradition demands that a man seeks his bride from well outside his own area, hence many brides come from a totally different *milieu*. As a result, in their social intercourse as well as their public life in their husband's village, they are 'foreigners' and perceived as such. This state of affairs may be aggravated by a poor understanding between them and their mothers-in-law or the co-wives, or by their being barren and under the impending threat of being charged with witchcraft. A childless couple, it is believed means that one or the other practises sorcery; since the man cannot be the guilty one in the eyes of his family, the woman will bear the brunt. She tends to react to this by joining some church where she feels she is a full-rank subject of the 'Kingdom' as she is given many responsibilities, may take the initiative and above all enjoy a status which does not depend on her family position.

All the independent Churches of Africa tolerate polygamy, even though they do not regard it as an ideal institution; one of them, the Mamya Church, even approves unreservedly of polygamy. Interestingly these churches, whose success some believe is due to their toleration of polygamy, are, nevertheless, successful in managing to restrict it. In effect, social pressure is more easily brought to bear on a small group and the Christian ideals which are put into practice in a small community make the resistance to the family pressures more effective. If a man takes a second wife, he is not excommunicated, but certainly loses prestige and in most cases is not allowed to fulfil any public religious function in the community.

The accent placed by African churches on the conjugal relationship aims at giving the wifely status its due. Some believe, for instance, that the Congolese movement known as *Jamaa* helps 'realize the emancipation of the African woman'[24] by stressing respect and comradeship as forging a vital bond between man and wife. The women of the *Jamaa* movement seem less inhibited than others as they show a greater willingness to speak out and to fulfil various social functions. Some husbands belonging to the movement even help with domestic duties. Yet, the fact is that the movement makes it easier for a woman to emerge from her conventional shell and that makes men suspicious and finally alienates them.

> ... many men refuse to have anything to do with the movement, as they have no intention of giving up what they regard as a traditional male preserve, namely the right to be *bwana*, the household head, who reigns over his woman and his children. At times, such is the man's opposition that the woman, if she happens to be a *Jamaa* member, prefers quitting it to having her marriage brought to ruin.[25]

Indeed customary marriage has so far successfully resisted missionary efforts to change it, and this in virtue of it being not a mere formal act but a rite intimately associated with the overall idea of the family as an institution rich in economic and social implications.[26] The Roman Catholic marriage ceremony for instance has had little success to date: the Legio Mariae and the Légion Catholique Africaine, which have maintained the ceremony in its established form, have not celebrated a single marriage yet.

Other churches have instead tried to Christianize and incorporate customary marriage into the religious and social life of the community. For example, the Roho Church followers meet for prayer in the young bridegroom's house; later, when at least half of the dowry has been paid, the elders and the bridegroom's father fetch the bride from her father's house and take her to her husband's.

Likewise, each Johera sectarian church has its own version of the Luo Christianized customary marriage: on the occasion of a Pentecostal meeting, a betrothed member is expected to inform the elders, and possibly, the minister. The marriage will take place within two or three months and meanwhile part of the bridewealth cattle are transferred, since it is a local custom to pay bridewealth in instalments over a number of years. On the appointed day the bride is taken to the church, where the marriage is consecrated by the prayers of the elders and the whole community.

Marriage, as it is celebrated by African churches, seems to bestow a few advantages: the ceremony is linked to the traditional stages of marriage, in particular as concerns the bridewealth and the bride's transfer to her bridegroom; it is in fact the community that moves for prayer as far as required to Christianize the various wedding stages. In addition, such marriage rests on flexible conditions and this allows the bridegroom to undertake a *bona fide* union without commitments, say, of the monogamous sort, which he would find hard to keep in a traditional setting.

For all this, messianism institutionalized through churches or sects has largely lost its liberating function for women as it has reinstated deteriorated and distorted traditional values and, moreover, a new kind of female potentially degrading subordination as shown by the following inquiry in a Lusaka suburb.

> ... Mr Henry Mpofu from Marrapodi suburb ... has been married for more than 10 years and has four wives and five children. He lives in a four bedroomed house and earns a living as a carpenter, while his wives make baskets and embroider towels ....

'Surely you have problems in your home', I asked him, 'Jealousy, maybe?' 'Not at all', replied the man, whose family believe in the Gospel of the Church of God, otherwise known as the basket-makers' Korsten sect. 'According to our Church, men may marry as many women as they like. And the women must refrain from mutual jealousy, *or they will fall victims to a mysterious malady.*'

I asked him about such mysterious malady, but all he could tell me was that nobody knows what it is: 'It is accepted as a decision of the Church, and the faithful don't like breaking the rules and committing sin.' Nonetheless, there should be no misunderstanding about the whole thing: there is love, real love in these marriages. As I went on voicing my misgivings about the purported understanding within the family, Mr Mpofu said, 'It is not all that bad, really. You know, we basically apply the principle of tolerance and practise what may be described as pacific co-existence. Even though, to be sure we must make sacrifices and show a good deal of understanding.' Leaving his work for a minute, the man looked at me pensively and said: 'Of course we have problems occasionally, but they are no different from those of any other family.'

When I asked him what sort of ceremonies his fellow members performed, he beamed all over as he explained to me that they adhered to the typical evangelical ritual of the Church of God: 'You see, marriage is a straightforward affair in our Church. No ceremonies, no fuss, no jumble. All our minister does is to give the announcement to the congregation and there, you're as good as married. And, then, you may wed as often as you choose: there is no limitation to the number of women a man can marry. Mind you though, if ever one of your wives is pronounced guilty of unfaithfulness, *she will be immediately expelled from the Church*, and from then on she will be an outcast.'

Maybe it is the dread of this that keeps women tied to the same man. Or maybe, something else. As I wondered, one of Mr Mpofu's wives came in and shyly took a seat beside him. While she gave the finishing touch to a towel she was sewing, she said to me: 'No, it is not because we're afraid of being ejected from the Church that we keep faithful to our husbands. When we married, we placed all our hopes in marriage; since then, we have learned tolerance and with our husbands' help, we have also learned how to share the cooking without jumping at each other's throat.' Then she added: 'When a woman marries, she ought to forget about other men and only think of her husband. It is God's will that no woman should have more than one man.'

Yet, as she also explained to me — the fact that a man chooses to marry another woman does not imply that there is something amiss with his other wives: 'We all accept the fact that if a man fancies another woman, he may come forward in the right manner and wed her. Only one thing is not permitted to him, and that is to have sex with her before his marriage has been officially announced by the elders.' Mr Mpofu's wife finally told me that most men let their women know about their intention to bring another woman into the family: 'They do not leave us in the dark about this and it is such honesty that enables us to trust them. Besides, the fact that men are prohibited to marry outside our Church makes us feel much more secure.'[27]

It does seem that African sects are undergoing a process of regression, as they grow laden with neo-traditionalist and conservative overtones, which often have also political connotations.

A case in point is Alice Lenshina's Lumpa sect, which openly defied UNIP, the only party in today's Zambia. On 25 July 1964, there was some skirmishing between Alice's followers and UNIP plus Government forces. Out of this a real war soon broke out with clashes in and around the ward of Chinsali for over five months. According to official reports, 710 people died during the unrest, but to all appearances the actual dead were more than that. In the aftermath of the disorders, a great number of Lumpa left the country and sought refuge in Zaire and, according to the *Times of Zambia* 19,000 of them took refuge at Mukambo camp; the official estimate was 15,000. In the opinion of the same newspaper, the overall number was 44,000: 'This may seem a rather high figure, but only if we accept it, can we find a reason for the extraordinary migration from the Chinsali Ward and the nearby area.'[28]

Unfortunately,

> The reactionary spirit of this movement and others of the kind finds fertile ground in the no-man's-land between the rural masses cut off from the process of modernization and yet urged by contact with the West to step out of tradition, and the ruling élite: a far-away no-man's-land which portends serious class tensions. The rural masses express their discontent with the 'colonized' and 'colonizing' élite in their traditional ways, and engage in a controversy mainly at a social and religious level . . . . A sort of African 'self-colonialism' takes shape as an ally of Euro-American neo-colonialism. Within such setting, villages and lumpenproletariat . . . represent pressure groups against the deculturizing and depersonalizing policies of some ruling élites.[29]

Understandably, far from attempting a revolutionary solution of the social problem at the root of the rebellion, the nationalist authorities endeavour to bribe the charismatic leaders of the various movements — not always without success.

On the occasion of the rebellion in Eastern Zaire following the fall of Kisangani, the rebel capital, Mama Marie Onema[30] the High Priestess of the rebellion was captured by central government forces. Victor Nendaka, Chief of the Secret Police, induced her to choose new 'allies', and as a result the rebel areas were before long teeming with government posters announcing Mama Onema's shift of ground.

Women's Involvement in Social Struggles and Political Movements

African women's involvement in the many wars and revolts against the colonial conquest has been by no means minor. A history of this involvement, in resistance movements and liberation battles, would be out of place here, but some examples and considerations of this are necessary for a comprehensive view of the position of women in Africa today.

African women have fought against colonial enslavement and exploitation. Anna Zingha, the Queen of Matamba 'the finest political brain in Central Africa', fought in Angola before anybody else, she fought against the Portuguese in the 17th Century.[31] In Nigeria, in 1929, 'the Aba riots' greatly impressed public opinion in Britain because of the strength and solidarity displayed by the women concerned; the men merely put in an appearance, arguably under some apprehension about their women's high degree of self-mobilization. It was provoked by the rumour that recent taxation, so far only levied on men, would soon apply to women. 'In a matter of days the rumour spread everywhere, causing resentment and dismay; more so since just then the price of palm oil products had fallen and the new customs taxes on many important articles for everyday use had been increased.'[32]

At the end of a large assembly, the women decided to take action and in their tens of thousands marched on the main trade centres: they cut telegraph wires and attacked banks, European shops and the prisons, freeing the inmates. The army moved in and they fired at the women, killing or wounding scores of them.[33]

Women also turned against the Native Authorities accusing them of corruption and subjugation to the colonial authorities; and in so doing, demonstrated that they clearly understood what was going on in the country and where the responsibility lay.

> To the members of the Native Courts who argued that the white man had brought peace to their country, they replied that they were determined to chase the white man out and remove the railway, and their chief complaint was that they were no longer as happy as they had been of old: we are complaining — they said — that the country has changed, and we are all dying.[34]

In more recent times, women have played a fundamental role in the struggle for national independence. Far from backing the conservatism of the rural native authorities, they have shaken and even broken their prestige and power. In Zambia, Heisler noted: 'Both individually and collectively through their own brigades, women had a role, even a violent one, in disrupting the rural system.'[35]

The nationalist agitations in the 1960s were a great blow for the traditional male stance towards women, whose combative spirit came as a surprise to everybody. These women were fighting not just for the political independence of their country nor for generic 'civil rights', but for clearly defined objectives based on their specific needs.

Betty Kaunda, the then secretary of the Chilenjie section of the African National Congress Women's League, recounted the struggles of Zambian women in those days:

> In Lusaka, we decided to fight on two issues directly affecting us as housewives. The first was about our shopping conditions. A woman has a right to choose what to buy for her family. But butchers' shops, as most other shops in town, were owned by whites. An African was not permitted to enter a butcher's and choose. A black man or a black woman was required to stay outside and hand the monies over a small window to the assistant, who would pick a piece at random out of a heap of cheap meat and throw it to the buyer through the window, shouting 'next one' . . . . The meat, if it ever deserved the name, sold to the Africans in such a manner, was not even wrapped . . . . At Chilenjie, as in any other urban suburb, women had to get up very early in the morning and walk for miles to the shop where they would queue in front of the window. Getting there late often meant a few hours' wait in the queue. This was very humiliating . . . . And so, the Women's League organized the boycott of all the butchers in town. For a better result, we chose the right time, that is to say, the wet season, since there are plenty of vegetables then and we could do without meat. In December 1954, with a few men we marched into the butchers' and demanded to be served inside . . . .[36] Of course the shopkeepers were shocked, but after nine weeks they were bound to give in. Unfortunately, the second action was not as successful.
>
> The Women's League decided to put up a fight on a second issue. In conformity with African custom, a woman may brew beer for her husband or sell it if she can, in order to lessen hardships within her family. We were not allowed to do so in Lusaka and in many other urban areas of [then] Northern Rhodesia . . . . A woman beer-brewer would be arrested if caught in the act, fined ten pounds, and the beer would be confiscated. A ten-pound fine was a heavy one, for only very few men were raising ten pounds per month in those days. At the League meeting it was decided that we would all march on the Ward Commissioner's Office to protest against the by-law forbidding us to brew beer. The morning after, a large number of women went on the march. Six of us were deputed to speak on behalf of the others: we went inside and the crowd waited outside. We put our case to the Commissioner. He told us to report to the women that the question would be looked into and the decision made known in due course. We did so, but the women didn't like the words 'in due course' . . . . We were sent in again to ask where and when the law would be abolished. The Commissioner refused to give any further details. Outside the crowd waited, noisily. It was the natural noise of a crowd, especially of

a crowd of women carrying crying children on their backs, and in the heat of the sun the noise grew louder and louder. Before long, we were surrounded by the police: twice they fired upon us from the east, and also used teargas. The crowd dispersed. In spite of the Commissioner's promise, the question was never looked into, and so women went on brewing beer under the counter, albeit many of them were arrested and punished.[37]

There are many more women of distinction in the history of Zambia's struggle for independence, among whom are Makatindi Nganga Yeta and Julia Mulenga. The former is a princess, a granddaughter of Litunga Lewanika, the king of the Lozi who, in 1890, signed the first agreement with the British South Africa Company; she was the first member of an ancient aristocratic family to join Kaunda's political party. A leader of the Women's Brigade, she was also the first woman to be elected as an MP.

Julia Mulenga, better known as Mama Unip, is a Bemba woman, who in 1938 moved to Lusaka with her husband. There, she contributed to the family budget by selling vegetables at the local mart. That was the time when political parties were budding, and before long Julia made a name for herself in the political circles for her drive and courage. They say she used to go around by night shaking a tin full of pebbles as a call to women to go to their secret venue. If necessary, she collected money for her party, and on a demonstration she was always in the forefront singing impromptu slogans and songs of freedom. She had been nicknamed *chikamoneka*, which means 'we shall see', for such was her rejoinder to an officer enquiring about her name and activities.

Over the same period, the Congress Women's League organized imposing demonstrations in South Africa: 'The ferment was so widespread that it went well beyond the organizational capacity of the League.'[38]

At the October 1958 demonstration in Johannesburg, over 2,000 women were arrested. Still, the history of the struggle of South African women has not been written yet.

The mobilization of women in the years of the nationalist revolution has certainly brought them the status of full citizenship, but no more than that. Although now as in the past, a wife's contribution to the family budget is direct and essential, particularly in rural areas, now as in the past it does not entail the wife's social emancipation. Neither her labour nor her political rights have given the African woman real power and autonomy.

Unfortunately, the action of women's organizations, born out of the nationalist revolution, is often chaotic and contradictory. An accurate analysis of the political role of official women's organizations and of the suggestions put forward by them in various countries needs to be articulated and documented. Here, there is only space to stress that African women's organizations tend to stake claims that reflect the position of compromise and insecurity of African women. They fear to make demands that are too progressive to be acceptable to their African 'brothers', also their desire is for a stabilization of the legal and general social position of women, which only too often accords with a non-critical or inadequately explained acceptance of Western models.

As a counterweight to the ideological and political uncertainty of women's organizations, African governments' are fully aware of the importance of controlling womens' masses.

On the one side are progressive states such as Tanzania, which afford vast scope to womens' organizations, which may be a pivotal factor — even an economic one as was shown by the Ghanaian tradeswomen's support of Nkrumah's party — in attempting a new departure in society. On the other, we have fascist regimes, such as Mobutu's, which happen to 'discover' the female masses.

Mobutu took part in the campaign for the International Year of the Woman travelling up and down the country to 'talk with women'. In the course of a 21-day long tour, he met the female élite of the main inland localities. The undoubtedly ingenious demagogy of the 'Father of the Nation' deceives nobody. It is enough to read some national newspapers, a faithful mirror of the regime, to understand what the 'emancipation' of the Zairese woman is all about.

> Contrary to the tenets of the WLM, a woman is not necessarily promoted by engaging in some paid work outside her home. A woman is a woman. If she wishes to stay at home, she must be put in a position to realize herself as a bride, a mother and a woman. The co-operation of the man constitutes a determinant in her liberation. Let a woman choose . . . . It would be a mistake to believe that a housewife wastes away through her domestic cares. A housewife, too, may 'create' and fulfil herself in a thousand different ways, such as decorating the house or inventing cooking recipes. She may also find her accomplishment in nurturing her children or making herself pretty.[39]

The female presence in the guerrilla war in the former Portuguese colonies as well as through organizations born in and out of this struggle merits special mention.

In Guinea-Bissau, in Angola, or Mozambique talk *of* and *on* the woman is clearer than elsewhere: its clarity springs from the quality of the struggle that the peoples from these countries had to wage, an armed struggle which went on for many long years and deeply involved the whole population, upsetting and questioning ways and patterns of life: this had not been necessary during the nationalist struggle, which had been essentially and even exclusively a political one.

Nevertheless, it is not merely the active presence of women in the armed struggle that seems to be the most interesting fact.[40] The choices and the political speeches which were made as the fight went on, seem far more interesting and promising. At the First Conference of the Women of Mozambique, which was held from the 4 to 16 March 1973, it was underlined that:

> While in the past it was the women's duty towards revolution that was constantly emphasized, now Frelimo itself is talking of duties towards women. In many countries, women have been a crucial factor in liberation struggles; yet, after victory, they have been rewarded for their splendid militance with the mere bestowing of a slightly higher status than the one they had before. Frelimo women are not prepared to be caught in the trap, and on this they are supported by the leaders of the liberation movement.[41]

Unlike those of other African women's organizations, Frelimo women, as well as PAIGC or MPLA women, do not hesitate to talk of exploitation and oppression of the woman even in pre-colonial times; consequently, they proclaim, in Amilcar Cabral's words, the necessity of 'cutting off the dead branches of tradition':

> The situation of women as oppressed and exploited human beings is not a phenomenon only related to Mozambique. In several countries and in each continent women are, one way or another, being divested of their most basic rights, prevented from participating in political life, confined to their duties as reproducers and homemakers, and subjected to tyrannical authority. But it is in countries like ours, *where the traditional concepts of woman's subordination and colonial concepts have been combined or juxtaposed* that oppression and exploitation take on extraordinary dimensions.[42]

Carmen Pereira, a member of the PAIGC executive council and vice-president of the National Assembly of the New Republic of Guinea-Bissau, told a woman journalist visiting the liberated areas of the country: 'We say that women have now to fight against two colonialisms, one from the Portuguese and the other from men.'[43]

Far from being sectarian or corporative, this struggle is an essential part 'of the general struggle for the construction of a new society'[44] such revolutionary process of material and ideological reconstruction is the hope, the only hope, African women now have.

Albeit there are many ways in which the process of women's liberation manifests itself and develops in diverse countries and in diverse situations, one is the root of the exploitation and oppression of women, hence the problems deriving from it are equal. Domestic labour, a marginal wage labour, 'black' labour, motherhood, abortion, sexuality, a social lower status, all these are issues common to all women or at least to all those living in a capitalist or capitalist-ruled area — even though at differing levels and degrees of articulation.

Truly enough, the African woman lives in a context of 'general' dependence. Someone has put the question:

> What is the meaning of female emancipation in such a context? Can a

movement for the emancipation of women ever be envisaged in a political context heavily conditioned and man-manipulated? Also, has the declaration of the UN General Assembly on 7 November 1967, abolishing the social and professional discrimination against women, any real value? And, can the celebration of the International Year of the Woman make any sense to the millions of black women who have lapsed into the oblivion of history?[45]

Many women ask themselves the same disturbing questions as they fight on. It is high time somebody said that African women have not lapsed into the oblivion of history, but rather into a wishful oblivion of the official history, much the same as the 'remote African campaigns' are not so remote as we are led to believe. What is rhetorical and mystifying for the women of Africa is equally so for us, the women of the West. Finally, we must reverse the terms of the question and ask: 'Shouldn't we expect that a heavily conditioned and man-ruled country will sooner or later be visited by "the wind of revolution and in the same breath by the wind of the emancipation of women?"'[46]

Notes

1. 'La Donna in Africa', in *Terzo Mondo Informazioni*, op.cit.
2. From a resolution of the first conference of Mozambican women, as reported in the Italian edition of *Mozambique Revolution*, June 1974.
3. 'In the presence of all her disciples, the aunt performs various body motions, says words of sweet kindness, shows how the eyes ought to be moved, so that a girl may win the heart of her husband and be pleasing to him.' M.N.T., *La Circoncision: un rite?*, op.cit. Much the same happens among the Akan, as Kwabena Amponsah has reported in *Topics on West African Traditional Religion*, mimeo, Cape Coast, 1974.
4. P. Just, 'Men, Women and Mukanda: a Transformational Analysis of Circumcision among Two West African Tribes', in *African Social Research*, No.13, June 1972.
5. Nange Kudita Wa Sesemba, 'Tshikumbi, Tshiwila et Mungonge — Trois Rites d'Initiation chez les Tutshokwe du Kasai Occidental', in *Cultures au Zaïre et en Afrique*, No.5, 1974.
6. Female puberty rites are sometimes characterized by the excision of the clitoris to coincide with the sexual and social maturity of the girl. Since there is no excision in the case on the Tapis, we have to assume that it was unknown to the Tutshokwe.
7. *Ibid*.
8. *Ibid*.
9. *Ibid*.
10. *Ibid*.
11. *Ibid*.

12. J.C. Caldwell, op.cit.
13. FAO, op.cit.
14. According to Virgina Cutler, a teacher of domestic science at the University of Ghana, Legon, girls' school attendance is adversely affected by the fact that their average age for marriage is 17.9 years; at the age of 20, 10% of the rural girls are already wives and mothers. At the age of 34, the average woman has four children, and at the end of her reproductive age, usually more than six. The average number of children for each woman of procreative age is 6.9, which gives Ghana one of the highest birthrates in the world. *Woman Power, Social Imperative and Home Science*, Accra, Ghana Universities Press, 1969.
15. In *Salongo*, 6 May 1975.
16. V. Lanternari, op.cit.
17. L. Mair, *La Stregoneria*, Il Saggiatore, Milano, 1969.
18. See M-F. Perrin Jassy's analysis, *La Communaute' de Base dans les Églises Africaines*, Centre d'Études Ethnologiques, Bandundu, 1970.
19. H. Debrunner, *Witchcraft in Ghana*, Presbyterian Book Depot Ltd., Accra, 1961.
20. L. Mair, op.cit.
21. H. Debrunner, op.cit.
22. V. Lanternari, op.cit. Nevertheless, women have at times been able to avail themselves of their Christian beliefs as a means of personal redemption: 'A far-reaching survey among the Mossi of Upper Volta has enabled Sister Marie de l'Assomption, in the world Marie Le Roy Ladurie, to amass a useful documentation of the motives drawing local women to the Christian religion . . . . Agnese, a Mossi woman, hears people at the market say that there is 'a good white man who is prepared to talk also to women and takes care of children's health.' When the 'good white man' pays a visit to her village, she hears him speak and is converted . . . . We see in a case like this the maternal concern for the children's well-being and a woman's desire to liberate herself from a traditional condition of humbleness (she had been impressed by the fact that the white man was prepared to 'talk also with women'). Eugenia narrates: 'The missionary had been kind and good to me. So, when he asked me to go to catechism, I felt that I couldn't be unkind to him by saying no, and here I am". Here too, "being good and kind" becomes a significant and socially pregnant act for someone who is holding a minority status, as she is, in an authoritarian and feudal society of the Mossi kind. For the local girls, the mission may well be the way out of a forced marriage; they are welcomed to the "sisters' court", given some tuition and practical training, and may also attend catechism. There, they may find help too in case they wish to follow their Christian fiance' . . . . The Mossi woman, more than the man, is keen on Christening because subdued, anxious and of low-status as she is, she finds liberation and security in Christianity. In the light of this, the expression used by a woman trying to explain why she has chosen to be a catechumen sounds like an attempt at social ransom. She said she had entered a convent "to receive plenty of life".
23. M-F. Perrin Jassy, op.cit.
24. E. Van Loock, 'La Jamaa, Vue dans le Concret', in various authors,

Le Mariage La Vie Familiale, l'Education Coutumière, Bandundu, 1966.
25. *Ibid*.
26. 'The man is usually keen on a religious marriage as on something bound to last at least as long as he is given a child by his wife; otherwise, he may take a second wife.... Only between 30 and 40 marriages are celebrated in the Nyarombo Parish yearly, out of a Catholic population increasing by 500 souls every year.' M-F. Perrin Jassy, op.cit.
27. D. Chishiba, 'Life in a Polygamous Family', in *Zambia Daily Mail*, 23 January 1975.
28. M.E. Jackman, op.cit.
29. V. Lanternari, op.cit.
30. Mama Marie Onema has been portrayed as 'a wrinkled, one-breasted, exceedingly short woman' whose horrid countenance would add to the efficacy of her magico-religious practices. See M. Crawford Young, 'Rebellion and the Congo', in various authors, *Rebellion in Black Africa*, Oxford University Press, 1971.
31. Ibrahima Baba Kake, *Anne Zingha*, Ed. ABC, NEA, CLE.
32. See S. Leith-Ross, *African Women – A study of the Ibo of Nigeria*, London, 1965. Her reconstruction of the episode basically draws upon the *Report of the Aba Commission of Inquiry* (1930) and from Margery Perham's book *Native Administration in Nigeria*.
33. 'In January 1930, a Commission comprising the governor of the Lagos colony and the Privy Council, which had been appointed to probe into the responsibilities for the massacres, decided that no responsibility was to be attached to those who had fired.' *Ibid*.
34. *Ibid*.
35. H. Heisler, op.cit.
36. S.A. Mpashi, op.cit.
37. *Ibid*.
38. A. Luthuli, *Let my People go*, London, 1962. About South African women's struggles, see Z. Dhlamini, 'Women's Liberation: a Black South African Woman's view', in *Sechaba* (African National Congress official publication), VI, No.9, September 1972. Also E.S. Landis, 'L'Apartheid et les Handicaps Qui en Résultent pour les Femmes Africaines en Afrique du Sud', 1973 (abridged in two parts in *Elima* of April 1975).
39. 'La Deuxième Naissance de la Femme', in *Zaire*, 10 March 1975.
40. Even though we should bear in mind that 'taking up a shotgun' is no mean achievement for a woman: 'Men were not that happy to know that we were preaching the emancipation of women and the equality of sexes. They were not very happy either if someone suggested that women should take arms: for, while in the CIR, women learned how to handle weapons and now they can do so just as well as men. As I was about to leave the area, I received a communique to the effect that three women had taken part in an attack. I convened the population and read it out. The women were delighted to hear it, while the men were beginning to understand that it could work.' From a statement by Lucio Lara of MPLA, as reported in M. Albano's *La Rivoluzione in Angola*, Sapere, Milano, 1973.
41. 'La Donna Mozambicana', in *Terzo Mondo Informazioni*, V, No.3,

March 1974.
42. 'Organizzazione Femminile e Processo Rivoluzionario — Risoluzione della prima conferenza delle donne mozambicane', in *Mozambique Revolution*, June 1974, Italian edition.
43. S. Urdang, 'Lottiamo contro due Colonialismi', in *Donne contro il Colonialismo Invisibile*, IDOC internazionale, March 1975.
44. *Ibid*.
45. M. Glisenti, op.cit.
46. S. Machel, 'Per un Nuovo Rapporto Donna-Societe', in *Nuova Rivista Internazionale*, July-August 1975.

Bibliography

General works
Authors, various, *African Agrarian Systems*, London, International African Institute, 1963.
Authors, various, *L'economia dei paesi sottosviluppati*, Milan, Feltrinelli, 1966.
Authors, various, *Readings in the Applied Economics of Africa*, Cambridge University Press, 1967.
Authors, various, *Antropologia economica*, Milan, F. Angeli, 1974.
Althabe, G., *Les fleurs du Congo*, Paris, Maspero, 1972.
Balandier, G., *Le societa communicanti*, Bari, Laterza, 1973.
Bohannan, P. and Curtin, P., *Africa and Africans*, New York, 1971.
Cohen, A., *Custom and Politics in Urban Africa – A Study of Hausa Migrants in Yoruba Towns*, London, 1969.
Davidson, B., *La civilta africana*, Torino, Einaudi, 1973.
Davidson, B., *Which Way Africa?*, Harmondsworth, Penguin Books, 1973.
Davidson, B., *L'Angola nell'occhio del ciclone*, Torino, Einaudi, 1975.
Gulliver, P.H., *Social Control in African Society*, London, 1963.
Hanna, A.J., *Storia delle Rhodesia e del Nyasaland*, Florence, Sansoni, 1963.
Hodder, B.W., *Economic Development in the Tropics*, London, 1968.
Hoebel, E.A., *Il diritto nelle societa primitive*, Bologna, Il Mulino, 1973.
Kamark, A.M., *The Economics of African Development*, New York, 1967.
Lanternari, V., *Occidente e terzo mondo*, Bari, Dedalo, 1972.
Lanternari, V., *Antropologia e imperialismo*, Turin, Einaudi, 1974.
Mayer, P., *Townsmen or Tribesmen*, Citta del Capo, 1971.
Meillassoux, C., *L'economia della savana*, Milan, Feltrinelli, 1975.
MPLA, *Storia dell'Angola*, Rome, Lerici, 1968.
O'Connor, A.M., *An Economic Geography of East Africa*, London, 1966.
Segers, J. and Habiyambere, A., *Les conditions de la croissance economique*, Kinshasa, Centre d'etudes pour l'action sociale, 1973.
Vignes, J., *Sguardo sull'Africa*, Milan, Feltrinelli, 1968.

Society and Women
Authors, various, *Seven Tribes of Central Africa*, Manchester University Press, 1968.

Authors, various, *L'organisation sociale et politique chez les Yansi, Teke et Boma*, Bandundu, Publications du Centre d'Etudes Ethnologiques, 1970.

Authors, various, *Rebellion in Black Africa*, Oxford University Press, 1971.

Authors, various, *La donna un problema aperto*, Florence, Vallecchi, 1974.

Adetowun Ogunsheye, 'Les femmes du Nigeria', *Presence Africaine*, No. 32-33, 1960.

Allott, A.N., *The Place of African Customary Law* in *Modern Africa Legal Systems*, Accra, 1964.

Alberti, E.M., *Women of Burundi: A Study of Social Values*, in *Women of Tropical Africa*, London, 1963.

Baleka Bamba Nzuji, 'Que signifie au juste la liberation feminine?', *Cultures au Zaire et en Afrique*, No.1, 1973.

Bolanle Awe, 'Women's Liberation Movement and African Women', *Presence*, VI, No.1, 1973.

Caldwell, J.C., *African Rural Migration*, Canberra, 1969.

Census of Population and Housing, 1969, Final Report, Lusaka, Government Printer, 1973.

Comhaire-Sylvain, S., *Femmes de Kinshasa*, Paris, L'Aia, Mouton, 1968.

Cutler, V., *Woman, Power, Social Imperatives and Home Science*, Accra, 1969.

Cutrufelli, M.R., 'Trasformazioni e prospettive della condizione femminile in Zambia', *Terzo Mondo*, VIII, No.27, gennaio-marzo, 1975.

Debrunner, H., *Witchcraft in Ghana*, Accra, 1961.

Dhlamini, Zanele, *Women's Liberation: a Black South African Woman's View, Sechaba*, September 1972.

Diarra, Fatoumata-Agnes, *Femmes africaines en devenir*, Paris, 1971.

Diop, C. 'Gardienne de la tradition, pionniere du progres', *Elima*, 11 May, 1975.

'La donna in Africa', *Terzo Mondo Informazioni*, V, No.3, March 1974.

Falade, S., 'Women of Dakar and the Surrounding Urban Area', *Woman in Tropical Africa*, London, 1963.

FAO, *Report on the Possibilities of African Rural Development in Relation to Economic and Social Growth*, Rome, 1962.

Fougeyrollas, *La condition de la femme senegalaise*, Dakar, 1969.

Gatto Trocchi, C., *Le giumente degli dei*, Rome, Bulzoni, 1975.

Glisenti, M., 'La donna africana nel contesto della dipendenza', *Politica Internazionale*, No.12, December 1975.

Gnali, *La femme africaine*, 1968.

Heisler, H., *Urbanisation and the Government of Migration*, London, 1974.

Houyoux, J., *Budgets menagers, nutrition et mode de vie a Kinshasa*, Kinshasa, Presses Universitaires du Zaire, 1973.

Independence et cooperation, IDEF, December 1974.

Jackman, M.E., *Recent Population Movements in Zambia*, Lusaka, Institute for African Studies, University of Zambia, 1973.

Jassy Perrin, M.-F., *La communaute de base dans les eglises africaines*, Bandundu, 1970.

Kay, G., *Chief Kalaba's Village*, Manchester University Press, 1964.
Kay, G., *Changing Patterns of Settlement and Land Use in the Eastern Province of Northern Rhodesia*, University of Hull, 1965.
Kay, G., *A Social Geography of Zambia*, University of London Press, London, 1967.
Kay, G., 'Agricultural Progress in Zambia', *Environment and Land Use in Africa*, London, 1969.
Kilolo, B., 'Le droit coutumier des successions de la ville de Kinshase', *Cahiers zairois de la recherche et du developpement*, XVII, 1971.
Lebeuf, A.M.D., 'The Role of Women in the Political Organization of African Societies', *Women of Tropical Africa*, London, 1963.
Leblanc, M., *Personnalite de la femme katangaise*, Lovanio, 1960.
Lefancheux, 'The Contribution of Women to the Economic and Social Development of African Countries', *International Labour Review*, II, 1962.
Leith-Ross, S., *African Women*, London, 1939.
Leith-Ross, S., 'The Rise of a New Elite Amongst the Women of Nigeria', *Int. Soc. Sci. Bulletin*, Vol.8, 1956.
Levine, R.A., 'Sex roles and Economic Change, in Africa', *Black Africa, its Peoples and their Cultures Today*, London, 1970.
Little, K., 'Voluntary Associations and Social Mobility among West African Women', *Canadian Journal of African Studies*, VI, No.2, 1972.
Little, K., *African Women in Towns*, Cambridge University Press, 1973.
Machel, Samora, 'Per un nuovo rapporto donna-societa', *Nuova Rivista Internazionale*, July-August 1975.
Mbilinyi, M.J., 'The New Woman and Traditional Norms in Tanzania', *Journal of Modern African Studies*, X, 1, 1972.
Mitchell, J.C., 'The Woman's Place in African Advancement', *Optima*, September, 1959.
Mpase Nselenge Mpeti, *L'evolution de la solidarite traditionnelle en milieu rural et urbain du Zaire*, Kinshasa, Presses Universitaires du Zaire, 1974.
Mpashi, S.A., *Betty Kaunda*, London, 1969.
de Negri, P., 'Yoruba Women's Costume', *Nigeria*, No.72, 1962.
PAIGC, 'Report on the Politico-Socio-Economic Role of Women in Guinea and the Cape Verde Islands', *Presence*, VI, No.1, 1973.
Plisnier, L., *La condition de l'africaine en Afrique noire*, Brussells, 1961.
Preston Thomson, B., *Two Studies in African Nutrition*, Manchester, University Press, 1968.
Report of a conference, *Kitwe Squatter Conference* (cyclostyled), 12 August, 1972.
Report of a consultation, *Making Our Towns Liveable* (cyclostyled), April 1969.
Report of a consultation, *Women's Rights in Zambia* (cyclostyled), Mondolo Ecumenical Foundation, 1970.
Report of a seminar, *The Place of Land Settlement in National Development* (cyclostyled), Mondolo Ecumenical Foundation, 1969.

Richards, M., *Histoire, tradition et promotion de la femme chez les Batanga*, Bandundu, 1970.
Riviere, C., 'La promotion de la femme guineenne', *Cahiers d'Etudes Africaines*, VIII, 3, 1968.
Staub, H., 'The Changing Role of Women in Tanzania', *Rural life*, XVI, No.2, 1971.
Suttner, R.S., 'The Legal Status of African Women in South Africa', *Africa Social Research*, No.8, December 1969.
Seth Twum, *The Worker, the Employer and the Law — A Comprehensive Study of Ghana Labour Law*, Teller International Publications, 1973.
Urdang, S., 'Lottiamo contro due colonialismi', *in* Donne contro il colonialismo invisible', *IDOC Internazionale*, March 1975.
Vincent, J.F., 'L'evolution feminine dans les villes', *Afrique documents*, Nos.70-71, 1963.
White, C., 'The Politico-Legal Status of Women in Uganda', *Presence*, Vol. No.1, 1973.
Wills, J., *A Study of Time Allocation by Rural Women and Their Place in Decision-making*, Makerere University, 1967.
Wipper, A., 'The Politics of Sex', *Presence*, Vol. No.1, 1973.
Wipper, A., 'The Role of African Women: Past, Present and Future', *Canadian Journal of African Studies*, Vol. No.2, 1972.
'Women and the Mozambican Revolution', *CFM news and notes*, September 1973.

Women and work

Addae, G., *The Retailing of Imported Textiles in the Accra Markets*, West African Institute of Social and Economic Research, 1954.
Aguessy, *La femme africaine et le marche dakarois*, Universite di Dakar, 1963.
Byangwa, M., *The Muganda Woman's Attitude Towards Work Outside Home*, Makerere University, n.d.
Boserup, E., *Women's Role in Economic Development*, New York, 1970.
Brunger, A., 'Women in Dahomey', *Women the Struggle for Liberation*, World Student Christian Federation, 1973.
Burawoy, M., *The Colour of Class on the Copper Mines*, Lusaka Institute for African Studies, University of Zambia, 1972.
Burnley, E.G., 'Women's work in the West Cameroons', *Women Today*, Vol. No.1, 1964.
Capelle, M., 'The Industrial Employment of Women in the Belgian Congo', *Inter-African Labour Institute Bulletin*, March 1959.
Central Statistical Office, *Employment and Earnings 1966-68*, Lusaka, 1970.
Chishiba, D., 'The Plight of Bar Waitresses', *Zambia Daily Mail*, 6 December, 1974.
Comhaire-Sylvain, S., 'Le travail des femmes a Lagos', *Zaire*, Nos.2-5, 1951.
ECA, 'Women: the Neglected Human Resources for African Development', *Presence*, Vol. No.1, 1973.

Gluckman, M., *Economy of the Central Barotse Plain*, Manchester University Press, 1968.
Gugler, J., *The Impact of Labour Migration on Society and Economy in Sub-Saharan Africa: Empirical Findings and Theoretical Considerations*, Lusaka, African Social Research, University of Zambia, 1968.
Hodden, B.W. and Ukwu, V.I., *Markets in West Africa*, Ibadan University Press, 1969.
ILO, *The Employment and Conditions of Work of African Women*, Geneva, 1961.
ILO, *The Employment and Conditions of Work of African Women*, Geneva, 1964.
ILO, *Report to the Government of Zambia on Incomes, Wages and Prices in Zambia*, Lusaka, Government Printer, 1969.
ILO, *Policy on Employment of Women in Developing Countries*, Geneva, 1971.
ILO, *Employment in Africa*, Geneva, 1973.
ILO, ECA, IWCA, *African Workshop on Participation of Women in Handicrafts and Other Small Industries*, Kitwe (Zambia), December, 1974.
Institut de Science Economique Appliquee, *La femme africaine et les marchees dakarois*, Dakar, 1963.
Lacroix, J.L., 'Les poles de developpement industriel au Congo', *Cahiers economiques et Sociaux*, No.2, 1964.
Lacroix, J.L., *Industrialisation au Congo. Transformation des structures economiques*, Paris, 1967.
Lacroix, J.L. 'Evolution de l'economie et transformation des structures economiques au Congo depuis 1960', *Revue francaise d'etudes politiques africaines*, No.58, October 1970.
Le Cour Grandmaison, C., 'Activites economiques des femmes dakaroises', *Africa*, XXXIX, No.2, 1969.
Ligan, G., 'Women in Business', *Entente africaine*, March 1972.
Mabogunje, A.L., 'Yoruba Market Women', *Ibadan*, No.9, 1959.
McCall, D.F., *Trade and the Role of the Wife in a Modern West African Town*, London, 1961.
Marshall, G., *The Marketing of Farm Produce: Some Patterns of Trade Among Women in Western Nigeria*, Ibadan, Nigerian Institute of Social and Economic Research, 1962.
N'Dongala, E., 'Mutations structurelles de l'economie traditionnelle dans le Bas-Congo sous l'impact de la colonisation et de la decolonisation', *Cahiers economiques et sociaux*, No.9, March 1966.
Nypan, A., *Market Trade — A Sample Study of Market Traders in Accra*, Accra University College of Ghana, 1960.
Oberschall, A., 'African Traders and Small Businessmen in Lusaka', *African Social Research*, No.16, 1973.
Ohadike, P.O., *Development of and Factors in the Employment of African Migrants in the Copper Mines of Zambia 1940-66*, Lusaka, University of Zambia, 1969.

Peil, M., *The Ghanaian Factory Worker: Industrial Man in Africa*, Cambridge University Press, 1972.
Report of the Regional Meeting on the Role of Women in National Development, Addis Ababa, March 1969.
Richards, A.I., *Land, Labour and Diet in Northern Rhodesia*, London, 1939.
Rourke, B.E. and Obeng, F.A., 'Seasonality in the Employment of Casual Agricultural Labour in Ghana', *The Economic bulletin of Ghana*, No.3, 1973.
Sikaneta, C., 'It's Back to the Land for Urban Women', *Zambia Daily Mail*, 2 January 1975.
UNICEF, *Conference de Lome — Enfance, jeuness, femmes et plans de developpment*, 1972.
Westergaard, M., *Women and Work in Dar-es-Salaam*, University of Dar-es-Salaam, 1970.
White, C.M.N., *A Preliminary Survey of Luvale Rural Economy*, Manchester University Press, 1968.

The Family

Authors, various, *The Family Estate in Africa*, London, 1964.
Authors, various, *Le mariage, la vie familiale, l'education conutumiere*, Bandundu, 1966.
Barnes, J.A., *Marriage in a Changing Society*, Manchester University Press, 1970.
Colson, E., 'Family Change in Contemporary Africa', *Black Africa, its Peoples and Their Cultures Today*, London, 1970.
'Christina, Jane, Christiana, Three Young Women Speaking', *Presence*, Vol. No.1, 1973.
Date-Bah, E., *Some Features of Marriage Patterns Among the Members of One Elite Group in Ghana*, Accra, University of Ghana, 1973.
Deniel, R., 'Images de la famille en Cote d'Ivoire', *Jeune Afrique*, 18 April, 1975.
Diallo, Assiatou, 'Recrudescence de la polygamie', *Anima*, August, 1975.
Diallo, Assiatou, 'Le celibat des junes filles en Afrique', *Anima*, September, 1975.
Gutkind, P.C.W., 'African Urban Family Life: Comment on and Analysis of Some Rural-Urban Differences', *Cahiers d'Etudes Africaines*, 3, No.10, 1962-63.
Gutkind. P.C.W., 'African Urban Family Life and the Urban System', *Black Africa, its Peoples and Their Cultures Today*, London, 1970.
Guy, B., *Ville africaine, famille urbaine: les enseignants de Kinshasa*, Mouton, Parigi-l'Aia, 1969.
Hennin, R., 'Les structures familiales en milieu urbain (Elizabethville)', *Problemes sociaux congolais*, 1965.
Kamika Mwana Ngombo, 'La polygamie — de la legitimite a la legalite', *Zaire*, 13 October, 1975.
Lamy, E., 'Etude d'integration partielle: obligations derivant du mariage',

Problems sociaux congolais, No.72, 1965.
Lamy, E., 'La dot congolaise et ses prolongements directs et lointains', *Problemes sociaux congolais*, No.80, 1968.
Little, K., 'Attitudes Towards Marriage and the Family Among Educated Young Sierra Leoneans', *New Elites of Tropical Africa*, Oxford University Press, 1966.
Little, K. and Price, A., 'Some Trends in Modern Marriage Among West Africans', *Africa*, XXXVII, No.4, 1967.
Mair, L., *African Marriage and Social Change*, London, 1969.
Marris, P., *Family and Social Change in an African City*, Evanston, Northwestern University Press, 1961.
Martin, V., 'Mariage et famille dans les groupes christianises ou en voie de christianisation de Dakar', *Christianity in Tropical Africa*, London, 1968.
Mitchell, J.C., 'Social Change and the Stability of African Marriage in Northern Rhodesia', *Social Change in Modern Africa*, London, 1961.
Okediji, F.O. and Oladejo, O., 'Marital Stability and Social Structure in an African City', *Nigerian Journal of Economy and Social Studies*, VIII, No.1, 1966.
Oppong, C., *Marriage Among a Matrilineal Elite*, Cambridge University Press, 1973.
Phillips, A., *Survey of African Marriage and Family Life*, London, 1953.
Phillips, A. and Morris, H.F., *Marriage Laws in Africa*, London, 1971.
Pierard, J.P., 'La dot congolaise, sa situation actuelle et son avenir', *Bulletin ARSON*, No.3, 1967.
Richards, A.I., *Bemba Marriage and Present Economic Conditions*, Manchester University Press, 1969.
Schapera, I., *Married Life in an African Tribe*, London, 1971.
Sofoluwe, G.O., 'A Study of Divorce Cases at Igbo-Ora', *Nigerian Journal of Economy and Social Studies*, VII, 1965.
Tufuo, J.W. and Donkor, C.E., *Ashantis of Ghana*, Accra, 1969.

Reproduction and Sexuality
Ampofo, A., *The Family Planning Movement in Ghana*, Accra, 1971.
Caldwell, J.C., *Population Growth and Family Change in Africa*, Canberra, Australian National University Press, 1968.
Chishiba, D., 'Are Nurses Cruel to Expectant Mothers?', *Zambia Daily Mail*, 31 December, 1974.
Froelich, J.P., 'Les societes d'initiation chez les Moba et les Gourma du Nord Togo', *Journal de la Societe des Africanistes*, XV, 1945.
Gross, B.A., 'Pour la suppression d'une coutume barbare: l'excision', *Notes africaines*, No.45, 1950.
Guena, R., Ch. de Preneuf and Ch. Reboul, 'Aspetti psicopatologici della gravidanza nel Senegal', *La Donna – Un problema aperto*, Florence, Vallecchi, 1974.
Henry, P., 'La clitoridectomie rituelle en Guinee: motivations, consequences', *Psychopathologie Africaine*, I, 1965.

Kerharo, J. and Bouquet, A., *Sorciers, feticheurs et guerrisseurs*, Paris, 1950.
Lestrange, De, M., 'Societes secretes, circoncision et excision en Afrique noire', *Le Concours medical*, November, 1953.
Lestrange, De, M., 'Meres en enfants en Afrique noire', *Le Concours medical*, 1954.
Okediji, F.O., 'Some Social Psychological Aspects of Fertility Among Married Women in an African City', *Nigerian Journal of Economy and Social Studies*, X, No.1, 1967.
Owens-Dey, T.G.K., 'The Right to be Born', *Ideal Woman*, June, 1974.
Makonga, B., *La position sociale de la femme mere*, Elisabethville, 1951.
Makonga, B., *La mere en Afrique*, Brussells, 1964.
Romaniuk, A., *La fecondite des populations congolaises*, Paris, 1967.
Rouch, J. and Bernus, E., 'Note sur les prostituees 'toutou' de Treichville et d'Adjame', *Etudes eburneennes*, VI, 1959.
UNICEF, *L'enfant dans le Tiers-Monde*, Paris, 1965.
Zanotelli, A., 'Female Circumcision: a 'Barbarous' and Immoral Rite', *Insight and Opinion*, XI, No.1.
Zwane, B., 'Birth Control or Social Justice?', *Africa*, December 1974.

Education: Traditional and Modern
Foster, P.J., *Education and Social Change in Ghana*, London, 1965.
Just, P., 'Men, Women, and Mukanda: a Transformational Analysis of Circumcision Among Two West Central African Tribes', *African Social Research*, No.13, June 1972.
Lloyd, B.B., 'Education and Family Life in the Development of Class Identification Among the Yoruba', *New Elites of Tropical Africa*, London, 1966.
Mair, L., *La stregoneria*, Milan, Il Saggiatore, 1969.
Mwanakatwe, J.M., *Adult Education and Political and Social Change*, Lusaka, NECZAM, 1970.
Mwondela, W.R., *Traditional Education in North-Western Zambia*, Lusaka, NECZAM, 1972.
Nange Kudita Wa Sesemba, 'Tshikumbi, Tshiwila and Mungonge: trois rites d'initiation chez les Tutshokwe du Kasai occidental', *Cultures au Zaire et en Afrique*, No.5, 1974.
Nyirenda, W.P., *Adult Education and Development*, Lusaka, NECZAM, 1970.
Omari, T.P., 'Changing Attitudes of Students in West African Society Towards Marriage and Family Relationships', *British Journal of Sociology*, XI, No.3, 1960.
Peil, M., 'Ghanaian students: the Broadening Base', *British Journal of Sociology*, March, 1965.
Report of the Regional Conference on Education, Vocational Training and Work Opportunities for Girls and Women in African Countries, Rabat, 1971.
Richards, I.A., *Economic and Social Factors Affecting the Education of African Girls in Territories under British Influence*, Cotonou, 1960.
'Sur le scolarisation des filles au Dahomey', *Cahiers d'Etudes Africaines*, 1955.
UNESCO, *The Education of Girls in Tropical Africa*, Cotonou-Paris, 1960.